WOMEN'S WORK, MEN'S CULTURES

WOMEN'S WORK, MEN'S CULTURES

Overcoming Resistance and
Changing Organizational
Cultures

Sarah Rutherford

Director, Rutherford Associates

palgrave
macmillan

First published 2011 by
PALGRAVE MACMILLAN

Palgrave Macmillan in the UK is an imprint of Macmillan Publishers Limited, registered in England, company number 785998, of Houndmills, Basingstoke, Hampshire RG21 6XS.

Palgrave Macmillan in the US is a division of St Martin's Press LLC, 175 Fifth Avenue, New York, NY 10010.

Palgrave Macmillan is the global academic imprint of the above companies and has companies and representatives throughout the world.
Palgrave® and Macmillan® are registered trademarks in the United States, the United Kingdom, Europe and other countries

ISBN-13: 978-0-230-28370-1

This book is printed on paper suitable for recycling and made from fully managed and sustained forest sources. Logging, pulping and manufacturing processes are expected to conform to the environmental regulations of the country of origin.

A catalogue record for this book is available from the British Library.
A catalog record for this book is available from the Library of Congress.

10 9 8 7 6 5 4 3 2 1
20 19 18 17 16 15 14 13 12 11

Printed and bound in Great Britain by CPI Antony Rowe, Chippenham and Eastbourne.

CONTENTS

CONTENTS

FIGURE AND TABLE

Figure

Table

ACKNOWLEDGEMENTS

This book had been in my head for a few years now but it never seemed the right time to write it. Circumstances and a chance meeting with my publisher Eleanor Davey-Corrigan at another book event in early 2010 conspired to make what had been an intention into a reality. I was committed!

My first thanks go to Professor Sylvia Walby, who encouraged me to do an MSc in Sociology at the London School of Economics back in 1991 and later to do a PhD under her supervision at Bristol University. Her intellect and dedication to women's equality have been and continue to be an inspiration.

Thanks go to the openness and honesty of all my research subjects and the men and women who generously gave their time to talk to me about their experience and to share their knowledge, and often on more than one occasion.

The team at Palgrave Macmillan have been a delight to work with and I thank them.

My thanks go to my good friend Juliet Gwyn Palmer who applied her excellent editorial skills to the first draft, and gave many helpful suggestions and lastly and most importantly to Ian Annand who provided practical and emotional support during the whole process. This book is dedicated to all women everywhere who are entering the workplace with rightful expectations of achievement and success.

CONTEXT

SCOPE

This book draws on a broad range of materials, research, and experience. Many of the ideas and theories as well as the two main case studies came out of my PhD research, which investigated the ways in which different organizational (and divisional) cultures inhibited and/or marginalized women managers.[1] These organizations were interested in the subject matter and gave me unparalleled access to the highest levels of management, for which I am extremely grateful.

I approached the airline that here I have called Airco because of its history and commitment to equal opportunities. It employed nearly 30,000 people and I researched five of its divisions, Marketing, Finance, Human Resources, Cabin Services, and Cargo. These divisions were like discrete companies and their cultures varied hugely. Management was divided into managers and senior managers, and overall, 21 percent of managers were women.

Investco, the pseudonym I have used for a bank, was much smaller with only 3,000 employees and had no history of equal opportunities, although it was known in the City for employing a relatively higher percentage of women than other financial institutions – 15 percent of all managers were women. I researched three different divisions, Broking, Investment Management, and Corporate Finance, and there were three levels of management: manager, assistant director, and director.

Between these two organizations I had eight very distinctive cultures to analyse for their impact on women managers. The research involved a detailed survey sent to a random stratified sample of male and female managers (215 with a 72 percent response rate) and semi structured recorded interviews with a random stratified sample of male and female managers (15 men and 29 women).

Both companies have changed structurally and culturally a great deal since my research, and the practices described are not a reflection of their practices today. While this material is now some years old, the depth and detail of the data is invaluable for illustrating the very different ways in which cultures operate, and in providing substance to some theoretical considerations which are becoming increasingly relevant today. All interviewees in this research have been anonymized to protect confidentiality.

The original data and concepts have been developed and added to through subsequent research that I have conducted alone or with others, and examples drawn widely from my work as a consultant[2] as well as a whole body of academic material on gender and work. I undertook a number of interviews for the specific purposes of this book. The majority of interviewees are named in the text although a number requested confidentiality – particularly a group of young women starting out in their careers. Other unidentified sources are drawn from my consultancy work and for obvious reasons are heavily anonymized.

I have had the privilege of being a young employee of an investment bank, and more recently a non-executive director of a FTSE 250 company, also a bank. Without question these experiences in an elite and male-dominated area of finance inform my view of how organizational cultures can marginalize and exclude in obvious and tangible ways, and more and more in the most subtle and intangible ways. I bring my own reflections into my work, mingling them with the research and observations of others. And lastly my thoughts are developed from the many conversations I have had with professionals and working women both over the years as well as for the specific purposes of the book.

My research and consultancy has been largely UK-focused, as have been my own cultural influences. I use news stories and examples from my own culture not to exclude readers from other ones but to press home the interrelationship of organizations and the wider culture in which they operate. It would be impossible to do this in a meaningful way with more than one culture.

However, as is widely known and as the examples in the following pages will illustrate, the majority of leading organizations 'practising' diversity and inclusion, taking gender seriously, are global organizations. Gender issues, more so than any of the other strands of diversity, do cross boundaries. There is nowhere in the world where women earn as much as men, nowhere in the world where domestic violence is not a serious social problem, no country in which rape does not occur. In this way I suggest that women share the common bond of being less valued than men in all societies. However this is expressed in different ways. For example, in fundamentalist Muslim states, like Saudi Arabia, the majority of women live very curtailed public lives and even an education may be seen as inappropriate for women (under the Taliban in Afghanistan educating girls was treated as a crime). In other countries like China, the communist regime required women to take their place next to men in the workplace, but the devaluation of women has resulted in millions of baby girls being abandoned or aborted. A huge challenge therefore presents itself to global companies, anxious to rid themselves of the vestiges of cultural imperialism, and the associated hierarchy that involved. They strive to adapt their organizations to different cultures, to promote home nationals and not expats, and to acknowledge and respect local values and customs. When it comes to diversity, Western values about gender often collide with local practice.

While some of the details of the UK legal landscape and culture may be different from the United States, other parts of Europe, and certainly the Middle East, Africa, and Asia, I hope that the experiences described in this book will resonate with women managers and professionals the world over. The specific cultural barriers may vary from country to country, as they do from company to company, from division to division, but the model of culture described here can apply to any company anywhere.

My definition of culture is not finite. The model set out in the book can be adapted and added to for other strands of diversity. I am acutely aware of omitting to discuss race in a specific way. Black and ethnic minority women in organizations experience dual discrimination. While acknowledging this dimension I did not have sufficient research material to do this important and under-researched area justice. By using the generic word 'women' I do not mean to diminish the very material differences between us, but I believe that in order to make political, economic, and social progress feminism requires some element of shared experience of 'womanhood.'

Even when the path is nominally open – when there is nothing to prevent a woman from being a doctor, a lawyer, a civil servant – there are many phantoms and obstacles, as I believe, looming in her way. To discuss and define them is I think of great value and importance; for thus only can the labour be shared, the difficulties be solved.

Virginia Woolf, 'The professions and women' (1942)

From *The Essays of Virginia Woolf*, Vol. 1, © Quentin Bell and Angelica Garnett, published by the Hogarth Press. Reprinted by permission of the Random House Group Ltd and Harcourt, Inc., and the Society of Authors as the Literary Representative of the Estate of Virginia Woolf.

INTRODUCTION

INTRODUCTION

Diversity is now an accepted part of the UK corporate agenda, and of all the diversity issues, arguably gender is at the top. Or it should be. Women make up over half the population, 47 percent of the UK workforce, and 57 percent of all graduates, and yet they are still hugely under-represented at the top levels of almost all organizations.[1] This is a terrible waste of talent.

Organizations are faced with a dilemma. Either they do nothing, recruit the best and hope that their female talent stays and rises to the top. Or they recognize that by doing nothing they risk losing these women and potentially, because word spreads, missing out on future recruitment as well as business opportunities.

Many companies now see that as well as being a talent pool which can no longer be ignored, women are also an economic force, and they want to exploit this growing market. The majority favor a piecemeal strategy when resources allow, coupled with good intentions, a possibly enthusiastic leadership, and a passionate diversity head. Then there are the few organizations that have been in this game a long time, and have diversity and equality firmly embedded in their company values. This is true of most UK public sector organizations as well as a good selection of global blue chips – examples are IBM, Shell, BP, Lloyds TSB, GlaxoSmithKline, Procter & Gamble, Unilever, National Grid, and more recently the leading professional services firms and investment banks. Yet even these companies struggle to have more than 15 percent representation of women at senor management level, and their boards often have even fewer.

Why is this? Why does it take so many years of hard work to progress so little? Why does it feel like such a struggle to achieve true representation for women at all levels of organizations? Why are diversity heads complaining of fatigue? The answer is that the issues they are being asked to grapple with are more complex than a mere business case allows. Organizations are taking too simplistic an approach and consequently change is limited.

This book focuses on the mid to senior levels of management, often referred to as the 'glass ceiling,' which is actually more like a thin layer of cling film wrapped around the locus of power – wherever it resides. At these levels in organizations, competition is intense and people use whatever resources they have available to protect their interests. It so happens that men still have more of these than women. They have the material and cultural resources gained from a history of male domination at their disposal. This simple admission – that power bases and interests are being protected – is missing from most discussions on diversity. It must be brought in. Men's reluctance to share power in the workplace needs to be discussed. If historical inequalities, gender relations in wider society, and resistance on so many levels continue to be ignored, organizational change will remain tempered. Understanding the wider social issues will put organizational initiatives into context, and acknowledging resistance will reveal the attitudes and beliefs under the surface that really drive organizational behavior.

Meanwhile women are voting with their feet. Their expectations are higher than they were 20 years ago, and they are moving to more female-friendly environments, often setting up their own organizations. The waste of talent to business is phenomenal, the waste of opportunities in corporate life to women a disgrace.

Debates on the reasons for the glass ceiling turn this way and that, and the language of equality and diversity changes, but consultants, both internal and external, rarely draw on the huge body of academic research that has been done on gender, work and organization.[2]

I hope this book goes some way to fill in the gaps and provide some theoretical and historical underpinning to the key issues relating to women's progress in the workplace, and that it will contribute to the debate within organizations about what many agree is *the* issue of the business world today.

MY APPROACH TO CHANGE

People are now beginning to recognize that most work organizations in the past have been male-dominated and that this means most organization cultures are more suited to men than women. But how do we effect cultural change when it comes to diversity, and in particular when we are looking at gender?

There is no doubt that many organizations have made great progress through their internal gender initiatives. Yet the figures at the top remain much the same. What kind of approach to furthering women's equality should organizations be taking to get better results?

A psychosocial approach to culture change is required, and this means understanding your own culture and why it has developed the way it has, acknowledging resistance to change, and understanding wider social gender relations. All these elements are vital when implementing a change program. A holistic, systematic approach will ensure that all levels of the organization are reached:

- change on the organizational level – structures, policies, communication
- change on the interpersonal level – addressing behaviors and how people relate to one another
- change on the personal level – touching on deep-rooted and sometimes unconscious attitudes and beliefs.

The culture model set out in this book provides a blueprint from which to start. Data for each separate constituent, discussed chapter by chapter, can be collected through a survey and interviews which will establish in what ways your organization's culture is gendered, and identify in what areas there are barriers to progress. This information together with demographics will inform in what ways and where the organization has to change. The discussions in each chapter are intended to provide information and knowledge about the issues to give professionals and leaders a solid foundation from which to build/develop initiatives and start conversations.

It is important to ask the right questions. I argue that organizations need to engage in a much wider debate on the position of women in society. Of course one organization cannot change gender relations in the wider context, but any organization can choose to be part of the transition that is taking place anyway. However, half-asked questions will elicit half responses which in themselves will lead to partial solutions. Taking the business case as the sole reason for change, cut adrift from the roots of historical and current inequalities, discrimination, and sexism, is like painting a layer of lacquer on a badly tarnished table. Whilst useful in bringing issues to the attention of people who would otherwise not be interested, it will lead to a limited response and might even work against equality.

Addressing gender issues as merely one difference among many, as if it was the same as a different nationality, will not lead to any substantial change either. Nor will imploring men to learn and understand the female sex as if their inequality has been one giant historical misunderstanding. The popular trend of analyzing and understanding individuals' propensity to stereotype through unconscious bias is again only a partial solution to a much more complex problem. Without an understanding of why stereotypes of women are so often negative, resistance can and will remain unchallenged.

The assumption of every organization that is dominated at senior levels by men should be that it will be less comfortable and more difficult for women to make it to the top. I think we have enough statistics to be able to start with this premise. Of course every organization will have its own specific issues, depending on its history, geography, and business. Each is located in particular place, time, and culture. But every organization is capable of transforming its culture to be as inclusive as is possible in its own situation.

A good place to start is with self-reflective questions. What kind of an organization do we want to be? What is stopping us being that? What do we need to do to get there? These are big, wide questions, very different from the kinds of questions I regularly hear – How many women have we got on the board? How can we change this quickly? How can we avoid a legal case? How are we doing on diversity compared with our competitors?

There are a number of key factors for success, the most important being the will and commitment of leadership, and the fact is that leaders are simply not doing enough. Most do not see gender equality as an important enough business issue, because if they did, more would treat it as such.

1

WOMEN IN SOCIETY

INTRODUCTION

We cannot discuss the roles and position of women in organizations without looking at their place in society. Organizations do not operate in a fishbowl but are part of a wider social system. Indeed today many organizations are part of a global system, and as such affected by global issues. Women's emancipation is an unfinished global story, each country at a different chapter. In some countries equality seems a squeak away, in others women's freedoms are only just beginning. However, their standing in society, wherever that may be, has been hard won.

One hundred years ago there was only one country in which women had the vote – Finland, where women won the vote in 1906. Other countries followed; in the United States women were being granted the vote in 1920, the United Kingdom in 1928, Spain in 1931, France 1944, and Switzerland not until 1971. Nor were women allowed to enter the professions or receive a degree from university. The granting of these privileges came after long hard-fought campaigns by women and men who supported women's equality. In the United Kingdom they were allowed access to accountancy and the legal profession for the first time in 1920. During both World Wars women in the United Kingdom took on men's work roles while the men were away fighting. After each war there was an ideological backlash to encourage women back into the domestic sphere and out of the workforce. After the First World War, one man commented:

> I am certain I voice the opinion of thousands of young men when I say that if men were doing the work that thousands of young women are now doing the men would be able to keep those same women in decent homes. Homes are the real place of the women who are now compelling men to be idle. It is time the Government insisted upon employers giving work to more

men, thus enabling them to marry the women they cannot now approach.[1]

After the Second World War the backlash was subtler but every bit as effective. Nurseries were closed and a spate of concern around the way children were being raised was expressed by professional child psychologists. The ideology of motherhood as a career strongly emerged to deter women from the world of work. Women returned to the home.

The 1960s saw intense political pressure from women for women's equality in the West – the women's liberation movement, which lasted through to the end of the 1970s. In the United Kingdom it was legal to discriminate against women in the workplace and pay them less than men until the Equal Pay Act and Sex Discrimination Act came into force in 1975. Since then, legislation piece by piece has given women full equal rights with men. It was not until 1980 that women in the United Kingdom could legally apply for a loan or credit in their own names. In 1994 rape in marriage was made illegal after 15 years of campaigning by women's groups. In the same year equal employment rights were given to part-time workers, 87 percent of whom were women. Birth control gave women the freedom to control their family size and with that the opportunity to enter the workplace. And they have – in droves. Change for women in the workplace in countries all round the world has been dramatic when put in its historical context. However in the workplace and elsewhere formal exclusion has slowly been replaced by informal exclusion, workplace cultures still remain dominated by men, and women have only made small inroads into positions of power.

WOMEN IN EMPLOYMENT IN THE UNITED KINGDOM

Women are poorer than men. In the United Kingdom the bare facts are that despite Equal Pay Act 1975 (now the Equality Act 2010), women working full time are paid 12 percent less on average than men working full time. The gap is much wider in the private sector. And women working part time are paid on average 37 percent less per hour than men working full time. This is important, as over three-quarters of part timers are women. Benefits make up 21 percent of the average woman's income and just 8 percent of the average man's income.

A gender audit of the UK Coalition government's emergency budget of June 2010 showed that more than 70 percent of revenue raised from direct tax and benefit changes was to come from female taxpayers. Of the nearly £8 billion net revenue to be raised by the financial year 2014–15, nearly £6 billion was to come from women, and just over £2 billion from men. This did not take into account public spending cuts which disproportionately affect women because they make up more of the public sector workforce.[2]

A large part of this pay gap is accounted for by job segregation as 90 percent of women are employed in service occupations. Women are concentrated in what Kat Banyard, author of *The Equality Illusion* (2010) and founder of UKFeminista, calls the five Cs – cleaning, caring, clerical work, cashiering, and catering.[3] Even in well-paid managerial and professional jobs women will usually be crowded in the lower-status and lower-paid areas of work. The Equality and Human Rights Commission (EHRC) found that there were large pay gaps in the financial services sector, with women working full time earning 55 percent less than male full-time staff. When bonuses and performance-related pay are accounted for, the gap is even higher at 80 percent.[4] Two-thirds of low-paid workers are women, and an estimated 30,000 women still lose their jobs every year in the United Kingdom simply for being pregnant.[5]

Women's savings are worth 33 percent less than men's, according to research from the UK lobby group, the Fawcett Society. Fawcett's research uncovered a worrying picture: women's saving is much more likely to be disrupted than men's by life events such as childbirth or divorce.[6] According to the Fawcett Society, one in five single women pensioners risks being in poverty in retirement, and retired men on average have between £50 to £100 per week more private pension income than women of the same age. The numbers of women who are saving for retirement halve when they have a baby. The figure for men remains unchanged when they become new fathers.

Organizational cultures are shaped around these structural realities of low pay, marginalization and disposability which characterize most women's work, and these realities underpin the different symbolic values placed on male and female work. If women's work is devalued compared with men's (and we only have to look at the gender pay gap, the percentage of women in poverty, and the proliferation of women in low-paid work, plus the devaluation of unpaid housework, to justify this view), then the recurring refrain that women feel they have to work much harder than men to compete with them or be noticed or do well begins to make sense.

There has been a huge influx of women into employment over the past 30 years. Of the 8 million new jobs created in the European Union since 2000, 6 million of them have been filled by women. Yet there is impatience with the lack of representation at the top of organizations both public and private, which has changed very little over the past five years. (The numbers are well documented – only 5.2 percent of FTSE 100 executive directorships are held by women, rising to 12.5 percent including non-executive directors. For the FTSE 350 this is only 7.3 percent. A fifth of FTSE 100 companies still have exclusively male boards, and over half of FTSE 250 companies do.)[7]

We are living in a global age, and consumers and shareholders are increasingly aware of conditions in which global organizations operate. The progress and improvements in opportunities and living standards of Western women have not been matched in other parts of the world. Although women do two-thirds of the work in the world, and produce half the world's food, they earn 10 percent of the world's income and own 1 percent of the world's property.[8] There is no country in the world where women's wages are equal to those of men.[9]

However women are getting richer and more powerful, and this is giving them a voice that is being heard in societies all over the world for perhaps the first time. It is being heard too by governments and powerful businesses, which recognize that it is in everyone's interests for women to be brought into greater parity with men. As well as economic inequalities there are still cultural inequalities to be overcome.

WOMEN AND VIOLENCE

Writing about violence at the beginning of a book on workplace cultures may jar for some readers, but domestic violence, which has for so long been confined to the private realm, is now in many countries acknowledged as a social ill. It is also an issue for organizations, as its effects are felt in every workplace. It is a world phenomenon, and the charity Womankind describes violence against women and girls as a problem of pandemic proportions. At least one out of every three women around the world has been beaten, coerced into sex, or otherwise abused in her lifetime, with the abuser usually being someone known to her.[10] In the United Kingdom one in four women are victims of domestic violence, and many of these have suffered on a number of occasions. One incident of domestic violence is reported to police every minute, two women a week are killed by a current or former partner,[11] and 54 percent of UK rapes are committed by a woman's current or former partner.[12] Around 21 percent of girls and 11 percent of boys experience some form of child sexual abuse. Twenty-three percent of women and 3 percent of men experience sexual assault as an adult. Five percent of women and 0.4 percent of men experience rape.[13]

Many of the women and men involved in this violence will be

employees in an organization. Once a taboo topic, companies are now engaging with domestic abuse and violence. They need to. UK business is affected profoundly by this epidemic, which costs UK employers £1.9 billion annually.

The Corporate Alliance Against Domestic Violence[14] (CAADV) was founded in 2005 by Baroness Scotland in an effort to encourage UK employers to support employees who endure violence. In 2004 Dr Sylvia Walby, UNESCO Chair in Gender Research, published a report sponsored by the Department of Trade and Industry (DTI), which showed that domestic violence impacted the workplace in absenteeism, tardiness, and loss of productivity. At that time, the cost was calculated to over £3 billion annually. There was also a dynamic risk to employers, as one-third of all domestic violence homicides happen at workplace parking/garage facilities.

Although this is often seen as a private issue, the sheer numbers involved mean that organizations cannot escape the implications. Over 33 million people work in the United Kingdom, and one in four women and one in six men will experience domestic violence in their adult lifetimes. As 56 percent of abused women arrive late for work at least five times a month, 53 percent are absent from work at least three days a month and 75 percent of domestic abuse victims are targeted at work, it is clear that addressing this epidemic is everyone's business.

CAADV offers simple, low-cost high-impact tools that empower employers to address the needs of people who endure violence as well as those who perpetrate it. In 2010 CAADV took the strategic position to move from a loose alliance of over 160 employers to a formal charity and registered business, ensuring it was addressing the needs of business throughout the United Kingdom. Employers such as KPMG, the law firm Wragge and Co, the NHS Employers Organisation, and The Body Shop, are part of the alliance that reaches well over a million employees in the United Kingdom.

In February 2010 Melissa Morbeck was seconded from KPMG as Chief Executive of CAADV. A founding member of several organizations in the United States that deal with employer response to the issues relating to domestic violence and the impact to business, Melissa brought well over 18 years of public sector advocacy and leadership experience to CAADV. Melissa came on board to help build the foundations of the charity, and to reach out to new members and private sector employers who have an opportunity to create dynamic change in their organizations. Melissa says,

We are now a strong professional body which aims to provide

organizations with simple, low-cost high-impact information, training tools, help with policies and be a place where they can cross reference with others. There is a great deal of interest from companies wanting to engage with the issue and train their staff. It is an exciting and wonderful time for the organization that ultimately will save lives.

Melissa herself blows the stereotype of a 'battered wife' out of the water. A business graduate and a highly successful professional, she left her abusive husband 20 years ago and went into hiding for three years. She was hired by a unique advertising company, Hill Holliday, under an assumed name, and her new employer gave her the courage and professional integrity to seek a new life based on respect and free from violence. She worked with Hill Holliday for over 13 years, moving from strength to strength as a productive employee. She went on to become the first woman in the state of Connecticut to sue for divorce on the grounds of battering, then became a well-known media and advocacy figure in the United States. Hill Holliday recognized that something was wrong in her life, and had the courage to build her confidence and then work with her to help her realize she was not alone and could be supported. After several months, someone questioned her and she told them everything. It was the patience, care and respect Hill Holliday gave to Melissa that helped her have the courage to change her life. She says, 'there is a stereotype that victims of domestic violence are weak. We are so strong and often endure years of leading double lives.' It was the support, help and encouragement that she received from her employer that led her to get involved in making domestic violence a corporate issue, first in the United States, then when she came to live there, in England.

As Melissa explains, 'although there are a number of excellent specialist agencies and charities dealing with domestic violence, it is important for employers, which are unquestionably affected to play their part.'

Having the support and understanding of your employer transforms the situation for the person who is abused.

WOMEN AND THE SEXUALIZATION OF CULTURE

In her book *The Living Dolls: The Return of Sexism* (2010), Natasha Walter describes her disappointment and alarm at the growing culture of sexualization and sexual objectification of women and young girls. Like many earlier feminists she thought that educational equality would be followed by economic equality, and that sexual objectification would, if not disappear, become marginal in our culture. She was forced to reassess this position as she watched the 'hypersexual culture getting fiercer and stronger and co-opting the language of choice and liberation.'[15]

She sees the increasing sexualization of women in our culture at a time when women have more economic independence than ever as a backlash, a new sexism. The 1990s saw the emergence of the new man – the metrosexual, in touch with his feminine side, a regular gym attendee and a ready consumer of the new ranges of male beauty products. Another growth trend tapped into the darker side of male masculinity – the rise of the new lads' magazines, pornography by any other name but more deadly because they are accepted into the mainstream and sit as if by right on the middle shelves nestling between the music and motoring magazines for all to see.[16] Pornography is now the biggest industry in the world, worth an estimated $98 billion, largely owned and used by men.

Stripping for photographs has almost been legitimized, heralding a celebrity lifestyle as a glamour model. Lots of little girls aspire to this career, which now by necessity involves breast enhancement out of all proportion with most 'real' woman shapes. The pressure on young girls to perfect their bodies and look like real-life Barbies comes at a time when educationally they are overtaking boys. Parents and the present UK government have expressed grave concern at this sexualization of young girls.[17]

The growing sexualization of culture in the West cannot help but infiltrate the workplace. Arguably progressive organizations should be demonstrating their values and speaking up against this trend which devalues and objectifies women. The law acknowledges that the display of sexual imagery at work can create a hostile working environment for female employees, but it is deemed acceptable for women to endure a hostile environment when they leave the workplace. Most organizations have some kind of sexual harassment policy but a few organizations are breaking a taboo and engaging with this issue externally. Both British Telecom and Barclays Wealth have signed up to the Fawcett Charter – a public statement of principles that demonstrates employers' commitment to promoting an inclusive work environment by challenging the objectification of women at work (see Chapter 7).

There has been a huge increase in media images of women in sexualized poses, in advertisements, music videos, magazines and films. As stated above, many, many women and some men face the reality of everyday violence in their lives. Yet in the West we are witnessing an increase in images of sexual violence as a form of entertainment.

Charting the rise in film and media depictions of violence to women, writer Natasha Walter has argued that we are becoming immune to the horrors of misogynistic violence, 'The disturbing new trend of women as objects of sexual violence is tedious – and very dangerous – misogyny.'[18]

Another symptom of this sexualization of women is the depiction of prostitution as an acceptable way of living for women. Books and television (such as the book *The Intimate Diary of a London Call Girl* (2005) and its TV adaptation *Secret Diary of a Call Girl* (2006)) have portrayed prostitution as glamorous and lucrative. These tales show the top end of prostitution as being little different from dating, but getting paid for it. The reality for most prostitutes is very different. A 2002 study found that 74 percent of women involved in prostitution cited poverty, the need to pay household expenses and support their children, as a primary motivator for entering sex work.[19] A UK report cites studies which record the high level of violence experienced by women involved in prostitution. They found that 63 percent of women reported experience of client violence over their lifetime, 37 percent had experienced a client attack in the last six months, 47 percent of women in street prostitution reported being kicked or punched, 28 percent reported attempted rape, and 22 percent of the women in street prostitution in Leeds and Glasgow had been raped.[20]

WOMEN AND ORGANIZATIONAL CULTURE

What do all these social statistics on women have to do with organizational culture and change? Everything. This small smattering of largely UK data provides some of the social and cultural background in which our organizations operate. Women are poorer, less powerful, more abused and less valued in our society. I do not intend to be pessimistic or to position women as victims. I am being realistic, and drawing attention to some unpalatable aspects of gender relations which continue, despite the progress women have made in public life over the past 30 years. If anything, these facts attest to the strength of women and their ability to overcome hardships in their lives. These same women are entering organizations to compete on the same terms as men. Cultural meaning attached to gender follows men and women into organizations. It is not fixed or immutable, and will vary enormously from one region to another and from one country to another, but 'sex role spillover' has been identified as central to gender relations at work.[21] If women are not valued and respected in wider society, organizations have a steep hill to climb if they are to insist on value, respect and fairness within their own workplaces. Organizations committed to creating an inclusive culture for women need to acknowledge and understand the influence on behaviors of gender status in wider society.

Organizations that are aiming to be more inclusive of women need to make reference to historical inequalities, discrimination, or the wider social systems in which organizations are located. James Wolff, writing in 1977, recognized then that limits set by organizational life were insufficient to explain women's position in organizations. The constraints operating on women in organizations originate not merely in the organizations themselves but in society. From the perspective of organization theory, it is acknowledged that long hours and inflexible working time mitigate against the employment of women with 'two roles,' but no one discusses the basic question why women have two roles.[22]

In the same way, organizational work on stereotypes or unconscious bias has little meaning without taking into account wider social inequalities. Why is it that stereotypes of women are given as a reason for women's lack of progress in the workplace but stereotypes of men are not cited as barriers in the same way? If it is because the stereotypes of women are largely negative in the workplace, then rather than simply making people aware of them, we need to understand how they came to be negative in the first place. Negative stereotypes of women are the outcome of inequalities, not the cause.

The rise in importance to organizations of sustainability and corporate social responsibility is evidence of the fact that organizations now recognize that they are part of a wider social system and are influenced by external material conditions. What goes on in outside society is now organizations' business. Gender inequalities are part of that. The increasing role that organizations are taking in our lives – we are working longer hours and for more years – and the mindfulness of corporate social responsibility means that some of the manifestations of women's inequality in wider society are being recognized by some organizations. It is no coincidence that supporting women's charities at home and abroad and celebrating International Women's Day is now a common activity in companies that promote diversity.

However, feminism is not a word that is used in organizational life. The relentless media attacks on feminists and feminism in the 1970s and early 1980s resulted in a wholesale rejection of the word despite its aim being to end gender inequalities. I look at the language of equality in Chapter 3, and note that language and the naming of things is wrapped up in power. A straightforward definition of feminism is that it is a movement and a theory 'for the social, cultural, political and economic equality of men and women.' These are goals that today are hard to argue against.[23] However women have often been punished for identifying themselves as feminists, which means that even now when speaking on issues of inequality and wanting to be accepted and heard, it is necessary to start with 'I'm not a feminist but ....' This anathemization of feminism has influenced what it is possible to say on the issues of gender, and has hindered real debate both inside and outside organizations.

However, there is a new young feminist movement. And some of the young feminists are in the mainstream media.[24] Over the past two years (to the time of writing in spring 2011), there has been a growth in blogs and websites, activist women and men's groups, and these have really escalated in the past nine months.[25]

'The resurgence in grassroots feminism and feminist writing is a direct response to the lack of progress and indeed the increase in sexualisation and objectification of women in our culture,' says Kat Banyard, Director of UK Feminista[26] and author of *The Equality Illusion.*[27]

Organization's cultures, then, are shaped around the wider culture in which they operate. Chapter 2 will examine what we mean by organizational cultures, how we define them, and their relationship to gender.

2

BELONGING: MEANINGS OF ORGANIZATIONAL CULTURE

It was 1983 and I was in Tokyo working for a British investment bank. Women in the City (of London) were still a fairly rare commodity. I had joined the bank as a graduate in 1981, and attended a one-week introduction course with all the other graduates of accepting houses (as they were then). We were 16 women and 86 men, and the organizers called the event 'The Year of the Woman' as they had never been so many women entering the merchant banks before. Well, if there were not many women in the City of London, there were even fewer working in Tokyo. Japanese women could only work in a professional capacity in foreign (*gaijin*) banks. Even if they had a degree they could only find employment in Japanese companies as tea ladies.

I knew no one on my arrival, but was immediately immersed into the work life in the financial district of Tokyo. There was a lot of after-hours entertainment which I found a struggle, as no doubt did the Japanese businessmen who were my hosts or guests. After discussing business, I would ask them about their families and travel, but after a couple of hours it became hard work. If they had spent some time out of Japan it was easier, as we could find more common ground. I wasn't enjoying myself. There were few Westerners around because it was the summer, I disliked the crowds and was unusually homesick. One afternoon I was in a meeting with a pharmaceutical analyst at Yamaichi Securities when I felt the trickle of tears falling down my cheeks. I knew this kind of display of emotion was quite beyond the everyday experience of this young man, but once started I couldn't stop. He ignored me for as long as he could, then asked me if I was unwell, to which I replied no (I should have said yes). I continued crying. At this point he backed out of the room, and returned some minutes later with his superior, who had spent five years in New York. Neither Western women nor their tears were foreign to him, and he took me away and called one of my colleagues. I went to the English doctor that evening and described my feelings of disorientation to him. He told me, 'It is quite common for Westerners living here to feel like this. It's culture shock.' Hunt refers to culture shock as 'the experience of being a stranger in an alien and unfamiliar world.'[1]

Reflecting back on this experience I do not think my reaction was just to the Japanese culture. After all, I had traveled widely, often alone, and normally enjoyed experiencing other peoples' customs and ways of life. It was the combination of the strange land, language and the particular culture of Tokyo's financial district with which I felt so uncomfortable. I did not share their values, did not really know how to behave, certainly couldn't be myself, and I felt very alone.

Although this was also true to some extent about my work in the City, there at least I shared with my colleagues a language, an education, and had friends and family. I was familiar with many of the customs and rituals even when I felt excluded from them. My father had been a stockbroker, and I knew the streets and buildings, the language and customs. I didn't really feel I belonged, and as a woman I was still very much an outsider. Of course in those early years in the 1980s there were no equality policies in the City despite the law, and the working environment was sometimes very challenging for a young woman. At the end of the 1990s during my research on senior women managers in the City I came across the same themes of alienation that I had felt in Japan and in my own time in the City. Women talked of their efforts to fit in, the stress of being different but not wanting the difference noticed, not being able to discuss the anguish they felt at leaving their children for so long, the adaption of their communication and ways of being, of not being able to be themselves. Judi Marshall wrote a book on women managers in 1984, called *Women Managers: Travellers in a Male World*.[2] More than 25 years later, as I am writing this book – how far have we traveled?

WHAT IS 'ORGANIZATIONAL CULTURE'?

> Much of the challenge is not so much to change the legal framework but to change practice and where, necessary culture.[3]

As formal barriers to women's equality in the workplace, for example unequal pay, discrimination, and being barred from specific work, have been removed by law, they have been replaced by less tangible barriers. Consultants, academics and chief executives all point to 'culture' as the reason for women's lack of representation at the top of organizations.[4]

In the 2010 Gender Gap Report for which organizations from

16

30 countries took part, a masculine/patriarchal corporate culture was the second most cited barrier to women's progress. Certainly 'culture' is used to explain the failure of equality legislation and diversity programs, and the term 'male culture' or 'macho culture' is used to convey a working environment that may be difficult for women to work in. Many reports and books devoted to the subject describe the culture as 'male,' or in a more male dominated industry 'macho,' but there is little detail on that means or what organizational culture actually is. To be successful, leaders and change agents need to have a clear understanding of their culture, and be able to identify in what ways it is male or masculine, in what ways it may be excluding or marginalizing of women in the organization.

Many authors and commentators writing on women in management use the concept of organizational culture without any attempt to define what they mean by it,[5] or they import definitions from management writers without further discussion.[6] The meaning, definition and impact of organizational cultures on organizations has, however, been thoroughly discussed in the managerial literature, although none of the influential writers include any specific discussion of gender in their analyses.[7] They are of practical help in identifying which aspects of organizational life make up its culture.

Organizational researchers have been investigating the informal side of organizational life since the Hawthorne Studies first made their impact in the 1940s and 1950s.[8] These studies were the first to demonstrate that workgroups were social systems and that informal ways of working affected productivity. They provided the rationale for human relations to be actively managed. The studies signaled a shift from a modernist emphasis on bureaucracy and function to a more people-oriented view of organizations. The culture literature evolved concurrently with the equally large and still burgeoning literature on human resources management. Taken together they represent a refocusing on people in organizations as the means by which 'sustainable competitive advantage can be achieved.'[9] As the quote suggests, most studies of human behavior in organizations have been top-down, with the agenda derived from senior managers for whom problems existed on the shop floor. The development of the culture concept that has followed has also been a management-led phenomenon.

The rise of the multinational company fueled an interest in national differences of company cultures. Hofstede's (1980) classic book *Culture's Consequences* was one of the first to draw attention to these differences in national structures and behaviors. Anxiety about the future of Western-dominated capitalism turned management writers' attention to the phenomenal success of the Japanese corporation and the reasons behind it, which they attributed to strong company cultures. There were descriptions of employees in uniforms, chanting corporate songs and swearing their allegiance to the company. Often without regard to the particular history, geography and economy of the country, management writers began to promote the theory that a strong corporate culture was a prerequisite to success or 'excellence' in any company.[10] These observations have been enormously influential in management despite criticisms of this managerial approach.

Organizational culture was in the early stages discussed as an integrated whole, whereas it is now more widely recognized that organizations may be made up of many cultures, divisional, professional, functional, employee, management, and hierarchical.[11] Although the tone of a company organizational culture is usually set by leadership, individual departments develop their own local cultures, For example the marketing department of an organization may have a very different culture from the finance department, and senior management culture will be very different from junior management culture. Identifying the different subcultures in an organization is an important part of any analysis of gender and diversity.

In some traditional management texts culture is depicted as a passive field waiting for managers to act on it. This makes it difficult to explore the dynamic qualities of cultural change and the tensions these produce. Cultural barriers to women are very much more fluid and flexible than the image of the glass ceiling portrays. Seeing culture as a process is important as it allows us to see that people are involved in the making of culture.

> While people are working they are not just producing goods and services, pay packets and careers, they are also producing culture.[12]

There is a source of confusion that surrounds the terms used. 'Corporate culture' and 'organizational culture' are often used interchangeably, but whereas corporate culture usually pertains to the management-led company values and attitudes imposed on employees in myriad ways like mission statements and target goals and is always tied to business needs, organizational culture is a much wider concept, embracing all aspects of organizational life, including corporate culture. When trying to effect culture change with regard to diversity, the wider approach of organizational culture is required.

There were early criticisms of writers who defined culture as residing in the minds of people, in their values and attitudes, thus neglecting behavior and practice. More commonly now management writers include both beliefs and behaviors. Perhaps the most influential writer on organizational culture, Edgar Schein, suggests that culture should be studied on three levels:[13]

- the level of its artifacts, which may take the form of stories or rites and rituals
- the level of beliefs, values, and attitudes
- the basic assumptions.

The artifacts, which include architecture as well as language, stories, rituals, and so on, are easy to observe but harder to decipher. Espoused beliefs and values may only reflect aspirations, so Schein says that it is the level of basic assumptions that is the essence of the culture. More recently some organizations have started to address diversity and equality at this unconscious level, enabling them to see prejudice and bias as outcomes of people's unconscious thought processes.[14]

CULTURE AS EXCLUSIONARY

Most of the organizational culture literature refers to the inclusionary *nature* of culture, yet its *function* is also exclusionary. Boundary characteristics have been applied to class cultures and national cultures but less with regard to organizational cultures. Boundaries have been of great importance in social anthropology, separating the sacred from the profane[15] or the clean from the polluted.[16] In society, rituals are often used to reinforce the separation of insiders and outsiders. This also happens in organizations. Grint says that:

> What is important is the way culture is constructed as a boundary device to mark off insiders from outsiders; the privileged from the unprivileged; men from women; and 'us' from 'them.' Culture in this sense is largely if not mainly about distinguishing one group from another on the basis of where the boundary lies, culture is an exclusionary mechanism as well as an inclusive one.[17]

Grint notes the usefulness of this boundary approach to culture in discussing subcultures of organizations, where boundary devices are constructed to keep the 'other' out, and through this exclusionary practice to formulate the identity of those within. How do we know that the marketing department is different from the finance department? We can differentiate them on the basis of the actual work that is done, but we are more likely to do so on a broader set of attributes. 'I hate walking into finance. They all make me feel so uncomfortable.' This statement was not made on account of a difference in the type of work being done. The speaker had crossed a boundary, and knew that in some intangible way she did not belong.

Seeing cultures as drawing boundaries is extremely useful in helping to conceptualize culture as an active exclusionary concept. This approach emphasizes the way a group keeps out others, which is in contrast to the current trend for focusing on the individual's unconscious bias. Even the early corporate culture writers noted the exclusionary aspects of culture, although they did not identify them specifically:

> The exclusion of women and minorities from the rich and supportive life of an organization's culture begins the day they walk in the door. Most don't even know it's happening to them.[18]

Boundaries become more important the more similar the groups are. Think of football teams and their fans. From an outsider's point of view there is not that much difference between them, but from the fans' view the other team might as well come from Mars. They identify all their good parts with their team, and split off all their bad parts into the rival team. In reality both teams are made up of good and bad. Within an organization, emphasizing women's difference from men is one way of keeping the boundaries clear.

All cultures include some members while excluding others. Putting new company recruits through an induction process is both a conscious and unconscious acknowledgement of this. Women managers may be included in some aspects of an organization's culture and excluded from others at the same time. It is the job of the consultant/leadership to identify when this exclusion occurs and why. Divisional cultures and hierarchical cultures may also draw boundaries to exclude others within organizations. Analyzing the exclusionary aspect of organizational culture at all levels enables us to see where it is creating active resistance to women's equality.

One of the reasons for academic interest in the 'glass ceiling' is that it is an interesting insight into the male interests at work, because there is little in capital/business's interests to keep women below this ceiling. Even now, 35 years on from the introduction of equality legislation, speaking of men's resistance is pretty much taboo – and I am speaking here as a consultant. Blaming a hostile culture has become acceptable and is now quite common, but trying to talk about the practice of men's resistance to equality is not so popular. Cynthia Cockburn[19] was one of the first writers to identify the importance of cultural practices and resistance to equality programmes in organizations, and link these directly with the behavior of men. Many of the discursive and cultural practices discussed in the following chapters amount to men's resistance.

THE PSYCHODYNAMIC APPROACH

Organizational and management theorists have adopted the concept of culture to explain the more intangible aspects of organizational life. A psychodynamic approach to organizational culture puts more focus on why cultures develop and what happens when they change.[20]

Individuals form groups, and cultures develop within groups and give them their identity. Some of these developments are conscious and some are unconscious.

Let's take the experience of arriving for a week's residential course along with 11 other delegates, all unknown to each other. Within a very short period of time the group will take on particular characteristics. These of course will depend on the personalities and characteristics, including gender, of the participants. Rituals like gathering in a certain place for tea, or having an evening drink, together with in-jokes, will bind the group, with the dominant characters leading the process. We do this to reduce the anxiety of being in a group and try to create conditions in which we feel most comfortable. On holiday people from the same country and often class will immediately be drawn together, no longer so estranged from their unfamiliar surroundings.

The central premise of a psychodynamic approach to culture is that 'members of a group, organization, or society will produce forms of behavior that will be psychologically advantageous to them under the conditions imposed by the environment.'[21]

In any one situation there will be a dominant culture, which is developed around the interests of the dominant group. The dominant group both in society and in many organizations is male. They have more access to more resources than women do in order to perpetuate this culture. This culture can be challenged by other non-dominant groups, but for radical change to occur it needs to be in the interests of the dominant group. We will see in the following chapters how this results in tortuous efforts by change agents to get buy-in from leadership to make the culture more inclusive.

A psychodynamic approach to culture sees group membership as psychologically essential but also a great source of discomfort when it is challenged or changed. The desire to belong and be accepted is a strong urge in all human beings. Such is the strong identification with a group that a slight to the group can affect individual group members personally. Many BP employees, following the Gulf of Mexico oil disaster, felt devastated at the fall from grace and tarnished image of their firm, and suffered this as a personal loss. In other situations employees may well feel 'sold out' or betrayed when they are told about a merger or takeover with another company, or abandoned at the departure of a charismatic leader. A psychodynamic approach does not see organizations as centers of rationality as espoused by Max Weber, but often as activities driven by emotion and the unconscious. Groups form cultures in order to stave off anxiety, to reduce uncertainty, to reduce conflict and to promote ease of communication.

> In developing a culture the members of an organization develop a structure of meaning. Any change is liable to undermine the very structure of meaning on which it has come to rely for its sense of continuity consistency and confirmation.[22]

A psychodynamic approach to organizational culture is particularly useful when addressing culture change. It argues that attention must be paid to the beneath the surface feelings. Schein says that challenging basic assumptions will release anxiety and defensiveness. Culture can provide members with a basic sense of identity and defines the values that provide self-esteem.

> Cultures tell members who they are, how to behave towards one another, and how to feel good about themselves. Recognizing these critical functions makes us aware why changing culture is so anxiety provoking.[23]

Change brings with it anxiety, then. It is to fend off this anxiety that change might be actively resisted. The Catalyst Research work on *Engaging Men in Gender Initiatives* showed that 74 percent of male interviewees identified fear as a barrier to men's support of gender equality – fear of loss of status, fear of making mistakes and fear of other men's disapproval.[24]

Anxiety and resistance can best be seen as people clinging to existing institutions because changes threaten existing social defenses against deep and intense anxieties.[25]

A board of 12 men might, in principle, believe that having several women around the table would enhance their discussions and benefit the business. However, on a deeper level they might also have fears of their in-group being broken, of being exposed as lacking, their incompetence exposed, or their masculinity questioned. Some of these unconscious fears are socially and culturally informed; others are more personal, again, rooted in early infancy experiences; but both drive behaviors. An in-depth psychodynamic approach can reveal the individual resistance of some men even when intellectually they may be committed to the principle of equality.

This brief theoretical overview of organizational culture begins to explain how hard it is to change cultures, but what we also need is a wider social theory of power to explain why women should be considered the outside group, and for further clarification of the ways in which the dominant (male) group draw on resources to mark off their prized areas in the workplace and beyond. Only then will we be able to understand how to effect real change.

POWER

Today we talk of 'inclusive culture' and acknowledge that there are zones of exclusion but we rarely discuss exactly what it is that people want to be included in, or what women and minorities are being excluded from. The answer is power and privilege. There are many theories and definitions of power which may apply to organizational life, the best known being that of Max Weber who described power as 'The probability that an actor within a social relationship will be in a position to carry out his own will despite resistance, regardless of the basis on which this probability rests.[26]

For Weber and organizational theorists after him, power was located in the position – whoever had the job, held the power. ' Men have power in the organization and women do not because they do not have access to the same opportunities for power and efficacy through activities and alliances.'[27] This depiction by Kanter of men and women in an industrial company in the United States has stood the test of time in its description of both formal and informal power relations. However, for Kanter women's exclusion was based on their difference from the dominant group, not their being women. She saw male domination as being irrational – the job makes the person and power wipes out sex. But she failed to see the continuing process of exclusion as a material practice, and also failed to tie in the concept of power within the organization to the power that men hold in relation to women outside the organization.

So we need a concept of male power in wider society that ties in to explain the cultural exclusionary practices at work. Organizational problems cannot adequately be grasped without an appreciation of wider gender relations. Both within and outside organizations more men have more power in terms of access to resources and the ability to control these resources than do women. This is not to neglect the very real material differences in both men's and women's lives. Women managers may indeed have more in common with male managers than with women lower down the organization, but looking at the social facts of women's lives around the world today, there is enough evidence to suppose a system of male order, or patriarchy, sometimes called 'gender regime,' which is a system of social structures and practices in which men may dominate, oppress and exploit women.[28]

Power is often synonymous with money and status. Where there is a lot of money and high status there will be few women. Power is highly prized and protected. We need to identify the cultural practices that act to exclude outsiders (including women) from the elite areas in organizations. 'Organisations whether we are talking about banks and businesses, armies universities, hospitals or city councils, are significant concentrations of power .... We should not expect men to relinquish their privileged position voluntarily.[29]

Hegemony is a useful concept to explain women's participation in practices that may not be in their interests. When we talk of a dominant group imposing a culture on outsiders, it is not necessarily a coercive regime. Hegemony designates a process whereby cultural authority is negotiated and contested – the result being that the dominant ideologies that come into being are accepted as 'normal' and common-sense by the non-dominant group. One of the key aspects of hegemony is that, once established, cultural authority can be perpetuated through institutional means like the media, law, and religion, yet the dominant group will always make concessions to other groups up to a point.[30]

Turning to gender relations, we might ask why during the struggle for the vote many women argued against it. How was it that Chinese women had their daughters feet bound, with all the pain and crippling effects that entailed? Why do some Muslim women participate in the genital mutilation of their young daughters? Why do women blame prostitutes for prostitution rather than the men that use them? How can it be that young women today fail to recognize that their freedom has been won through the struggles and efforts of feminists? Moreover, many young women denounce this feminism as being irrelevant to their lives. They are not forced to accept this belief for, as Dorothy Smith says, 'At the interpersonal level it is not a conspiracy among men that they impose on women it is a complementary social process between women and men. Women are complicit in the social practices of their silence.'[31]

GENDERED CULTURE

There are common themes (in male cultures) one of which is that ... men continue to underrate and undervalue women in general.[32]

Although feminist writers broke the myth that organizations and jobs were gender-neutral many years ago, this is how they are still largely perceived by those who work in and around them. In her ground-breaking 1990 article 'Hierarchies, jobs and bodies,' Joan Acker depicted organizations as imbued with masculinity.[33] The fact that organizations are gendered is now being recognized by those active in diversity and change, and diversity professionals are now looking more specifically at the ways in which the maleness of the workplace makes it hard for women to progress. Calling the culture 'male' does not adequately convey the ways in which cultures that serve the interests of men act to exclude women.

Since 1990 there has been a prolific output of research on gender and organization[34] (see the journal *Gender, Work & Organization*). Many feminist academics have noted the existence of cultural barriers in their analyses of specific organizations.[35] Other writers have concentrated their efforts on decoding organizational culture for its 'genderness' and have explored different approaches of analyzing gendered cultures.[36]

Linda McDowell's *Capital Culture* (1997) provides rich data on gender at work in the City, seeing work as an embodied performance and the playing out of masculinities and femininities. This approach will be explored further in Chapter 4 on style.

Drawing on the symbolic order of gender,[37] Gherardi develops a theory that gender can only be defined 'by default' since what we attribute to one gender is implicitly denied by the other gender. She says that the meaning of gender is constantly deferred and negoti-ated in discourse while we simultaneously acknowledge the deep symbolic order of gender. Thus she sees the way we 'do gender' at work as helping to diminish or increase the inequality of the sexes. 'We use ceremonial work to recognize the difference of gender and remedial work socially to construct the "fairness" of gender relationships.'[38] She argues that gender is located at the level of inter-actional and institutional behavior (the gender we do), and also at the level of deep and trans-psychic symbolic structures (the gender we think). She argues that women entering the male workplace feel they must be discreet, and 'take their place' in segregated jobs, so they collaborate with men to render the female presence feminine, discreet and almost invisible. She calls this 'remedial work' because the symbolic order has been broken.

Her examples of remedial work are immediately recognizable: women's use of apologies before speaking, hesitant speech and allowing themselves to be interrupted, working harder and not drawing attention to themselves. The current vogue is to see these traits as innately feminine rather than developing out of structural positions of inferiority and superiority. They show the subtlety of cultures and the ways in which both men and women interact in accordance with them. While I acknowledge the importance of the private/public order as a problematic divide for women entering the workplace, I think that it is also the hierarchical gender order of dominant/subordinate that is particularly challenged when women enter management and professions. This is what creates the cultural paradox of female leadership and makes it so prob-lematic. The power of both the external gender order and the intra-psyche gender order explains women's reticence in claiming their place in the public world and men's resistance to their doing so.

Some writers have attempted to go beyond calling the culture male and try to identify different types of cultures. All the cultures in Maddock and Parkin's six-point typology[39] are readily identifi-able to all who have worked in organizations – the gender blind, the gentleman's club, the barrack yard, the locker room, the femi-nist pretenders and the smart macho. Collinson and Hearn also identified five different masculinities and linked them to different management styles: authoritarianism, paternalism, entrepreneur-ialism, informalism, and careerism.[40] The theme running through all these masculinities is the importance of the workplace to men's identities.

In-depth analyses and descriptions of male cultures provide profes-sionals with much material to identify with, investigate further and in practice target for intervention. Whatever the approach, there is consensus that cultures are gendered, and that although male cultures vary enormously from organization to organization, the recurring theme is the devaluation of women and women's skills.

It is important to tie in the cultural obstacles women face in organizations with the wider social devaluation and material situation of women.[41] Such a psychosocial approach to culture emphasizes the following characteristics:

- Members of a group or organization produce forms of behavior that will be psychologically advantageous to them under the conditions imposed by the environment.
- Organizations are open systems and will be affected by societal dynamics.
- Every culture is gendered.
- Every culture and subculture is unique.
- Cultures are developed to exclude and to protect the interests of the dominant group.
- Culture is a dynamic process and thus open to change.
- It is influenced by conscious and unconscious processes.[42]

A WORKING DEFINITION OF ORGANIZATIONAL CULTURE

Having established some of the purposes and characteristics of an organizational culture, we need a more detailed working definition for the purposes of analyzing cultures and in order to implement culture change.

> Little work has been put into identifying the values and attitudes, accepted codes and patterns of behavior at various levels of management within organizations and industries. If change is to occur, the cultural dimensions that prevent women from reaching the top need to be identified.[43]

Given that organizational culture is a concept borrowed from anthropology and applied by management writers, organizational theorists, sociologists, geographers and psychoanalysts, there are literally thousands of definitions. However none of these definitions specifically include gender. Andrew Brown gives a very comprehensive study of organizational culture saying that how we choose to define culture has implications for how we attempt to examine and study it. His definition is:

27

Organizational culture refers to the pattern of beliefs, values and learned ways of coping with experience that have developed during the course of an organization's history and which tend to be manifested in its material arrangements and in the behaviors of its members.[44]

The neglect of gender in most of the mainstream organizational culture material means that a wider net must be cast than has been to date in the culture field. Gender issues like sexual harassment, the same/difference debate, the work/life issue, and old boy networks all fall into the ambit of culture. Instead of seeing each issue as a discrete area outside of culture that can be addressed on its own, each issue can instead be seen to be one constituent of organizational culture.

Drawing on some of the management literature,[45] my definition of organizational culture for the purposes of gender analysis is the following:

the attitudes, values, beliefs and patterns of behavior of organizational members. It is expressed in the management style, work ideologies (what is and isn't work), language and communication, physical artifacts, informal socializing and temporal structuring of work, and in the gender awareness and expression of sexuality.

This working definition of gendered organizational culture has informed a model for implementing a culture gender audit so that organizations can map out for themselves the constituents they need to look at in their quest for an inclusive culture.

The boundaries of each constituent are not as definitive as set out in the model on page 29. For example, sexualized language may be part of language or part of sexuality, meetings can be a part of communication or management style, sexual entertainment may be part of sexuality or informal socializing, but keeping the constituents as conceptually distinct as possible makes for a clearer audit process. All these constituents of organizational culture have a direct or indirect impact on gender relations. By taking each constituent separately and analyzing each with reference to a specific division in an organization, it becomes possible to reveal the more subtle cultural barriers that may exist for women managers. In this book I incorporate the data on language and communication in Chapter 4 on style matters and in Chapter 8 on sex in the office.

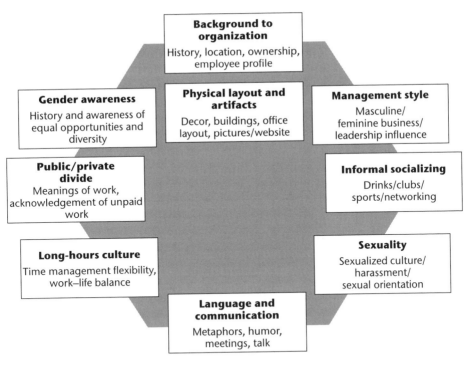

Figure 2.1 A model of gendered organizational culture

© Rutherford Associates 2011

THE INFLUENCE OF HISTORY, OWNERSHIP, AND ARCHITECTURE

In the same way that personal change requires an understanding of the self, culture change requires an understanding of the culture, and by analyzing these constituents one by one a holistic picture can be obtained. Before I go on to analyze some of these constituents and their impact on gender in more detail in the following chapters, there are two constituents, the aspects of which are beyond the scope of this book to explore in detail. The first is the starting point for any cultural audit – the organization's history and geography – its ownership and employee profile. These historical facts inform the culture of an organization from the start and can remain a strong influence even after many years.

Hofstede's work gives particular attention to the importance of nationality to an organization's culture.[46] This is particularly pertinent for global companies rolling out initiatives in different

29

countries. As any global diversity head knows, programmes need to be adapted to the particular region in which they are implemented, taking account of cultural and religious differences. The history of women's liberation and their role in public life is different in different cultures. There are a number of different aspects to pay attention to:

- the labor market
- the role of the state in society
- the recent history of women's employment
- the religious and cultural values around women.

An organization's culture is also heavily influenced by its past and its environment. Schein showed that a founder of a company has the opportunity to build in their own values and attitudes.[47] If the company is successful these will remain until they are challenged by a change in the environmental situation or the leadership. Subsequent leaders then have their own opportunity to influence the culture. Littlewoods, a mail order company was founded by the late Sir John Moores, who was a strong advocate of equality, with the result that Littlewoods was at the forefront of equality for many years. The Cadbury family were Quakers, and this influenced the culture, which emphasized social responsibility, throughout their company's history.

Every organization is located within an industry which itself has its own culture, and this will also have a bearing. A relatively new industry like marketing will not be imbued with a long history of male-only practices and traditions as is the case of older industries like engineering or banking. I found that the culture of one of the companies in which I carried out my PhD research, Airco (a pseudonym), was heavily influenced by the location of the airline offices, which were at an airport, and so employees were constantly reminded of their business. They were also isolated from any different types of businesses and activities, as everyone around them worked in the airline industry. This made work life more intense and urgent. The culture of, Airco was also influenced by the fact that it had developed out of the RAF and still carried military overtones, obviously masculine. Its military beginnings had left traces of military life, such the importance of rank and status. It had been state-owned and then privatized, and was still very bureaucratic. It was also heavily unionized, which again informed aspects of the management style and culture, particularly in the Cargo division, which had a history of difficult employment relations.

The organization that was the subject of my second case study, Investco, was founded 150 years ago and had been part of an elite group of 11 accepting houses – where discount bills from the Bank of England could be accepted. Traditionally a place of work for gentlemen of a certain class, this culture lingered despite the arrival of a more global, fast-moving, and highly educated set of employees. However, many of the senior employees came from private schools and a privileged background. Investco was still family-owned and harbored paternalistic leanings towards its workforce. Women had arrived very recently as graduates and professionals. It is not hard to see how these constituents had an indirect gendered impact. The traditional feel of the bank was formal and distinctly masculine in comparison with Airco, which had employed many women for a long time and so had never been an entirely male domain.

BUILDINGS AND ARTIFACTS

Buildings, artifacts, and the physical layout of work are key expressions of an organization's culture, and can provide the first clues to an outsider about the values of a business.[48] We often ignore the physicality of a workplace as being nothing to do with gender yet we readily describe a room as 'masculine' or 'feminine'. Physical surroundings are important to how we work.

In Airco, Cabin Services was housed in a modern glass building known as the C Centre along with Flight Operations, the pilots' division. The C Centre was the flagship building of the airline, and looked like an updated version of the Pompidou Centre in Paris, with bright blue steel tubular designs and lots of blue glass. Walking into the huge atrium, with its sleek modern café opposite the reception area, felt more like entering a smart hotel, particularly with the continual flow of cabin crew wheeling their luggage in and out. Inside the facilities were excellent, with computer terminals dotted around so that cabin crew and pilots could check their flight schedules. Many buildings are designed to offer this feelgood factor as you walk in to work.

The importance of buildings to culture in Airco's case was illustrated by the fact that the cultural change program in the Cargo division was focused around its new state-of-the-art cargo center – the modern building symbolizing modern values and an end to old practices. Airco had recently moved many of its staff to a new development, a mile up the road from the airport. It gave the impression of being in an enclosed and airy shopping mall, the cobbled streets providing a feel of a comfortable country market town. The center provided dry cleaners, a gym, and shops. The message was clear – work hard for us and we will look after you. Many organizations today require their employees to work very long hours, leaving little time for leisure or basic chores like shopping and cleaning (see Chapter 5 on the public/private divide). By providing facilities for all their domestic needs, companies reduce the time staff need to spend on chores at home.

Investco was set in more opulent surroundings, a series of smart buildings in the City of London which lent a traditional and wealthy feel to the organization's culture. Two uniformed men greeted you in the reception area. 'Restrained grandeur' was the way I would describe the working environment. There were huge mahogany dining tables in the offices of corporate finance, the elite section of the bank, whereas the meeting rooms for the broking department were much smaller with just a coffee table. Portraits of family members hung on the walls and there was little in the way of color. The interior décor implied power, money, and men. The head office lay in the heart of the City and was of classic architecture, with a plain, marbled reception area. The meeting rooms got larger and smarter the higher up the building you went – the seventh floor was corporate finance, smart mahogany table, lovely views, and tea brought in porcelain cups. Many of the big City institutions are now based in Canary Wharf – its iconic skyline a symbol of the wealth and power contained in the skyscraper glass buildings, no longer held back by family holdings or even traditional banking functions, the opportunities for profit endless – unbridled greed for profit encased in rocket-shaped buildings – the sky was indeed the limit until the credit crisis revealed the vulnerability within.

All kinds of physical conditions can be analyzed here, from the layout of the offices, to whether secretaries sit as gatekeepers to the important men in their private offices, to the car parking facilities and safety procedures for women working at night. One highly successful property company has a very understated head office, which looks more like a garage than a building. This symbolizes a lean business focused on the bottom line with restraint on costs. Clients often walk straight past the building but once in, know where they are, as they are greeted not by a garage mechanic but by an attractive female receptionist. All these physical expressions of culture will be saying something about gender.

One of the first things I do as a consultant going in to an organization for the first time is browse its website for clues to its values and culture. You can learn a lot. It is immediately clear whether it is people-oriented or not, whether it is proud of its diversity or hiding the fact there are too few women and minorities at senior levels. The tone of its commitment comes through, and the physical positioning of information is also an indicator – how many pages you have to go through before reaching information on its values and diversity in particular.

Companies spend huge amounts of money on the development of their image – erecting and promoting corporate logos, mottoes and websites. Organizations, particularly global ones, have in recent years realized the importance of presenting a diverse image to the public. They may highlight their values and mission statements – and some of these may include diversity. A first glance at these symbols will to some extent reveal the organization's commitment to gender equality as well as how established it is. Is it among the key business principles, as, for instance, at global oil company Shell? Images, pictures and increasingly personal stories may portray women and minorities extolling the virtues of working for X and the opportunities that are on offer to them. The real evidence, though, will be how many women are on the drop-down list of partners/directors.

The above constituents provide the more material aspects that both inform an organization's culture and express it. The next six chapters will be devoted to six constituents of culture that I consider to be the most relevant for their revelation of an organization's attitude to women in the workplace.

3

THE GENDER AGENDA

PART 1: EQUAL OPPORTUNITIES, DIVERSITY, INCLUSION – WHAT'S IN A WORD?

INTRODUCTION

When I began studying gender and organizations in 1991, equal opportunities was the dominant discourse when addressing inequalities in the workplace. Now in the United States and the United Kingdom private-sector companies predominantly refer to equality issues through the discourse of diversity, or diversity and inclusion. In the United Kingdom, the public sector has held on to the notion of equality, and this is still the dominant concept used in Europe. Although there are some differences in meaning, these are not universally understood, and the word 'diversity' (unlike equal opportunities) has literally hundreds of definitions. It is important to pay attention to the language, as the naming of something is itself a political activity. It is no accident that certain words gain the status of knowledge over others for language and power interact.[1] Sinclair notes that words like diversity resist one set of meanings and take on others that better suit elite interests: 'The point about terminology and language reveals a deeper point about power and who appropriates language.'[2] There is no doubt that business has embraced diversity in a way that it did not equal opportunities.

When people ask what I do at social gatherings, and when I was a director of a small bank and I replied 'diversity consultant,' 90 percent (unless they worked for a US investment bank or a large blue chip) would look blankly at me. As people are usually asking out of politeness and not interest, I shoot back a speedy reply, 'It's is the new equal opportunities,' which stretches the truth, but not by that much. At that point they are either very interested or look alarmed or bored – but the point is that they know roughly what area of work I am in. And some may respond with, 'Women have got everything now, it's boys who are doing worse at school,' or 'We've had a woman prime minister,' or another suggestions that there is no further need for equal opportunities and my work is not needed. In the same vein when I ask participants attending their first ever diversity training workshop whether they know what it is, I'll usually get the same blank look. If I push, they may reply that it is something to do with political correctness.

How useful is a term that does not have a common definition or understanding among the general population? Diversity is itself a contested concept, and there are signs that its usefulness in addressing inequality issues is being challenged.[3] Part of the problem, I suggest, is that the concept itself emerged out of frustration with the limits of equal opportunities, and had neither a consensus definition, nor conviction of particular outcomes. Diversity, as we shall see, is defined as being about acknowledging and valuing difference, and has no inherent reference to increasing representation of particular groups.

Equal opportunities emerged in a climate of liberalism in the 1970s driven by employee pressure, feminist and left-wing politics and as a condition of joining the European Economic Community (the EEC, via the Treaty of Rome), which led to UK legislation covering discrimination on the grounds of sex (Sex Discrimination Act 1975) and race (Race Relations Act 1976) and making unequal pay illegal (Equal Pay Act 1970). (These have now all been replaced by the Equality Act 2010.)

The Equal Pay Act 1970, which provided for equal pay for men and women working in the same jobs, came into force on 29 December 1975. It was recognized that the differences in pay between men and women could not be corrected overnight, and a period of five years was set to allow employers and unions to bring women's rates of pay into line with those of men. Although the gap in pay has narrowed considerably over the past 35 years, it remains at 12–17 percent.

The principal reasons for persistence of the gap are the unequal impact of women's family responsibilities, the vertical segregation of men and women, such that women tend to occupy the lower-status jobs in a firm's hierarchy, including part-time employment, and limitations by a form of 'glass ceiling' or horizontal segregation, which places women in particular lower-paid occupations.[4]

The neglect of part-time workers (later rectified by an EEC directive) and the persistence of occupational segregation (which the Equal Pay amendment of 1984 tried to ameliorate), combined with the inability to bring class actions, also tempered the impact of the equality legislation. The European Union has been a major influence on the development of equality law in the face of the reluctance of the United Kingdom to extend rights beyond the minimum or to redress any anomalies of the original law (for example extending employment protection rights to part-time workers in 1995 and extending maternity provisions to all pregnant women). In addition to the legislation mentioned above, there was further legislation relating to other types of discrimination – the Disability Discrimination Act 1995, Employment Equality (religion and belief) Regulations 2003, Equality Employment (sexual orientation) Regulations 2003 and Employment Equality (age) Regulations 2006. All of these Acts have now been replaced by one Act, the Equality Act which came into force in October 2010.[5]

LIMITS TO EQUAL OPPORTUNITIES

The limits to the approach of treating women the same as men soon became apparent. The fact that men and women were segregated into different jobs meant that there were few direct comparisons, so the Equal Pay Act was amended in 1983 in order to comply with Article 119 of the Treaty of Rome. The Directive on Equal Pay and Equal Treatment was introduced to provide for claims to equal pay for work of equal value. This has proved to be an invaluable (if lengthy and complex) route for women, challenging as it does the notion that skills and value can be measured objectively.

In the United Kingdom in 2010, female council workers from Birmingham won their equal pay case based on work of equal value. During the seven-week hearing the tribunal heard how a man doing the same pay-graded job as a woman could earn four times more than she did. Under a bonus scheme male refuse collection staff sometimes received up to 160 percent of their basic pay. In one year a refuse collector took home £51,000 while women on the same pay grade received less than £12,000.[6]

However the deeply entrenched gender segregation, both horizontal (in different parts of an organization, in different industries) and vertical, whereby women are crowded into the lower-paid end of an organization, cannot ever be adequately tackled by legal measures.

By the end of the 1980s there was despondency as the progress of women and minorities had not improved as much as had been hoped. There were several reasons for this. Most importantly, apart from the public sector and some of the largest employers of women like the retailers, the majority of UK companies failed to introduce equal opportunities at all. In 1988 a British Institute of Management survey of 350 member organizations showed that although about half were committed to the concept of equal opportunities, less than one-third were taking active steps to ensure they were put into practice.[7]

Despite efforts from lobby groups like Opportunity Now (a membership organization for employers who are committed to creating an inclusive workplace for women) emphasizing the business case for equal opportunities, organizations did not see its relevance to business, and its association with the left wing and feminism, combined with legal obligations, resulted in some hostility to the concept. Organizations with large numbers of female employees that did implement initiatives often marginalized them, and there was ongoing resistance and resentment to their implementation. In her book *In The Way of Women* (1991), Cynthia Cockburn demonstrates clearly the resistance by men to equal opportunities programs through a myriad of cultural practices.

The neglect by the majority of UK companies to take equal opportunities seriously was also because the law lacked serious sanctions – class actions, which allow for a group of workers to bring about a lawsuit, were not permitted, and the payout for discrimination cases was capped at £11,000 until 1994. Gaining legal redress for a complainant was costly unless sponsored by the Equal Opportunities Commission (EOC) or a trade union, and the ensuing stress of taking on a sex discrimination or equal pay claim meant that only the most determined attempted it.

It was, though, the more fundamental limits to the philosophy of equal opportunities that caused the frustration of further progress. Equality legislation was premised on the liberal ideology of fairness, and treated discrimination against women in organizations as an aberration of rationality. The ethos of equal opportunities was to remove formal barriers, with the intent that people should be recruited, selected, and promoted purely on merit.

Trying to create conditions for women to compete with men 'on a level playing field' assumed that the structure of work and organizations themselves are in some way neutral, unaffected by gender, and need not be questioned. In fact, this was merely 'giving women an equal chance under the men's rules.'[8] The emphasis on culture change in the diversity discourse now acknowledges the gendered nature of organizations.

Research into the gendered nature of work reveals how masculine even the very notion of work is, and that the whole working day is suited around the lives of men,[9] whose domestic lives are taken care of for them by women and whose time is made available to them by women. Research on women managers reveals the stresses that women suffer adapting to a male working pattern, and frequently carrying the dual roles of work and family.[10]

The shift from formal barriers to informal barriers which still prevent women from reaching senior levels of organizations means that 20 years on much more attention is now given to the role of culture in the success or not of equality and diversity policies.

RECOGNITION OF DIFFERENCE

There was some recognition of women's difference to men, acknowledged by the inclusion of indirect discrimination in the Sex Discrimination Act 1975 (now Equality Act 2010). This refers to situations where a condition of work is applied to all, but in practice a larger proportion of one sex would find it hard to comply. Early examples were physical requirements, but later considerations like insistence on full-time work were deemed to discriminate against women, who were more likely to be carers. So, despite the emphasis on equality of treatment and sameness, legislation aimed at equalizing men and women recognized that in some situations treating men and women as the same would result in unfairness.

Women's biological difference was also recognized in tandem with the equal treatment discourses through state maternity provisions and the introduction of family-friendly policies by some companies, committed to the retention of their female employees. Women's role as homemakers was never in question. The extension of state maternity rights in recent years emphasized this difference further, when the United Kingdom allowed for up to one year maternity leave and only two weeks paid paternity leave. However the Labour government's commitment to improve paternity allowances was followed through by the Coalition government, and additional paternity leave entitlements came into force in April 2011.[11] This is discussed further in Chapter 5.

This tension between equality in the workplace and the maintenance of traditional gender roles in the private sphere continues today, and has not been solved by the development of different discourses like diversity and inclusion.

The introduction of family-friendly policies may have met a need, but it also meant that men could ignore the issue because it had no direct impact on their working life. Many women with ambition did not and still do not take these policies up, as they know they will drop down the career ladder if they do. In the United States, where maternity leave has always been much shorter than in Europe, women returners opting to take time out or work shorter hours found themselves on the 'mommy track,' signaling to the organization that their career was on hold. Some US research showed that 49 percent of women earning over $100,000 did not have children, illustrating the harsh choice women still have to make.[12] Although many organizations today encourage both men and women to take up work/life policies, there is still little evidence that anything other than career standstill will occur (see Chapter 6 on the long hours culture).

There was no need for men or masculinity to be problematized by the introduction of equal opportunities, nor was there any need to change organizational structures and ways of working. Arguably the shift to diversity has left men and masculinity/gender power relations even less challenged.

THE MOVE TO DIVERSITY

There was a fundamental change in the political landscape in the United Kingdom in the 1980s as trade union power was broken and the Conservative government ushered in an era of individualism. The philosophical shift to postmodernism and difference in the early 1990s reflected this disillusionment with group politics and the search for individual identities. The 'grand narratives' which included concepts like truth, equality, and even feminism were being challenged along with other enlightenment thinking.[13] The prevailing ideology of individualistic consumerism continued through the 1990s, and even the credit crisis of 2008–9 failed to challenge it. Diversity needs to be seen as a reflection of this wider social philosophical current, along with the changing demands of an increasingly fluid and global economy, where skilled labor, particularly knowledge labor, was privileged, and with an aging workforce in Europe, supply was running out.

Diversity's focus is not specifically on women, nor even on inequality, but fits in with a trend in human resources management (HRM), which speaks of capabilities, potential and empowerment. It encompasses every form of difference – age, disability, race, religion – yet does not necessarily recognize inequality around these differences. The focus in diversity has been the individual, although the law is still drawn up around social categories.

Globalization and the changing demographics of labor markets demanded a shift in corporate awareness, so that businesspeople could see the business world could no longer afford to remain Anglo-Saxon male in its orientation. Writers and consultants saw diversity as breathing new life into equal opportunities, and some saw it as offering a radical new approach:

Managing diversity is about the realization of the potential of all employees ... certain group based equal opportunities need to be seriously questioned, in particular positive action and targets.[14]

Diversity was perceived by its advocates as benefiting the organization, while equality programs had often been seen as favoring one group over another. Consultants listed the differences in the approaches on their websites. Littlewoods, one of the first companies to promote equal opportunity policies in the United Kingdom, announced in 1995 that equal opportunities was seen as an initiative which favored women and ethnic minorities at the expense of white men (whereas diversity favored everyone).[15] This led some to argue that the move to diversity was part of a backlash to women's gains in the area of employment.[16]

Pitting diversity against equal opportunities was not a constructive approach, nor was it realistic. Where diversity as a concept has been successful is in introducing equality issues and initiatives into a previously reluctant UK private sector. It was noted above that in the UK businesses had a deep distrust of equal opportunities but many have since embraced diversity with vigor. Its focus on business benefits and positive spin was much more attractive than an approach which, for many, had too political an overtone. Cynicism would add that this coincided with the removal of the limit for sex discrimination payouts, and the introduction of further legislation on sexual orientation, age, disability and religion.

Increasing globalization has encouraged and to some extent required a focus on difference and inclusive cultures. The diversity approach has its roots in the United States but is now established in most UK organizations, although some still refer to equality and diversity, acknowledging that without equality of opportunity, diversity and inclusion are meaningless. The diversity management approach may differ from the 'equal opportunity' approach in several significant ways.

- It emphasizes difference rather than sameness.
- It focuses on the individual rather than the group.
- It prioritizes the importance of the business case.
- Social justice is no longer a key objective.
- The legal element is rarely mentioned in definitions of diversity despite the fact that the law is now much more comprehensive than it was ten years ago.

INCLUSION

Organizations are often by their nature diverse. The addition of inclusion was recognition that it was necessary to change cultures in order to achieve the outcome of diversity being valued in an organization – a culture that included everybody. Different organizations use different words – inclusiveness, inclusivity or inclusion. There are hundreds of definitions of diversity and inclusion. Global professional services firm Ernst & Young define diversity as 'the demographic mix in a given environment which includes both seen and unseen differences.' It uses inclusiveness, which it defines as 'how we make the mix work by creating an environment where all people feel valued and are able to achieve their potential.'[17] Whilst the words inclusion and inclusiveness again avoid notions of inequality, they implicitly recognize exclusion and their focus is entirely on culture.

The diversity approach distanced itself from the law, but the laws that refer to inequalities, legislation and discrimination remain the backdrop to all work on diversity in the workplace, including disability and work–life balance. However much companies say they would implement diversity regardless of the law, that is said with hindsight. There were precious few companies taking steps to promote equality before the legislation. Equal pay and discrimination were legislated for, flexible working rights and parental rights are enshrined in law. The threat of legislation on gender pay audits and boardroom quotas is further focusing attention on gender in 2011.

Diversity has no political overtones, and no direct links to the concepts of inequality or discrimination. It was a name change and shift in approach for the same issues. The problem with using the concept of difference is that it requires a norm from which others are deemed different. This can inadvertently reinforce social categories, permitting diversity to be seen by dominant groups as being something to do with other people. Ten years on, diversity, just like equal opportunities before it, has become connected in many people's minds with 'political correctness' and the law, and further name changes are afoot. The goals of diversity are hard to challenge yet do not seem to be reached easily.

GENDER AND DIVERSITY

While the original equal opportunities accommodated women's biological difference with the introduction of family-friendly policies, diversity's main premise is on women's difference from men in all areas. The common language in the United Kingdom and United States now is gender diversity, whereas in Europe is remains gender equality.

Diversity's appeal lay in its evident acceptance of difference, and fitted neatly into the idea that there are different styles of working. It has been argued that the equality approach, based on gender neutrality, aimed at helping women to be like men and to compete on their terms. Diversity, it was argued, allows for difference and in fact celebrates it. But as Liff pointed out,[18] there is a need to do more than merely acknowledge difference. When does difference matter and how can these differences be valued equitably? Would the outcomes of a diversity approach be better than those of one based on equal opportunities? The main thrust of academic critique of diversity management was that it de-emphasized the conflicts, problems and dilemmas in developing meaningful initiatives and failed to acknowledge resistance to change.[19]

> The significance of acknowledging diversity is to see that it is not a case of the happy existence of neutral difference, but that it is bound up with power relations (this is totally neglected by recent literature on the subject) whereby masculine codes are rewarded more highly than feminine in organizations, therefore rationalizing and justifying continued male dominance.[20]

Has the diversity discourse served gender well? One of the concerns about 'losing' gender equality in the pool of diversity was the loss of focus that might have ensued. This concern was shared by other strands of diversity such as disability and sexual orientation. But by slipping gender under the umbrella of diversity, organizations took note when they had not done so before.

Advocates of diversity blamed the language and tone of equal opportunities (emphasizing sameness) on the failure for women to make substantial inroads into positions of power in business and public life. Now some commentators are blaming diversity for the same failure, arguing for gender to be taken out of the diversity strand umbrella.[21] Wittenberg-Cox and Maitland, for example, cite the growing importance of women in the economy as reason alone for businesses need to start championing women in their work-places. They argue that diversity has not served the gender issue well, and that women are not a minority but half the population, and therefore deserving of their own agenda. The authors claim to be 'reframing the gender debate, taking it out of the various boxes into which it has been awkwardly pushed for the past decades – whether as a women's issue, a dimension of diversity or an equal opportunity argument.'[22]

This is a denial of the many years of hard work and struggle, which have resulted in what progress we have today. There have unquestionably been huge gains made during the 35 years since the first equality legislation in 1975. Anne Watts CBE, Chair of the Appointments Commission, relates the story of how when she complained of progress being slow to her male colleague at NatWest (from where she founded Women in Banking 30 years ago), he replied, 'What to do you expect? You cannot end 10,000 years of discrimination overnight'. Watts says, 'In those days we weren't talking about women in management issues because there weren't any women managers! So if you look in most organizations now there is a good core of women in middle management.'[23]

Yes, there is further to go, but women's opportunities in work have changed enormously – for the better. So the gender debate is very much a women's issue, a dimension of diversity and an equal opportunity argument – and it may be more. In the words of feminist writer Joan Smith, women's progress in work is part of an 'unfinished revolution.'[24]

In the United Kingdom in 2011 there is almost daily coverage of some aspect of women in the workplace, whether it is the pay gap, work–life balance, women entrepreneurs, the lack of senior women in organizations, or women in politics. The credit crisis (and subsequent blame on male bankers) in many ways brought attention to the paucity of women in senior public and private-sector positions, and a succession of UK government-led enquiries has kept the issue in the news – the Treasury Select Committee Report, the Equality and Human Rights Commission Report, and the Davies Review on women on boards.[25] It is now easier than it ever has been to talk about gender in business – and the universal acceptance that there are not enough women in senior positions means that the barriers have to be acknowledged.

Sarah Churchman, head of diversity and engagement at Price WaterhouseCoopers, agrees that gender is now 'out there' in the press and being talked about in business much more than before although she says that nothing much has changed fundamentally yet.[26]

Another reason for the attention on gender is that a new generation of women are being very vocal about it. With an equal education and the same expectations as their male peers, women have responded to barriers in the workplace by blogging about them, joining networks and professional groups, and generally making a noise.

Diversity as a word is even less common in Europe than it is in the United Kingdom. Like the United Kingdom, European Union (EU) member states have been compelled to adhere to the European directives on all aspects of discrimination. Some are still in the process of doing so, but the internal drivers from employees and other stakeholders have not been so critical in pushing diversity onto the corporate agenda as they have been in the United Kingdom. The word 'diversity' is often considered a US concept, associated with race and ethnicity, and organizations tend to regard immigrant issues as being a state rather than organizational responsibility. Indeed the word 'diversity' itself still has little meaning in most European countries, although it is being imported by global companies via their diversity initiatives. They are familiar with and refer to 'gender equality,' and this has been a key issue in the European political scene with reference to the workforce, as well as implementing it into all mainstream union policies.[27]

For global organizations, gender is the only diversity issue that companies can measure everywhere. Indeed from my own work in Europe I know that while there are certain cultural differences as well as labor market differences, the gender issues discussed in this book are common, in varying degrees, to all countries. Fleur Bothwick, director of diversity and inclusiveness for Europe, the Middle East, India, and Africa (EMEIA) at Ernst & Young, agrees. She has been 'surprised by the similarity of issues raised by senior women in the firm, whatever country they are in.'[28]

While gender inequality is an issue that crosses all countries and cultures, approaches to gender equality vary greatly. The proactive stances taken by some state governments with regard to quotas as a way of pushing ahead gender equality are discussed later in the book.

PART 2: THE BUSINESS CASE – REFOCUSED, RENEWED, REPEATED?

Although proponents of equal opportunities used the business case as a driver for change,[29] the shift to diversity management led to a much stronger focus on it. McKinsey's influential reports *The War for Talent* (1998) and updated *War for Talent Part 2* (2001) concluded that in the future the best talent would be harder to find and more challenging to keep.[30] This was not a time to be consciously or unconsciously excluding talent for reasons of gender, race, ethnicity, sexual orientation, disability or age. Lord Browne, former chief executive of BP, said that talent should be drawn from all sections of society, to access the widest most creative range of new ideas.[31]

Broadly speaking, the aim of diversity management is to harness the differences of people for the benefit of the organization. The focus on the business case has enabled change agents to appeal to leadership in a way that was impossible without it. The concerns from activists that diversity would result in a loss of focus on inequalities were overridden by the evidence that business was embracing diversity because it saw the business benefits of it. The ends justified the means. Research has shown that without the potential of positive business impact, leadership would lose interest in diversity as a strategy.[32]

It was shown in Chapter 2 how the dominant group of an organization develops conditions in which it believes its members operate the most effectively in any particular environment. If change can only be successfully implemented by the dominant group, then the change has to appeal to their interests. Diversity professionals have to articulate gender issues through the discourse of the business case in order to be heard and to influence the dominant group and persuade them to make changes. If a diversity professional walked into a boardroom and said, 'The women in this company are fed up with the way they are paid less, work harder and their home responsibilities go unrecognized, and they are constantly excluded from the male in-groups heading for the top. We demand change,' they would be out of a job. Appealing to the profitability or improved service delivery (in the case of the public sector) of the organization has been a vital argument for the introduction of diversity.

The first stage of the business case focused on the potential of women, their particular skills and the wasted investment in training women who then might leave the organization for family or other reasons.[33] This business case has broadened over time as women's economic independence has grown and their influence as other stakeholders is felt. Similarly the increase in immigration and the high educational achievements of ethnic minorities provided a clear business case for better recruitment and retention of ethnic minorities, as well as their power as consumers. Looked at like this, it is women's increase in educational achievements, their entry into the workforce, and ensuing economic power that are providing further rationale for the advancement in the workplace. The business case is a consequence of increased gender equality rather than the reason for it.

A big sea change in perception and increased focus on the business case occurred from 1997 onwards, influenced by the change to a Labour government which had diversity and equality as one of its six Modernising Government Agenda items. *The Business of*

Diversity (2002) research which surveyed 70 private sector companies and 70 public sector organizations reported that the business case was the most cited driver for equality and diversity for the private sector and the second most cited driver for the public sector.[34] The highest proportion of respondents (33 percent) reported that equality and diversity had become business priorities from 1997 to 2002. This was regardless of how long the organizations had actually been implementing equal opportunities policies. Taking the private sector alone, over half of them had only made equality and diversity a business priority in the last five years.

Claire McCarron, HR support leader, Cummins, said, 'What happened a couple or so years ago was that we moved from beyond the minimal attention we need to give equal opportunities to avoid breaking the law to actually building a business case for diversity.'[35]

The business case arguments for equality and diversity developed from the need to recruit and retain women and minorities to include other business drivers. These included:

- new markets
- client pressure – demands from female and ethnic minority clients
- understanding customers better
- investor pressure
- procurement – from the public sector and some big corporates
- brand reputation
- social awareness – rise for CSR which includes employee relations
- increase in creativity and innovation.

With more and more graduates being young women, businesses are being compelled to make efforts to retain them once recruited. Suzanne Bottrill, head of diversity and inclusion UK and Republic of Ireland for Ernst & Young, explains the business case for E & Y.

> More commercially this year we have taken in 45 percent female graduates. We spend £200,000 on formal training to get them to manager level and that's a lot to see walking out the door. The percentage has already dropped to 38 percent by manager level anyway. There is an expected attrition rate following qualification but more women than men leave. That near 50:50 split goes down at each level of career progression until partner level where female partners make up 18 percent of partnership. This has increased from 13 percent over just three years. Numbers here should

be improving as, of the latest partners made up in July 2010 29 percent were women.

Many in the firm don't see the need for a business case any more than it's the right thing to do. The other key business case is that our clients are increasingly demanding that we pass the diversity test. The minimum is ticking the boxes but as we are able to show we do much more we are also able to connect with clients on a business level. More and more are asking us what we know about gender and diversity issues. If we do a good job internally we can help other businesses.[36]

A more customer-focused business case urged British Telecom to recruit more female engineers four years ago. Customers, especially women, often prefer a female engineer, and BT wanted to reflect society and improve equality in the workplace. Its analysis showed, however that out of the 6,000 young people chasing apprentice-ships only 8 percent were women. BT set about trying to increase the proportion of female apprentices. A brochure and adverts featuring current young women engineers appeared in the press and on websites highlighting the benefits of being a BT engineer – a job 'which is not just for blokes.' The company aimed at recruiting 25 percent of women in new intakes, a target it has since reached.[37]

Innovation has become a key driver for certain businesses. Robin Schneider, managing director of Schneider~Ross, also sees innovation as being a business driver for those clients who are well advanced on the diversity journey, 'Innovation is critical to them in a tough market. They see that different perspectives are important and that having an inclusive culture is needed to ensure that the different views are heard and taken into account.'[38]

Oil giant Shell is placing innovation at the heart of its policy of diversity and inclusiveness:

The energy challenges we face are enormous – and we're endeavoring to put the best minds in the world to work on developing the solutions. Finding innovative and responsible ways to secure the world's future supply of energy can't be done by few. It's a monumental undertaking, and it's going to require the input, knowledge and creativity of people around the planet. This is why we don't look at inclusiveness as an act of corporate goodwill. We don't see it simply as 'the right thing to do.' To Shell, having a diverse workforce is the only way we can accomplish our greatest company objectives. Yet, even more importantly, we see it as a matter of global necessity.[39]

MEASUREMENT

For all the rhetoric around the business benefits of having a diverse workforce, few companies in Europe have done much to measure the impact of diversity initiatives. In *The Business of Diversity* (2002),[40] recommendations included exhorting organizations that had said diversity was a business issue for them, to treat it like one. This means committing resources to it and ensuring accountability and measurement of the impact of this investment. In the research 'Reframing diversity,'[41] the authors argued that real and measurable returns on each diversity-related investment were crucial to retain leadership commitment and support for diversity. One head of diversity said to me a few years ago, 'We have little enough resources, we are committed to increasing women and minorities' numbers and we don't want to spend our resources trying to prove what is ethically right.'[42]

Lucy Adams, director of people for the BBC, has argued that not enough has been done on the business case: 'We kid ourselves that there is a compelling and accepted argument for the business benefits of more women in top jobs but if this were true, things would have changed more than they have.'[43]

Sarah Churchman does not think that the business case has been definitively proved:

> There is research showing correlations but not causality. Like other people management issues it is hard to measure. What we can do and are much better at doing now is using data in a more sophisticated way for a better understanding of our demographics and correlating one measure with another.[44]

Sir Nicholas Montagu, chairman of the Council at Queen Mary, University of London and former chairman of the Inland Revenue, 1997–2004, thinks that not having hard evidence of its impact makes it easier for some companies to ignore diversity: 'Many large companies like GlaxoSmithKline and Procter & Gamble have made determined efforts on diversity; but it's all too easy for the doubters to attribute their success to a whole range of other factors.'[45]

In the United States accountability and measurement are embedded into equality and diversity programs. IBM's plan to expand minority markets by promoting diversity in its own workforces has become a masterclass in diversity strategy.[46] The strategy was clear, the business expansion from the diversity plans were expected, and results were measured to show the business improvement.

WOMEN – THE ECONOMIC DRIVER

The disentangling of gender from diversity (outlined above) that has occurred over the past couple of years has been encouraged by an increase on the business focus on women both as talent and increasingly as a market – like the BT example above. Women represent the fastest-growing client sector in wealth management, and competition for their funds is strong. Private banks like Coutts and Barclays Wealth understand the need to appeal to, understand, and empathize with their banking clients, and have focused considerable attention on their gender diversity efforts over the past few years.

Craig Jones, global head of diversity at Barclays Wealth, says, 'Women represent the fastest growing segment of the private wealth management market, mostly entrepreneurs. It is obvious business sense to meet their needs as best we can.'[47] The arguments for the recruitment of the best talent still hold strong, but as women are now in middle management positions in greater numbers, increasingly the argument for women to be in senior leadership, decision-making positions, directing strategy, and on boards, has gathered apace.

Michelle Brailsford, president of the London branch of the European Professional Women's Network (EPWN), is an advocate for the business case of gender diversity. As well as their importance as an economic power as customers, consumers, and clients, like Robin Schneider she sees the next step of the business case as being innovation. She says, 'Companies like Shell and Coca-Cola cite innovation as the key business reason for having more women in senior positions in their companies... new products are the life juice of these companies and they need people with different perspectives. They want women's perspectives to make men think differently.'[48]

Goldman Sachs, an organization with global influence, has been strongly promoting gender diversity based on the business case although its own internal practices are sometimes under scrutiny.[49] It has identified both the micro- and the macro-economic gains to be made as a by-product of gender equality. It rightly sees the education and employment of women as a key indicator of developing societies and growing economies, and coined the phrase 'womenomics' more than ten years ago, when it published a paper on the influence of women's growing economic power in Japan.[50]

Goldman Sachs has extended its theory to women in the workforce in India, and that was the basis of its innovative program, '10,000 women,' in which it partnered with business school courses internationally to provide some training for women entrepreneurs around the world. It won the Opportunity Now Gender education award in 2009. On a micro level as a business opportunity, Goldman Sachs has highlighted a basket of 30 companies for investment that stand to benefit from women's increasing purchasing power.[51]

Women are being positioned as the new global economic force, although they are the poorest, with only 1 percent of the world's assets being held by women.[52]

In an article in the *Harvard Business Review*, Silverstein and Syre[53] begin with the sentence, 'Women now drive the world economy,' and proceed to highlight how marketing to women could be so much better. Having women at senior levels of the organization would be one obvious way of improving it.

For people interested in the advancement of women and ending women's poverty, the reasons to promote equality for women are not simply so that companies like Goldman Sachs can make more money. In the gold rush that some companies see as an outcome of women's economic power, the business world would do well to acknowledge that women and their skills have been excluded from participating in business life, and in many parts of the world still are, to the detriment of us all. They should also address the myriad ways in which businesses still marginalize women as employees and clients.

Lobbyists Catalyst in the United States and Opportunity Now in the United Kingdom have always centered their arguments for the advancement of women in business around the business case, and have worked with many leading organizations for many years. A more recent twist to the business case argument for diversity is the impact that women's style of management or even their presence may have on boardroom decision making. A Catalyst study found that companies that had higher women's representation on their top management teams financially outperformed those companies that had a lower representation.[54] Global management consultant McKinsey's study 'Women matter' suggests that the companies where women are most strongly represented at board or top-management level are also the companies that perform best.[55] An influential paper in 2006 in the United States showed that a critical mass of three or more women could cause a fundamental change in the boardroom and enhance corporate governance.[56]

As well as contributing to profitability, women's talents could have been used to prevent the financial meltdown according to some commentators.[57] Craig Jones, global head of diversity at Barclays Wealth, certainly thinks that risk is more capably dealt with by a mixed gender approach, and that the male, competitive environment on bank boards led to some reckless risk taking.

The view that the lack of women at the top of banks may have contributed to the credit crisis was discussed widely in the media.[58] In the United Kingdom, the Treasury Select Committee, 14 strong with only one woman on it, investigated the issue of Women in the City, reporting in April 2010 – and concluded that:

> The lack of diversity on the boards of many, if not most of our major financial institution, may have heightened the problems of 'group think' and made effective challenge and scrutiny of executive decisions less effective.[59]

Whether the Royal Bank of Scotland would have bought ABN Amro or Lloyds TSB bought HBOS if more women had been on their boards we will never know. Are there now more women on our UK bank boards? No, there are fewer than before. The recomposition of the bank boards with greater attention to diversity following the credit crisis never happened. In Iceland the three main bank boards have been reconstituted with women making up 40 percent, 60 percent, and 100 percent. One of the banks saved by the state, Royal Bank of Scotland, still has no women on its board at all. In Europe, some countries, notably Spain and France, are following Norway's example and introducing gender quotas. At the European level, a strong case was made for the inclusion of gender in the recomposition of bank boards but was not taken up.[60]

Michelle Brailsford, as president of the Local London branch of the EPWN, which has 4,000 members, has her finger on the pulse of the environment for professional women. She sees the fallout of the financial crisis as a positive time because it 'enabled a debate about women – not that I believe boards of all women would have done differently but because we were able to talk about having more balanced boards.' The crisis highlighted the small percentage (12 percent) of women on boards in the United Kingdom today. However she says that corporates are already suffering from gender fatigue. They are apparently already tired of talking about it. Her response to them is, 'Well, we are all tired of talking about it, but I'll stop talking about it when we have made real progress and achieved some balance on boards.'[61]

Diversity change agents find themselves in a double bind. In order to capture leadership and the attention and interest of the dominant groups/leadership, they have to argue for the elimination of bias, discrimination, or prejudice, or the restructuring of work, or for flexibility of work within the discourse of the business case. Business and social justice do not always go hand in hand. Capital moves around the world, finding cheaper and cheaper labor. What happens if it is in business's interests to pay women less than men, keeping their costs down and increasing their profits? That is why the introduction of equal pay was necessary. The segregation of women into low-paid support work may also suit business.

Carolyn Lee, head of diversity at law firm Herbert Smith, says:

My own firm told me to stop bothering with the business case because it didn't stack up. (Argument: if you look at women, they are more likely to have long periods out/leave, so the business case would suggest that rather than recruit them, we should wait until they were beyond childbearing. It's debatable, but...) They were and are more interested in changing the culture because they think it's the right thing to do, it makes the workplace more interesting, and it positions better as a global firm with global clients (linked to the business case but impossible to ascribe numbers). I think people get too hung up on statistics to the extent it inhibits creative thinking.[62]

In investment banking competition for jobs is so fierce there is not in reality much of a war for talent. Jobs are now global. Does a lack of a business case justify discrimination? That is not to say that by leaving women to one side companies may be missing extraordinary talent – they will be, but then they always have. For a short-term culture, employing people who may take a year off and then another year off may not actually make business sense. In some ways, then, business-case advocates can be hoisted by their own petard.

In his book *The Value of Difference* Binna Kandola, an experienced diversity consultant, expresses exasperation with the insistence of proving a business case: 'the constant call for a business case mystifies me more and more.'[63] 'Diversity can be represented as an economic issue, but it is also a moral one based on values.' Kandola argues that 'diversity champions should not be looking to finesse a business case, but to challenge the very demand for a business case.'[64]

Diversity professionals are not usually in senior enough positions to do this. Although equal opportunities did recognize the business imperative, equality officers often also saw themselves as agents of social change. Meyerson and Scully coined the term 'tempered radicals' to describe change agents like diversity professionals, who are often committed to change on a personal and social level but are required to frame their arguments within the confines of business discourse.[65] Gill Kirton and her colleagues have used the term in their UK research, and suggest that diversity's neglect of inequality and emphasis on business benefit often requires a tortuous mind-bending for change agents to present their arguments in pure business terms.[66]

Indeed, Allison and Shapiro's excellent research on diversity professionals found that there was frequently a mismatch between diversity professionals and chief executives, and that certain business case arguments, notably ethical and legal ones, were of little of no interest to some of the senior executives interviewed.[67] They warned that executives' attention to diversity was likely to be sapped:

> It is only when they see diversity effort as a strategic invest-ment with deliberate intent to enhance profitability or service delivery, that executives are convinced of its worth They need "a consistently clear and tangible return on each diversity-related investment."[68]

Sarah Bond, head of diversity at KPMG, thinks the business case trips off the tongue a little too easily, and this has resulted in a loss of passion in the topic.

> You need passion for diversity. So although the business case has been very useful in engaging people in the debate for diversity, it can be translated into a dispassionate objective – almost the human element is removed and it can lose its power.[69]

DIVERSITY FATIGUE

The slow progress of women gaining positions at the most senior levels of organizations has led to some diversity fatigue in the same way as there was equal opportunities fatigue 15 years ago. Five years of diversity initiatives and focus have produced some promising results at accountancy firm KPMG, but there is still frustration about the low number of women partners. Sarah Bond said:

> The culture of the organization is changing in as much as there is much more ease in talking about diversity – so that door is open. But it hasn't translated into changing demographics, into the deep structures and processes of the organization. But there are so many to be done – we've done about five when there are probably fifty and that's just in recruitment! We have not seen much prog-ress at senior level. However the percentage of women partners has improved from 11 percent to 14 percent in five years. Really

this is in tandem with all moves at the highest level across the big corporates.[70]

The head of diversity at another firm commented, 'I also think that organizations can be fickle – always moving on to the next thing – be it diversity, corporate responsibility, sustainability, carbon footprint.'[71]

A diversity head in a law firm reports diversity fatigue and thinks it is caused by 'lack of progress, and lack of innovative and logical thinking in and around diversity.'[72]

Anne Watts, as a long-time equality and diversity activist, thinks that:

Intellectually there are no more hurdles because women have proved themselves to be equal. But if you ask, 'are we as a society making the most of our resource of women?' – the answer is no. There are still precious few opportunities for working flexibly at senior levels. The talent is just not reaching the top.[73]

Conversations with many women and diversity professionals suggest that the male cultures in elite parts of organizations have been left untouched by diversity initiatives. Carolyn Lee comments:

Lack of progress is very difficult. Many things have been tried; everyone knows things take time; women get tired of the macho culture, they get tired of the politics, they get tired of arguing for equal recognition and pay. And they reach a point where they are just not prepared to do it anymore. And society gives them permission to leave – children or no children – and do something else.[74]

The slowing, or as Kandola has put it, 'stalling of the diversity engine,' means a restart may be required.[75] In spite of embracing the concept of multiple identities in diversity, the reality for most organizations is that they have to focus on one strand of diversity at a time. And usually it is only one person looking at them all. Sometimes it is what is most pressing and important, sometimes it is what is easiest. The rhetoric of diversity as empowering individuals rarely travels from words into practice. In that sense managing diversity is simply managing people well. There is no need for any extra input from a diversity specialist. What is beginning to happen is some deeper work on bias in organizations, a measure of the realization that deep radical culture change is required.

One professional said to me, 'We have done all the broad diversity training and there is little to disagree with. But our numbers still do not look good. It has not translated into change so now it's back to basics.'[76]

In the words of one diversity head of a large bank, 'people get disillusioned and worn down and tired and frustrated by the constant uphill struggle to move organizations on in anything other than baby steps.'[77]

The dilemma is put neatly by Michelle Brailsford: 'If men hold the power what is in for them to change their organizations? Women are struggling to survive on a daily basis often running two jobs and have not got the energy to keep going.'[78]

Recent arguments have focused on the business reasons for the inclusion of women in corporate life. However the focus again is on the accommodation and understanding of women's difference from men, rather than the interrogation of why and how masculine cultures are perpetuated and continue to exclude/marginalize women and some men.

THIS is the conversation we should be having in organizations.

PART 3: GENDER AWARENESS IN ORGANIZATIONS

Although all the constituents of organizational culture that have been identified in the model set out in the previous chapter, have an indirect or direct impact on gender, it is important to start by looking at the history and specific situation of gender relations in an organization. How long have women worked there and in what capacity? This can also include the demographics: how many women and where are they? What efforts, if any, have taken place to ensure that women are a respected and valued part of the workforce? What is the level of gender awareness of employees? What discourse is used to discuss women in the workplace? Gauging how women are thought of in your organization can be informative, and these questions can easily be asked.

Can we assume that if an organization has active equality/ diversity initiatives, gender awareness will be higher than in an organization that does not? Indeed does gender awareness matter? It may not be an issue. As a consultant I have been told many times, 'We don't have issues here – so we don't need to bring the subject up.' This very often means that women working there have to put up or shut up. The existence or not of equal opportunities history, or more recently diversity and inclusion, is important, and so is the extent to which employees are aware of policies and link them to the organization's values. The organization may be committed to promoting women in the workplace but employees may not share this awareness. My research showed that the existence of a formal equality and diversity policy of which employees are aware is an indication of increased awareness of gender issues. Women are to a certain extent empowered by the knowledge that some of their concerns are on the corporate agenda. Indeed diversity heads have said that the introduction of women's leadership programs or maternity coaching gives out a positive signal to female employees. The consequence of this higher level of awareness is that behaviors that are deemed to be sexist are picked up much more than in an organization where awareness is low.

The concept of discourse, as being what may be said of something at any particular time, is used in the analysis to illustrate how people can only interpret their own experiences through the discourses available to them.[79] Some discourses become so powerful that they appear as common sense, and these may be described as *hegemonic discourses*.

It was shown earlier that the discourses to tackle discrimination and inequality in organizations are in constant flux and change within and between organizations. Professionals working in a local authority will use different terminology to discuss diversity issues than those working in a top law firm. The framing of the problem will determine the type of solution. The two main case studies of my PhD research, Airco and Investco,[80] offer a contrast between an organization which recognizes equality and diversity issues and has active policies, and one which has a dormant policy but no real activity. In other words, in Investco there was no organizational equality and diversity discourse available for people to draw on.

A long history of equality and diversity provides the foundations even if there are periods of time when little activity on diversity takes place. However research has shown that it is not just length of time but rather the intent and integration with the business that determines the success or not of policies.[81] Carolyn Lee says that her firm, Herbert Smith, has been a late starter on the diversity journey, but that 'energy, passion and resource (financial and people) can push the agenda along very quickly.'[82]

The dominant discourse is the one through which all gender issues will be articulated. If there has been no real integration of diversity and equality into the business, then employees will not have the knowledge or language to engage constructively with the issues, unless they have a personal interest anyway. Workers who move from an employer with a strong history and commitment to equality and diversity, like those in the public sector, to a private-sector company with no such history, report on the difference. One man in a small financial services firm commented, 'I am amazed at how much is allowed to go on here. In my last job we wouldn't speak like that. You just know it's wrong. But here it's like stepping back in time.'[83]

Asking employees about gender relations, whether they have been made to feel unwelcome or experienced hostility in any part of the organization, can provide some revealing facts and pointers about the culture and its awareness of gender. In my PhD research[84] a high percentage (25 percent) of the women respondents reported feeling unwelcome and experiencing some hostility in some areas of their organizations because they were women, but interestingly the figures were higher for the airline than for the bank. An active equality and diversity agenda heightens awareness and makes employees more likely to complain of perceived injustices.

In the bank Investco, male-dominated and at the time of research with no history of equal opportunities, the culture was described by employees as meritocratic with little hierarchy. Once recruited, women were expected to compete on the same terms as men. It was a laissez-faire culture in which if you wanted to make money, you could, for results spoke for themselves.

The increase in the number of female graduates and the loss of trained women had caused the company to look at equality and diversity for the first time. The men in the organization took two different approaches to the subject of women working there. One was a no-difference 'gender blind' approach: 'I have no prejudice against women as long as they work as hard as men.' The other emphasized that women are different – 'The problem with women is that their biology is different, they do go off and have babies.' Very often they utilized both discourses at the same time, without realizing the conflict. Roper noted that men often used ideologies promoting marriage and motherhood to minimize competition with women. 'The supposedly fixed character of the gender order served as a reason for leaving resistance to women managers within the unconscious, unseen and therefore unchallenged.'[85]

At Investco there had been little opportunity and insufficient numbers of women to influence the culture and style, and there seemed little reason for men to question their attitudes and behaviors. More recently a graduate recruit in a small fund-management company described the situation:

The organization I work for does not make an effort to show their equality or diversity. There are no diversity policies that I am aware of in place. There are very few women in the company (1 in 15/20 employees is a woman) so I don't think they see much relevance in trying to display equality and diversity.[86]

The women managers who work in these male-dominated environments often accept the culture as if it were part of the job. In Investco women had to adapt to this culture to get on, which suited some more than others. For the most part the company employed women who could cope with the macho environment. Having to fit in to the prevailing style has been cited in a number of studies as being a key barrier to progress for women.[87]

TALKING ABOUT WOMEN – STEREOTYPES

If there is no available equal opportunities or diversity discourse, women's problems are treated as individual difficulties rather than organizational issues. The visibility of a few women (sometimes very few) at the top of a male-dominated organization can lead to a denial that there is any inequality or are barriers for women generally. Some of the few women in Investco had left shortly before I arrived, one because of bullying by a boss, and two others because they could not combine the long hours with family life. Although there was genuine concern by the chief executive, these cases were dealt with as individual problems specific women had – not an organizational issue. It was the job, which was tough, that made life difficult for women. In my research in the investment bank there was almost universal acceptance that banking, and in particular the more elite areas of banking, was tough and naturally more suited to men, and that women had to adapt. Some could. Most couldn't.

Thus the prevailing view was that only really exceptional women could cope with life at the top of the bank, and their exceptional natures were constantly highlighted. In Chapter 1, I noted the phenomenon of sex spillover, whereby roles in wider society spill over into the workplace.[88] This is much stronger in jobs where there has been a short history of employing women and gives rise to all kinds of unhelpful stereotypes.

Discussion of stereotypes is very popular in the diversity and equality field today, as research shows that damaging stereotypes of women are a barrier to their progress. But looking at stereotypes without taking into account wider social inequalities limits our understanding of their purpose. A stereotype is a commonly held popular belief about specific social groups or types of individuals. Stereotypes become prejudice when we make negative evaluations of an individual based on unproven and generalized beliefs about a group to which they belong. There are several different theories about the purpose of stereotypes, but broadly they serve two purposes. First, they make life simpler in the face of multiple complexities. Stereotyping is inexact but it is an efficient way to mentally organize large blocks of information. There is a human tendency to avoid processing new or unexpected information about each individual – it is more time saving to fall back on general group characteristics.

We make generalizations about nationalities all the time: for example that Germans like order and putting their towels on sunbeds by the pool on holiday, that Italians are excitable, that the French can be arrogant and the English reserved. But on meeting individuals we largely put aside these generalizations unless we do not want to get to know them better.

The second role of stereotypes is that they focus on difference and often exaggerate differences between groups, particularly when there is competition. This was illustrated in the previous chapter in the football club analogy (page 20). Stereotypes can make differences appear greater than they are. And this is certainly what happens in gender relations. In many ways men and women are more alike than different. Indeed there are more differences between individual men and between women than between the two genders taken as a whole, particularly when we look at individuals on the professional and management levels. Drawing on stereotypes to emphasize women's difference from men tends to occur at more senior levels of the organization. The differences lower down are minimal.

On a deeper level, we stereotype to make ourselves feel good. By designating our own group the standard or normal group and others as different and often inferior, we protect ourselves from anxiety. We know that when we say all Italians are excitable we are stereotyping, and sometimes it is scapegoating our own excitability. When men work with women and get to know them as individuals, the stereotypes are usually broken – or they should be. Very often male leaders become passionate about gender equality through personal experience of having a working wife or a daughter entering the workplace. But for many people unhelpful stereotypes of women represent their truth, and they are reluctant to alter their view, particularly in the absence of experience of working with women at high levels.

Cultural resources are drawn on to reinforce stereotypes, making them seem even truer. As an example the media's obsession with the supposed unfeminine appearance of some female politicians is an insidious undermining of female talent, as well as promoting restricted and derogatory stereotypes of professional women.

Stereotypes of working women are rife, but their short history in the workplace means that external stereotypes are often used as their basis. These very often draw on the reproductive or sexual nature of women and their inferior status in the social hierarchy. This is the spillover. Hence the powerful resistance from both men and women to accepting women leaders. Research has shown that women are more likely to be judged harshly for making one mistake than their male counterparts, more likely to be perceived as 'unlikeable,' and more likely to be judged as 'incompetent.'[89] The fragility of women's positions as leaders was reported as being well founded by researchers from Exeter University, who coined the phrase 'glass cliff' to describe the phenomenon whereby individuals belonging to particular groups are more likely to be found in leadership positions that are associated with a greater risk of failure and criticism.[90]

Amanda Sinclair raises one explanation for our ambivalence towards women with power: that we associate powerful women with the child–mother relationship, as our first female authority figure is our mother. This can provoke unconscious early feelings – a terror of dependence. Hence the need for female power to be controlled, and we deal with the presence of that power by trivializing, marginalizing, or sexualizing it.[91] The stereotype of a woman leader is almost always unflattering. Women are either feminine and make poor leaders, or they are good leaders but unfeminine. There is no similar punitive treatment of male leaders, as the stereotype of leadership is still male. So when we address stereotypes in our work on gender in organizations, we need to interrogate them and ask why stereotypes of women, particularly women in leadership, are so negative. I return to the restrictions on women's ways of managing and leading in Chapter 4.

When the topic of women arose in the interviews of my research, it often led to discussions of individual women who had succeeded in the organization. The stereotype of the 'Superwoman' finds favor particularly in male-dominated areas of work. Explanations for women's success or lack of it, setting aside the practical considerations of childcare, often rest on individual psychological traits, usually along the lines of 'She's very tough.' There seemed to me to reflect a desire by men to isolate 'successful' women, simultaneously singing their praises and distinguishing them from other (more ordinary) women. One senior director, discussing his company's investment management division's female managing director, said.

Women in the organization? Well. We've got a woman boss, S–. Haven't you met her yet? Do you remember when we first walked into the department there was a girl sitting at that first desk talking with another blond girl. Yes, well that was S. Very young, very bright. I've got a lot of time for S. She does an excellent job, extraordinarily clever, you know.[92]

A little later in the conversation I suggested that S– might also be a good role model for other women in the bank. He didn't like this, and almost denied that there were any other women who could be good enough to reach the top, saying, 'Well, S– is, of course, quite exceptional. Yes, quite exceptional ....'

This dialogue shows how this older man, who actually worked for S– and was thus accountable to her, simultaneously praised her abilities, yet in the same breath referred to her as a girl, establishing his male superiority. Then he proceeded to mark her out as apart from most other women, emphasizing her uniqueness and thus 'difference' from other women in the bank. Cynthia Cockburn found the term 'male right' useful in her book, *In the Way of Women*, as a way of showing that even when a man is junior to a woman he perceives some inherent 'right' through his sex to dominate.[93] This resonates with women leaders, who say they sometimes have difficulty establishing their authority. Kanter in her epic tale of Indsco says that power resides in the job and sex is deleted.[94] This is not born out by experience. An incident that was related to me by a senior female banker illustrates this. She and a female colleague had been out for a quick lunch and on their return walked through reception. The male uniformed receptionist said, 'Had a nice bite to eat and a chat then, girls?'

Men's power in the extra-organizational world, in the family, the state and civil society, enters the workplace with them and gives even the most junior man a degree of sexual authority relative to even senior women.[95]

Suzi Spink, chief operating officer of fashion retailer East, has noticed that there are some colleagues, particularly men, who perhaps treat her differently than they would a male boss, 'At times I have to reassert authority in a conscious way,' she says.[96]

The history of female leadership in business and the wider social world has only just begun, and I am sure we will see all kinds of different leadership from women, breaking stereotypes when they are given the opportunity. And why do stereotypes of men not hold them back? When it comes to race and ethnicity stereotypes are applied even more, often in the absence of real knowledge of individuals and cultures.

The stereotype of superwoman as a worker who also maintains traditional domestic functions is also prevalent in the media and in many organizations. The general message is that only exceptional women can cope, and thus all should strive to be exceptional rather than question the basis of striving. Arguably for highly prized and elite jobs this is still very much the same today. The most lauded superwoman in Investco was in corporate finance and had five children. Male directors loved to bring this example down from the shelf whenever the subject of women in the bank was raised. The director of corporate finance said, 'She is amazing. I've no idea how she does it. But she brings in the business. That's all we ask.'[97]

I found out how she did it – she got up at 4 am most mornings to catch up on work, because she left at the 'early' time of 6.30 pm. The younger women in the bank said that 'superwoman' did them no favors as they were constantly compared with her. Because she coped so well, it was assumed that combining family and work presented no problems.

HOW WOMEN SEE THEMSELVES

Without a discourse of equality and diversity, women may discuss problems in a fragmented way, accepting the status quo as natural. In Investco, one of the obstacles women acknowledged was difficulty in getting promotion. And the most oft-cited barriers in the bank to career progress for women were lack of training and lack of career guidance. Through these channels, women felt more comfortable and justified in expressing some resentment, although these issues were discussed as though they were unalterable facts of organizational life and not something that could be different. In all the divisions except for fund management, the women agreed that it was harder for them to get promoted than for men. There were all kinds of explanations:

Promotion is difficult for a woman, there is still a very definite attitude of 'Yes, but they are going off to have babies.' Or, 'We can't have a woman because we need someone who's a hustler, someone who's tougher.'[98]

Everyone wants to be a director. If you don't make it generally you leave so there is intense competition among your peer group. Women tend to have to wait longer. Men promote in their own image. You need to be ambitious and determined and put yourself forward – be proactive, perhaps project yourself more than most women would normally do.[99]

The insistence that the job was gender-neutral did not tally with women's own explanations. What is displayed in this data is a series of stereotypes of working women, an insistence on the bank and its work as being gender-neutral, yet an implicit acknowledgement of its maleness by women's acceptance of the difficulties of gaining promotion. It also illustrates the denial of inequality, with a combination of biological and psychological factors being cited to explain the absence of women in the senior ranks. In the absence of an equality or diversity discourse, women's difficulties were individualized by men and channeled by the women themselves into alternative discourses like promotion chances, which conveyed many different injustices. It was the work itself rather than men that posed problems for the women. Even with an active diversity policy in place, these competing discourses can explain away the lack of senior women in an organization. This individualism and 'free choice' explanation of women's lack of representation at senior levels has recently come back to the fore as commentators have pointed to a reluctance to attribute the problems to broader social and organizational discrimination.

I noticed that some of the more successful women in the bank were 'outsiders' in another sense besides their gender – they were foreign citizens. Linda McDowell also found a high ratio of successful foreign women in her research on gender in the City,[100] and more recently figures from Cranfield International Centre for Women Leaders, which compiles the *Female FTSE 100 Report*, showed that of the 14 women appointed to a directorship of one of the top 100 companies for the first time in 2009, only one was a British national.[101] My own hypothesis is that in some ways the 'difference' that these foreign women displayed gave them a greater degree of freedom than was available to UK women. Susan Rice, managing director of Lloyds Banking Group in Scotland, is an American who came over and joined the First Bank of Scotland in the United Kingdom in 1997, then Lloyds Bank in 2000. She says that she did not experience any specific cultural barriers at these male-dominated senior levels of British banking, and thinks her 'foreignness' may have eased her way, 'People were interested in my perspective as an American banker and seemed receptive to my ideas. Coming from overseas was a way for people to allow me in.'[102]

These women are not so constrained by the cultural stereotypes deployed at senior business levels regarding the appropriate roles and behaviors of English women of a certain class.

HIGHER LEVELS OF AWARENESS: AIRCO

As a large employer of women, both in the air and on the ground, the other company that featured in my research,[103] which I have here called Airco, immediately felt the impact of the 1975 Equal Pay and Sex Discrimination Acts. Air stewardesses had previously been sacked if they became pregnant, or grounded on reaching the age of 30. For the next 15 years, the airline complied with the law but did little else in promoting its own specific policies. It was at the instigation of the then chief executive that equal opportunities issues were put high on the organizational agenda. He felt that many of the women in the airline were of a higher caliber than the men, and saw the potential to make more of his workforce.

Given the timescale, the facts that equal opportunities had only began in earnest over the previous six years (though there had been 15 years since the law was passed, the most recent six had been more proactive), and that women had not been represented in management for even this long, the figures showed that women worked for the airline for as long on average as men. This, combined with the high return rate after maternity leave, meant that the biological discourse about the inevitability of women leaving to have children was never used in the airline. Women either fitted their family lives around work or did not have children (see Chapter 5).

All airline respondents were aware of the equal opportunities policies. However with the increased awareness of the issues comes an increase in objections that women expressed to certain behavior. They were sensitive to any sexist behavior, unlike the women in the bank – although (this is discussed further in Chapter 8 on sexuality) they did not report any sexual harassment. Their expectations of respectful equal treatment were much higher than those of the women in the bank, who saw the excluding behaviors they experienced as attributes of the job, not of the men.

The sheer numbers of women in the airline, at both middle management and senior levels, also meant that stereotypes were not as available as a resource for men and women to draw on when discussing women in the workplace.

CONCLUDING POINTS

The existence of a formal and active equality and diversity policy is a reflection or an indication of gender awareness. In my research, the airline and its employees were aware of most gender issues, as they were expressed within an equal opportunities agenda. This was reflected in the culture, in the way women were represented and talked about. In everyday conversation women were treated with respect, at least in mixed company. Women were expected to perform on a par with men, and there seemed little to stop them.

The formal embracement of equality and diversity does not however prevent other cultural means of resistance to women's progress from occurring, as the rest of this book will show. But women to a certain extent were empowered by the knowledge that some of their concerns were on the organization's agenda. At the airline there was a wide-ranging discourse on equality opportunities, which included the concepts of sexual harassment and targets, but there was no acknowledgement of wider social disparity or any discourse on feminism. The case was argued in terms of fairness and equality of rights, rather than on any notion of power, oppression and resistance. Both men and women can espouse a belief in the equality and diversity discourse. It can also run alongside other discourses, such as the one of 'competing practical considerations' around childcare issues and maternity, which are presented as unalterable facts, appealing to a biological inevitability or the nature of things. Or it can run parallel with a long-hours culture which stands outside the equality and diversity policy but counters its effectiveness. People draw on both discourses and do not necessarily see them as mutually exclusive. Indeed the contradictions are rarely noted by respondents.[104]

Investco, without an active equality or diversity discourse, allowed the men to deny the existence of gender issues, relying instead on individual psychologizing and stereotypes. When asked whether the bank was doing enough to create a culture that encouraged and nurtured women in their careers, every single male bank respondent replied that it was. In Airco, where life was much more accommodating of women, 43 percent of male respondents said that the airline was not doing enough to create an accommodating culture. This shows that unless awareness of gender is specifically raised in an organization, the majority of men can ignore it as an organizational issue. A denial of inequality is a form of passive resistance, and is a recurring theme in the book. Men are consistently less likely than women (in most cases half as likely) to recognize any of the barriers to gender diversity and women's progression.[105] A refusal or reluctance to acknowledge that there are barriers, and therefore an insistence that there is no rationale for any change, is hard to challenge.

Organizations with a long history of diversity and equality, and those that have a more recent strong commitment, are now developing a sophisticated corporate discourse on gender. New ways of working, different management styles, and inherent bias in workplace structures and practices have widened the debates, and are enabling a challenge to existing male cultures that was not possible before. Greater knowledge and understanding will promote better gender awareness in organizations, and together with more women role models, will diminish the power of negative stereotypes.

4

STYLE MATTERS

INTRODUCTION

Chapter 2 opened with a story about my time in Japan in the mid-1980s when the effort of socializing and doing business with the Japanese took its toll. I was young, *gaijin,* and female. In a culture that discriminated against women shamelessly it was nigh on impossible for me to gain respect, let alone any authority in the business world. I was not a man, but neither did I behave or talk in the deferential manner that was expected of many of the young Japanese women whom I met at that time – hesitant sentences, peppered with apologies and shy giggles with hands covering their mouths. Did the style of communication of these Japanese women reflect an innate feminine characteristic, or was it an outcome of women's unequal status in Japanese society?

My Japanese girlfriend and colleague, who like all the English-speaking Japanese women I met working in finance was employed by a foreign bank because Japanese banks would only have employed them as tea ladies, had two styles: a US one as she had been brought up for eight years in New York, which was confident and direct, and the Japanese one, eyes cast down, apologetic and deferential. According to the language she spoke and whom she spoke to, she literally changed in front of my eyes. Whether she used US or Japanese style, her status was made very clear on the two occasions when directors of companies we were visiting refused to see us. Because she was a Japanese woman, they would see me but would not do business with her.

Debates on women's different ways of communicating and behaving at work are currently very popular in the West, but too often neglect the role of status. Status influences the way people behave and communicate, and how they are treated.

MANAGEMENT STYLE

Management style is an important constituent of organizational culture, and is often cited as being a barrier to women's progress at work. In the management literature management style is often seen as interchangeable with culture. Indeed the classic *The Gods of Management* by Charles Handy described four different management styles, and was considered the bible on corporate culture.[1] For the purposes of this book the concept pertains to the manner in which the business of an organization is conducted. It may be identified in the decision-making processes, hierarchy and relating to subordinates, reward systems, and by looking at which work attributes are most praised. There are so many different characteristics to management that to refer to them all as a 'style' is itself misleading, but it is even more so when we refer to two distinct styles – masculine and feminine. Very often attributes of style are essentially skills – the two terms are often used interchangeably, particularly when talking about women's styles. This may explain why women's skills are often not rewarded. Is being a good listener a style or a skill? This concept is a mix of skills and behaviors.

Management style is influenced by a number of variables including the organizational structure, the nature of the business, the overall cultural history of the organization, and leadership.[2] The values and assumptions of those who occupy positions of power feed into the creations and perpetuation of organizational culture, norms, and practices.

In the equality and diversity field, management style has been much debated as a possible barrier that contributes to women not achieving progress on a par with men, usually because women find they have to adapt to the prevailing style, which is not naturally their own. The other side of this argument is that organizations do not value women's styles or indeed women. Indeed in the 2010 research *What Holds Women Back* by Opportunity Now, nearly half (48 percent) of all women respondents cite personal style differences as a barrier to progress.[3] However any debate on styles must take place within a theoretical framework which acknowledges inequalities of power, and economic and patriarchal interests.

The terms 'masculinity' and 'femininity' refer to the socially generated consensus of what it means to be a man or a woman.[4] They need to be kept analytically distinct from the biological categories of men and women, as women may display masculine characteristics and men can display feminine characteristics. The reason for this sociological distinction is often forgotten in business discussions on gender today, being replaced with an increasingly essentialist approach to difference. The same/difference discourse of the equal opportunity and diversity debates has been a central focus of analysis of management styles and gender. Like diversity itself, the difference argument has been gaining ground, fueled by the success of popular pseudo-science literature in which women's innate difference from men is increasingly being emphasized.[5] This genre of work is influencing organizational change practitioners and corporate education initiatives, and the implications of this are discussed in this chapter.

In the early years of equal opportunities women were judged by the 'norm' of management and found wanting. More recently this norm has been revealed and acknowledged as imbued with a masculine bias – through work on unconscious bias – and in some organizations there has been a shift in emphasis to include different (women's) ways of managing, although the masculine norms have gone largely unchallenged.

Masculinity and femininity are not fixed, innate characteristics but rather vary according to time, society, and culture. In current management terms, a masculine style is still usually associated with a command and control approach, and a distancing of the personal self from the professional role of manager, although arguably in recent years this has changed towards a more transformative style. Feminine style usually refers to a more communicative, collaborative approach to management, with an emphasis on people skills such as listening rather than mere performance of an abstract task.

MANAGEMENT AS MASCULINE

Management has traditionally been the preserve of men. At the end of the nineteenth century as ownership of organizations changed from being in the hands of one owner/manager to being owned by a number of capital holders in the form of a joint stock companies and they grew in size, management developed into a profession in itself. In his blueprint for bureaucracy, sociologist Max Weber emphasized the need for rationality, logic, and objectivity in order to eliminate personal feelings and bias from entering organizational thought. The rules and rationality of the new salaried management of large organizations replaced the hunches and intuition of the former owner-entrepreneurs. The earliest definitions of management emphasized precision, objectivity, rationality, and control, traits long associated with masculinity. The exclusion of feelings and emotions, the unpredictable and the uncertain, was vital to this new management rationale.

(its specific nature) is developed the more perfectly bureaucracy is dehumanized, the more completely it succeeds in elimination for official business love, hatred and all purely personal irrational and emotional elements which escape calculation. This is the specific nature of bureaucracy and it is appraised as its special virtue.[6]

In the twentieth century industry developed and organizations were structured according to Taylorism, which also emphasized rationality, objectivity, and impartiality.[7] When management was designated as a science, women, who were popularly considered as the antithesis of science by virtue of their closeness to nature, were further excluded.[8]

Weber's ideal-type bureaucracy has been criticized by feminist writers as having an implicitly gendered subtext, in that the apparent neutrality of rules disguises gender interests.[9] Pringle says it can be interpreted as a commentary on the construction of a particular kind of masculinity, based on the exclusion of the personal, the sexual and the feminine from any definition of 'rationality.'[10]

So the dominant model of professional management from its inception excluded the symbols of femininity and promoted characteristics of a type of exemplary masculinity (typically white middle class). These management practices assumed a gender-neutral professional norm, as have male-oriented patterns of behavior in the workplace, making masculinity invisible.

Kerfoot and Knights pointed out that masculinity and management are not two separate concepts but that the whole management discourse is imbued with certain notions of masculinity.[11]

Middle-class women were at that time confined to the domestic sphere, where their work was focused on reproduction. Because paid work was – and still is – the main social arena in which men act out their needs for status, authority, power, influence, and material rewards,[12] it has been argued that organizations are structured to protect male power and reward masculinity accordingly.[13] Even when the status of a job has been downgraded preserving the masculinity of a job is important.[14] Men's ability to hold on to management as a male domain is rooted in men's ability to construct the cluster of skills that make up management as being rooted in masculinity. This has become harder to do as women have developed the same skills and gained the same qualifications as men. Far from being an objective economic fact, skill is often an ideological category imposed on certain types of work by virtue of the sex and power of the workers who perform them.[15]

As an example, at the beginning of the computer age, computer programming was deemed eminently suitable for girls, who typically had nimble fingers for the keyboard, patience, and attention to detail. Computer programming was compulsory at my single-sex school in the early 1970s, and indeed at that time computer programmers were predominantly women. After all, typing had been considered a wholly feminine occupation, and programming was then seen as a mere extension of typing. Dame 'Steve' Shirley capitalized on the high numbers of computer-trained women who were unable to work full time because of their family commitments, and set up F International, a software development company, in the late 1960s. All of its staff were women working part time. In the West, as computers' importance rose, computer programming gradually became associated with science, rationality, binarism, and masculinity. It was adopted by male hobbyists, gamers, and later the dot.com entrepreneurs. Bill Gates and Stephen Jobs were heralded the 'kings of software,' and soon the image of a 'geek' became synonymous with a technology worker, and the shift from a feminine to a masculine skill was fully made.[16] There was an accompanying shift in definition from low-status work to high-status skilled work.

The gendering and valuing of skills was revealed clearly in the UK legal case discussed in Chapter 3, in which female council workers claimed their work was of equal value to male council workers on the same pay grade. Nearly 4,500 women working in traditionally female-dominated roles such as cleaning, care, and catering for made individual claims against Birmingham Council for which they worked, comparing themselves with male workers such as grave diggers, street cleaners, and refuse collectors. It was revealed that through bonus systems and overtime the men were earning up to four times as much as the women.[17] Currently in London, an underground train driver (in a male-dominated profession) earns £41,000 basic pay for a four-day week, while a nurse (a female-dominated profession) typically earns £24,000.[18]

It is important to pay attention to the wider concerns of management and the influence of the economic imperative on management demands, which can sometimes be neglected when solely focusing on gender. Management skills are socially constructed, and also change according to social and economic conditions.[19]

SOFTER SKILLS WANTED

The development of human resource management (HRM) happened in response to increasing global competition and the need to improve worker productivity. One means of doing so was to take more care of employees' welfare. The increase in emphasis on organizational culture was part of this shift, and management is now about winning the hearts and minds of employees as well as controlling them physically.[20] The feminization of management and the trend for more transformative leadership also coincided with the entry of women into management, and the shift from an industrial-based economy to a service economy

In the years following the equal opportunity legislation, when there was an the emphasis on sameness, women's real or perceived management style differences from the dominant masculine model were regarded by some as the reason for their failure to progress. This led to research being undertaken to see whether there were differences in styles of management, with some studies showing differences and other studies showing that there are no differences.[21] However perhaps of more importance were studies that showed that both men and women thought men possessed more of the characteristics that made a good manager.[22] A series of worldwide studies found remarkable similarities, but concluded that 'regardless of context, there appears to be a devaluation of women's qualifications among male students of management world-wide.'[23] When placed in the wider context of women's devaluation in society, 'the pervasion of managerial sex typing reflects the global devaluation of women.'[24] Rigg and Sparrow found some evidence of generalized differences between the managerial styles of women and men, as did Coyle, who put these down to a learned strategy within oppression rather than essentialist (innate) qualities.[25]

Organizations' response to the deficiency model has been a 'fix the women' approach to change. They have introduced women-only training courses and/or sent senior women to externally run women's leadership courses. There is undoubtedly great personal benefit to the individual women who attend these courses, and the organization is also sending a signal of its commitment to women's leadership. The courses can provide a supportive environment for women's self-development, and increase the self-confidence of the participants, but in themselves they do nothing to challenge dominant styles of management. It seems to be a key 'weakness' in women managers that they have a lack of self-confidence, which leads to a lack of self-promotion, which is itself a product of a wider social devaluation rather than any lack of specific management skill. A female assistant director in a bank commented:

The biggest single asset in this business is confidence. Men are given confidence, particularly certain schooling backgrounds which bestow confidence (Public schools). Women on the whole are taught self-doubt not confidence. If you don't naturally have high expectations of yourself, you have to create this attribute in yourself, because the men here already have it.[26]

The shift away from manufacturing to service industries and the ensuing changes in management requirements meant that communication skills became far more important, and that women might have had the right skills at the right time.[27]

At the same time that equal opportunities shifted to diversity, women's different styles were highlighted rather than minimized. Far from seeing women's different management styles as an obstacle to their progress, women management writers began to advocate the new feminine style as the approach for the 1990s and beyond. Hegelson called it the female advantage.[28] It was claimed that women's leadership involved more participation, motivation by inclusion, and power by charisma. However perhaps these feminine skills were in demand for management in much the same way as women's nimble fingers and patience made them 'suitable' for various types of monotonous factory work. Women were entering management to fulfill certain functions, and these were to be found in the lower ranks of management and in those areas most concerned with customer needs.[29] Women's 'difference' then was only valued to the extent that it contributed to profitability.

There was little evidence that women's superior skills were required in the upper echelons of management.[30] A change to a more 'feminine' or 'people-orientated' style of management does not necessarily mean an increase in the numbers of women reaching senior levels. Men can invest in feminine ways of leading and managing as well as women. Men have continued to dominate top management despite the big increase in women's participation, and the fact that the requirements of management are in a continual state of change.[31]

BUSINESS/FUNCTION NEEDS

In the management literature on corporate culture it is the business function and leadership that most influence the style of management.[32] Anna Wahl studied a woman-dominated company, and found that style was relevant according to the functional position of the manager: that is, the business area they were engaged in.[33] So, for instance, she found that the style of the marketing director was different from that of the finance director, and she put these differences in style down to the work the director was engaged in, and not whether they were male or female. Different businesses require different management skills. It could be argued that the business function itself sets demands on management style.

Judy Wajcman concluded that 'organizational constraints rather than individual personality traits determine management style', in her research into five global companies.[34] My own research also showed that it was the business function that was the most important influence on management style, followed by leadership and then gender difference.[35]

In a similar vein, linguistic researchers have reported that the nature of the work itself determines the style of workplace communication. For example in a study on police officers, both men and women adopted a level neutral tone, without smiling – an unemotive way to communicate calm and control in potentially dangerous situations, whereas in call centers both men and women used much more intonation in order to engage with customers.[36]

In my Airco research the airline's overall style, with its emphasis on status, meetings, and deferring decision making to senior managers, was found in all divisions, but the different business function led to completely different styles of management.[37] In Human Resources and Cabin Services, part of management's job was to find out what employees really thought and felt, not just that they were functioning and getting the job done. Where the goals of the division were not service related, the management style was one that reflected less personal involvement in employees' welfare. This was true regardless of whether the leader was a man or woman, and of the gender composition of the workforce. Many studies of female managers have been of organizations that employ a lot of women, such as retailing and retail banking, which are service industries. It may be that the 'feminine' style often found is a requirement of the business, not a consequence of the gender composition. The other strong influence was leadership. In my Airco research I found that in the Cabin Services division, the leader invested heavily in the new 'person-centered' style and emulated it.[38]

In the airline's Marketing Division nearly half of all senior managers were women (47 percent), but its dominant style could in no way be considered 'feminine'. It was results-oriented, fast, and communication skills were important. It was a relatively new division, and because of this men and women had arrived at much the same time. This meant also that this division avoided much of the historical status-oriented style that pervaded the rest of the airline. Of Marketing Division respondents, 57 percent thought that women managed differently, while the figure was 73 percent for the whole airline. The leader was a woman and her style was fairly abstract and detached. One male manager commented,

> I consider the style of management to be quite forceful here. It is a lot about pushing through your own ideas and you win through sheer force of character.[39]

And a female manager told me:

> I don't think there is much difference. There are so many women here. It s not an issue – we are all quite brash but we can work well in a team too.[40]

EMOTION LEGITIMIZED

Formerly banned from management discourse, emotion has now been included under the more legitimate and authoritative concept of emotional intelligence.[41] This is interesting because one of the recurring criticisms of women who aspired to be managers in the 1970s and 1980s was that they were too emotional, which was taken as evidence of lack of control. Can it be a coincidence that Daniel Goleman's best-seller *Emotional Intelligence* was published in 1995 after 15 years of women's presence in management?[42] It could be argued that before 1995 many women and some men used their 'emotional intelligence' but it was not recognized until a male writer packaged it up to sell it as a management skill. Even now the much-lauded soft skills that women are meant to have naturally do not seem to be valued as much as emotional intelligence, which can be learned at some cost in workshops. This is an example of the labeling and gendering of skills and consequent valuation of them. Intuition has been labeled feminine and not considered an appropriate basis on which to make a decision; gut feel however has more validity. Surely the fact that the top ten best-selling books (in 2010) on emotional intelligence were all written by men is noteworthy.[43] The surge in interest in emotion in organizations prompted Gherardi to ask whether they were being colonized by managerial man: 'One may legitimately suspect that emotionality is now undergoing a process of defeminisation with the intention of ascribing it greater legitimacy.'[44]

It is an extension of the trend towards regarding people as assets. The HRM approach of acknowledging employees' values and beliefs and trying to harness them to the needs of the organization is now being extended to emotions. In his book *Emotional Capital* (1998), Kevin Thomson states, 'organizations in the future will manage feelings, beliefs, perceptions and values – the asset of emotional capital – as the hidden resources with the power to translate people's knowledge into positive actions.'[45]

Hochschild's work *The Managed Heart* (1984) popularized the idea that emotional labor can be a public form of labor that is directly appropriated for commercial exploitation.[46] Originally recognized as the unseen work done by service workers to please and satisfy clients, emotional labor has now been extended and recognized as a management characteristic.

In the Cabin Services division in Airco, management did harness the emotions of both cabin crew and its management to further business ends. All cabin crew were being put through an intensive training course, based on existential psychology that sees the self as in charge of its own destiny. The emphasis was on 'being' as opposed to 'doing' and staff needed to understand themselves better so as to better relate to passengers. Managers were undergoing training in order to relate to cabin crew more effectively. A male manager said:

> It is a shift in leadership style that we are looking for: it's not doing, it's being and letting people free a bit more, freedom of choice, more spontaneity, being yourself, being genuine, being at ease with yourself, with colleagues, and with customers.[47]

Parker and Hall have said that people have personal identities and non-work roles and are more engaged in their work when they can express, rather than suppress these identities in the workplace.[48] One of the problems that women in management have encountered is this strict demarcation between home self and work self.[49] Working in the Cabin Services environment gave women some space to be themselves, but this was encouraged for business reasons, not because of diversity. A senior male manager thought that women 'brought themselves to work' more easily than men did, and 'what we are trying to do is get the men to do the same. They are still stuck on the professional kick.'[50]

This style suited the division, which was a very emotional work environment. The managers were managing cabin crew who as a group were comfortable with emotion and showing emotion. One female senior manager said:

> They [cabin crew] have to get to know people very well, often working in extreme conditions with a group they may have never

met before, and often dealing with difficult passengers. They have to be outgoing. Management has to adapt accordingly.[51]

This style was specific to the Cabin Services division though, as a male senior manager pointed out:

I'm not sure it is what the whole airline wants, but I think it works here. It is a simple message – it's really bringing yourself at home to work. You don't have to put on this cloak of professionalism, hierarchy and office.[52]

Men were being encouraged to invest in what has traditionally been seen as a feminine style of management – being in touch with their own and other people's emotions. This style was strongly influenced by the managing director, who introduced experiential workshops for management and went on one himself. The initiative came from him, and he wanted a change in style for the good of the business. As will be seen in Chapter 8 on sexuality, many cabin crew employees were gay men, and this had an influence on gender relations, the expression of sexuality, and arguably the management style.

Women might be thought to have an advantage in emotional intelligence, but many of the skills women managers have possessed 'naturally' are now suddenly being recognized as valued and being taught to men, akin to Linstead's 'colonisation of feminine skills.'[53]

Women in the airline felt that their 'emotional labor' skills were not explicitly valued, and one told me she thought emotional labor should have been recognized as a key performance indicator.[54] Elizabeth Kelan's work on IT workers in Switzerland found that when social competence was discussed as a characteristic of an ideal worker, it was not gendered and men claimed equal rights to it. However when women showed social competence, it was seen as gendered and natural to them: 'she did get credit for these skills – but as a woman for whom it comes naturally to display these skills, and not as a worker who displays skills as part of the job and who is remunerated for it.'[55]

EXPRESSION OF EMOTION

However the management of others' emotions is different from the expression of emotion in the workplace. The denial of emotion features in critiques of masculine management, yet Roper's classic study[56] of organizational men illustrates that men invest a lot of emotion in their work and their work relations.[57] Swan has argued that emotion needs to be located within specific historical and culturally specific discourses.[58] The appropriateness of how, why, when, and where we express emotion changes with time, place, and culture. A friend from the United States visiting England commented on the British reserve, 'Where do you Brits express your emotions? I don't see it anywhere.' She clearly hadn't been to a Chelsea football match when they had won 4–0. Watching football in the United Kingdom is one place where it is permitted for men to express the whole gamut of emotions, including joy and tears. Permission is much more limited in organizations.

At work, certain emotions are legitimate in some areas and not in others. Anger may be permitted in some places and circumstances, such as on a trading floor or from a boss to a junior. In the financial services industry, inflated salaries combined with job insecurity have resulted in fear and greed being motivating factors for many. There is a lot of emotion flying around when huge amounts of money are at stake. Anxiety about losing it, anger if someone makes a mistake, fear of losing one's job, are manifested every day on trading floors, but few would use the word emotional to describe traders. Psycho-dynamic approaches to culture acknowledge the key role of emotions in the workplace. It is often irrational emotion that drives behavior.

The expression of emotions such as love, sadness, fear, and expression of vulnerability is not generally considered professional. Most senior women know that to be called emotional is not a compliment. In both organizations I studied in my research, managers in all areas avoided showing emotions that implied difficulty in coping, such as symptoms of stress. Men and women saw crying as a sign of weakness, and as providing an immediate target for men to attack. A male manager in Airco said, 'Someone once cried but they had to leave the building to do it, so that gives you an idea of how acceptable that is.'[59] A female senior manager in HR told me, 'If you show weakness, that is regarded as a problem. That would include crying, or showing distress or signs that you could not cope with the job.'[60]

MANAGING DIFFERENTLY?

My research in the bank and the airline showed that a large majority of women respondents (84 percent) thought that they had a different management style from men, while 55 percent of men thought that women had a different style from them.[61] Even more marked were the statistics for the predominantly male investment bank, where 88 percent of women thought they managed differently but only

23 percent of men thought that women managed differently from them.

Opportunity Now's recent study showed a similar discrepancy in men and women's perception of different style as being a barrier to progress. While 48 percent of women said it was, only 21 percent of men agreed.[62] Can we put this down to lack of awareness?

Women I consulted in my research felt themselves to manage differently in three ways. Interestingly two of the differences refer to skills they felt they had, and one relates to status and politics:

- **Better people skills.** Many women respondents felt that women were better listeners, they were more relationship-oriented, more empathetic, more likely to take other people's feelings into account, and gave higher priority to human aspects of any situation.
- **Fewer status concerns**. Respondents felt that women managers were more consensus-oriented, more concerned with how decisions had an impact on others, less political, and more collaborative, with fewer status needs.
- **Better managerial skills.** Respondents said that women managers were stronger characters, tougher, more flexible, and that they were able to juggle different jobs at once. They were more demanding, more creative, found less obvious solutions, and had better organizational skills. They were more able than men to adapt their style according to their work teams.

In some ways these findings do not support the argument that women's different style prevents their progress. It is hard to see how difference can be penalized if it is not acknowledged by men. The airline was a very political environment, with networking vital for success. Women's stated dislike of status and politics, and the perception that they are not as political as men, may have acted to exclude them from positions of power in this organization, as both status awareness and politics were considered important for career progress. Women's exclusion – either voluntary or not – from internal networks is further discussed in Chapter 7. Lack of self-promotion and political networking, which becomes more important at senior levels, is still treated as a problem for women. These traits are not confined to the United Kingdom. Senior women from different countries in the professional services firm Ernst & Young are being put through the women's leadership course at the Centre for Women's Leadership Cranfield. According to Fleur Bothwick, director of diversity and inclusiveness for Europe, the Middle East,

India, and Africa. Their difficulties in the workplace are remarkably similar, and include 'believing that doing a good job is enough to be rewarded,' not paying enough attention to impression management, and not investing enough time in networking.[63]

My PhD research findings do support the trend towards problematizing masculinities of management in the workplace.[64] Perhaps it is time to challenge the usefulness of men's status concerns rather than ask women to adopt them too. These kind of political behaviors are usually signs of lack of confidence, and detract from the ability to do the job.

In my PhD research interviews many women said that they felt that the skills listed above were not recognized in organizations, particularly in the bank. The women felt themselves to be better managers than men, but undervalued in the organization. It may be hard to value women's skills in work when they are not recognized.[65]

The caring and communication skills women are expected to bring to their work are considered to be 'natural,' a part of their nature. In the same way, mothering is considered a natural skill, and the hard emotional and physical work that underpins it often goes unacknowledged. One female senior manager in the finance division of the airline said of her management style:

> We are more team players than men. But we can be very masculine if we want to. I can shout and bawl and swear if I want to, but I also can read people quite well – and then vary my approach accordingly. For instance, I may flatter X by saying, 'I'm having some difficulty with this plan and I wondered whether you could help me out with it.' We use many different approaches.[66]

Some of this 'adapting' seemed to involve taking into account particular male colleagues' needs, for example the need to feel more superior, the need to feel protective and so on, which requires conscious effort and falls into the category of emotional labor – and yet is invisible. Instead, it was factors like visibility, concern with status, and single-mindedness, all criticized by many of the women as having nothing to do with productivity or outcomes, and not 'good' management per se, which continued to be rewarded.

WHAT HAPPENED TO THE FEMALE ADVANTAGE?

Twenty years after US academics wrote of the 'female advantage,'[67] women's management style difference is still the focus of analysis of gender inequality in the workplace. A joint Opportunity Now and

Catalyst survey[68] on senior women managers in the United Kingdom showed that while the top career strategy for women's advancement was to consistently exceed performance expectations, almost as important was developing a style with which male managers are comfortable. This finding matched other Catalyst findings from research done in the United States and Canada. In Europe, findings from joint Catalyst and Conference Board research carried out in 2002[69] were less clear, with some difference of opinion over whether the survey item 'fitting your behavior style to what is typical at your employer' was an important component of getting ahead. Some respondents contended that the European work environment was more open to variations in personal style and that women can embrace their femininity. However more women (44 percent) than men (34 percent) reported adjusting their behavioral style to suit the organizational style.

The most recent Opportunity Now research (2010a)[70] reported that 48 percent of women respondents cited personal style differences as a barrier to progress, but only 21 percent of men thought they were.

So the 'female advantage' did not quite happen. Feminine skills did not carry women to the top of organizations. Instead it seems that these skills might not really be wanted at senior levels. In my research I found that some women in Airco observed a narrowing of the difference between men and women's management styles as women reached more senior positions, as was also found by Still and Wajcman.[71] A female manager in Marketing said:

> Junior women managers are more aware of and giving of recognition to their teams, they are less emotional and dictatorial and more open to discussion of different options. But of more senior managers I see no differences between men and women. And those attributes, which I consider positive, are seen by me in neither men nor women.[72]

Recently in the book *Why Women Mean Business* (2008), the authors Wittenberg-Cox and Maitland stated that 'Women, having entered companies in parity with men, still frequently find the culture foreign to their own leadership styles, particularly the higher they go.'[73]

DOUBLE STANDARDS

Although men can and do invest in feminine styles of management, when women invest in the more masculine styles there is a social penalty to pay.

An article in the *Harvard Business Review*[74] published the results of three studies, which showed that men negotiated for more money more than women did, and in different situations women always accepted less. When women did make demands the reaction was not always positive. The authors concluded that women who assertively pursue their own ambitions and promote their own interests might be labeled as bitchy or pushy. Throughout any organization, people respond in different ways to the same behavior in men and women, they argued. Behaviors that in a man might be called assertive or principled, in a women might be considered overbearing or strident.

In another study the same lead researchers found that men were less willing to work with a woman who had attempted to negotiate than with a woman who had not. So the authors concluded that women's reluctance to negotiate was based on an accurate view, and was a rational response: 'this isn't about fixing the woman. It isn't about telling women you need self-confidence or training. They are responding to incentives within the social environment.'[75]

What is the purpose of noting women's different styles when whatever style women use, they are liable to be judged by different standards? Women are obliged to walk what Janet Holmes calls a 'tightrope of impression management'.[76] Women need to come across as professionally competent but without losing their femininity.

Women can and do display the same characteristics as men, but they are often then stigmatized for being 'masculine.' We have so few models of women leaders that a leader who is a woman has automatically become less human. We saw in Chapter 3 on gender awareness how women leaders are often vilified, with research showing that women leaders are more likely to be perceived as 'unlikeable' and more likely to be judged as 'incompetent.'[77] Both women and men judge them harshly, and resort to criticisms of a personal nature, particularly around physical appearance, to explain their lack of femininity. When Ann Hopkins sued Price Waterhouse for sex discrimination for failing to make her a partner, the accountancy firm's defense was that she was unladylike, her behavior was macho, and that she should be more feminine in the way she walked, talked, and behaved.[78]

Female politicians are perhaps the most visual cultural leaders who are constantly judged against an aesthetic standard of attractiveness, and in the event of a mistake are vilified out of all proportion to the wrongdoing. Having authority, for a women, may mean accusations of being cold and aloof. Women and men both invest in these damaging stereotypes to repair the break in the gender order.[79] Even in 2010, a young female graduate working in the financial services industry told me that she had rejected an offer from a US investment bank after doing some work experience there and finding,

> I could not relate in any way at all to the 'role models' i.e. senior women who were told to spend time with the female interns. They dressed like men, didn't seem to have families and were aggressive. I just didn't want to end up like that.[80]

In my airline research there were negative comments from men about some of the senior women directors, such as the comment from a man working in finance, 'She is far too tough and aggressive. Some of these women overdo it when they get promoted. It is not very attractive.'[81] So it is not masculinity per se that is valorized in organizations, it is masculinity *in men*. By adopting male characteristics, women are not seen as extending their femaleness but as abandoning it. In contrast when men embrace a more 'feminine' way of behaving, it is considered an addition to male virtues.

One recently retired banker told me that she felt she had to present just one side of herself for her job, not something she was proud about, but she felt it had been a necessity. She now wonders why she could not have been herself more.[82] However there is a certain amount of professionalization that occurs, a growing into the job, which may require a certain distancing. Suzi Spink, 44, is chief operating officer of East, a ladies fashion retailer with turnover of £40 million and a staff of 600. She shares the running of the company with two other female directors. She gets feedback from people describing her style at work as focused and strong, and lacking emotional involvement:

> I take it on board but it's the way I have learned to operate in a business environment. You get to know what behaviors are effective. It's not conscious and I feel it is an appropriate style for work, although I think I am actually quite an emotional person outside work.[83]

LEARNING TO VALUE WOMEN

The 'difference' argument has continued throughout the 2000s in keeping with the diversity discourse and celebration of difference. The earlier stance that women were better suited to the new economic reality[84] gave way to an organizational emphasis on the need to recognize and value women's different skills. Women are now no longer better, just 'equal but different'. The problem lies in the failure of organizations to value this difference. Valuing difference, as we saw in Chapter 3 on gender awareness, is a hallmark of the diversity discourse. Rather than assuming that women need to change in order to 'fit' in with prevailing organizational cultures, some companies are now trying to shift their cultures to accept difference in style, and validating different ways of managing. If diversity initiatives aim to value different styles, they must first be recognized by men, who for the most part make up the leadership. At the same time some organizations are trying to eradicate the impact of negative stereotypes of women in the workplace through work on unconscious bias.

ONE BIG MISUNDERSTANDING – THE 'MEN ARE FROM MARS' PHENOMENON

In order to help organizations to recognize women's difference and accommodate it as well as value it, this difference has to be explained. And there has been no shortage of help. Enter the world of men baffled at what women want or even mean when they are at work or home, and women equally perplexed by the strange behaviors of men. The staggering success of the *Men are from Mars: Women are from Venus* books by John Gray[85] has given birth to an industry based on men and women's differences. The central theme is that women are different from men in styles, behaviors, and communication, and this leads to all kinds of problems in their personal lives and at work. If only men and women understood one another better, life/relationships/work/sex would be all be fine. And all you need is a book or a workshop.

John Gray has a lot to answer for. Men apparently gain a sense of fulfillment primarily from achieving results and doing an excellent job, while women experience fulfillment by sharing, collaborating, and cooperating in the process of achieving greater success. The business world has its own Mars and Venus groupies, and consultancies that claim to teach organizations how to understand women, or how men and women can better understand each other, are thriving. But more than that, the essentialist thinking is creeping into all areas of our understanding of gender difference, and we should be wary of this.

The linguistics writer Deborah Tannen is a leading proponent of the misunderstanding approach, and consultants draw heavily on her books, *You Just don't Understand* and *Talking 9 to 5*.[86] Before her work was published, the best-known approach to gender differences in language was the one pioneered by Robin Lakoff in the early 1970s, which treated differences primarily as effects of male dominance and female subordination: for example, 'I will speak in a facilitative way because you are more powerful and important than me.'[87]

Tannen instead takes a cross-cultural approach: that is, that the two styles are equally valid but the difference between them can lead to a misunderstanding.[88] Like the diversity approach, power is absent, the material conditions of men and women's lives are left unexplained – it's just one big misunderstanding caused by the fact that boys and girls spend their formative years in separate spheres. The differences do not stop at mere communication. Behaviors are very different too.

Pat Heim is another very influential figure in gender relations in organizations in the United States. An introduction to her workshop GenderSpeak says,

> Men and women grow up in different cultures. As a result we learn different lessons about 'appropriate' behavior. What seems natural to one gender can seem mysterious and baffling to the other. This workshop will help both men and women comprehend the rules of the other gender and value these differences.[89]

According to Heim and Tannen, misunderstandings between the sexes are treated in the same ways as misunderstandings between two different nationalities/cultures – each is unfamiliar with the other's way of doing things and puzzled by it. This is understandable when applied to different national cultures. We have no need to communicate with someone from another country until we go there or they come here. But boys and girls are brought up in the same households, and masculinity and femininity are defined in opposition to each other. Children are aware of the significance of gender distinctions from a very early age, and learn gender-appropriate behaviors. Everything in our society informs (screams at) us that boys and girls are different even before we have left the pram. There is a wealth of literature explaining the power of these differences, which are said to start literally from birth (even before, if we know the sex of the child). Dressing a small boy in pink will have you accosted in the street by strangers. We should be challenging these norms, not accepting them.

Although the Mars/Venus problem is presented as a mutual one, in reality the focus is more on men not understanding women. In my own research and consultancy I find that women understand only too well what men mean in the workplace. There is nothing baffling about them or their 'rules.' They may be unwritten but they are not particularly subtle. Women in business know that to succeed you have to still play by men's rules. Men still dominate senior management, not women. We have seen in all the work on styles that women can learn to play the rules very well, or they may have those characteristics anyway, but neither men nor women will approve of them. To talk of women's rules is nonsense. What are they? We have yet to find out. And why would men want to play them?

REASONS FOR DIFFERENCES

Following some research into why women were leaving the organization, consumer goods giant Procter & Gamble[90] (P&G) decided to introduce a number of initiatives to improve the retention and promotion of women managers. One of their findings was that the women managers said that the dominant management style was aggressive. To further explore this and bring it to everyone's attention, P&G developed an internal workshop, sex@workshop. Table 4.1 lists some of the management characteristics used in the workshop to facilitate discussion. These lists can be found in many different training programs. Any reading can see that the feminine list is on the whole positive, whereas the male characteristics are on the whole negative. The question that must surely be asked by everyone is that if they have all these positive skills and behavioral traits, why aren't women at the top of all successful businesses?

As an initiative, gender-difference-based training can be fun and

Table 4.1 Procter & Gamble's list of male and female management characteristics

Male	Female
Hierarchical style	Supportive coaching style
Directive	Multitask focused
Quick	Attribute success to external factors
Single task focused	Hedge, deferential speech
Status oriented	Unconcerned with status
Poor at reading nonverbal communication	Good at reading nonverbal communication
Bond through banter	Find banter rude
Dominate and compete in meetings	Involve others

Source: adapted from S. Rutherford, "Different but equal," in R. Burke and M. Matthis (eds), *Supporting Women's Career Advancement: Challenges and Opportunities*, Cheltenham: Edward Elgar, 2005.

provoke discussion in a relatively uncontroversial way, and avoid discussions around power, domination, and discrimination. It may also engage men in the debate. They may be mildly challenged without being threatened. However, many of the different skills on the list above look dangerously like perpetuating stereotypes, which are consistently given as a barrier to women's progress at work, and which organizations are actively trying to discourage.

Many of these differences can be explained through socially situated differences. Does not taking credit when it's due – or often when it's not due – mark a person out as lacking in ambition? Why should modesty not be rewarded, as indeed in other cultures it is?

There is a wonderful cartoon depicting a boardroom meeting with nine men and one woman sitting round the table. The caption coming from the chairman is, 'Thank you for that suggestion, Miss Smith. Now perhaps one of the men would like to make it.' It has been made into a cartoon because women laugh at it, and they laugh at it because it is so familiar.

Susan Rice, managing director of Lloyds Banking Group Scotland and the UK's most senior woman banker, is no stranger to board meetings. She is not only a senior executive in an industry where senior women are few and far between, she also sits on the board of Southern and Scottish Energy and the Court of the Bank of England, as the only woman. Even at these senior levels, she says, 'I speak quite deliberately and make sure that people are listening to what I'm saying. It's important to do that as a woman. It's easy to be overlooked.' She continues, 'I challenge in my own style. I may preface the challenging question with a "warning" like "I'm just thinking out loud but," or "it occurred to me that".....'[91] This prefacing could be interpreted by some commentators as being hesitant, as perhaps covering herself for a possible mistake or misunderstanding in the challenge. But it also acts to facilitate what may be a contentious subject. It is a softening of the atmosphere rather than a hardball direct challenge, and allows the person to whom it is directed not to reply.

Many of the male characteristics in the workshop list are arguably detrimental to conducting good business, certainly where managing people are involved. Hogging time at meetings, interrupting, taking credit when it's not due, and having status concerns are about self-promotion, not management.

This suggests that some of the masculinities performed in the workplace are an area that needs to be addressed. In some ways this process was started by the soul-searching that went on after the credit crisis. The largely male bank boards which contributed to the credit crisis of 2008–09 were criticized publicly for their reckless risk taking and failure. The collective mismanagement displayed by the banks has been explained either by 'groupthink' – that is having too many people of the same type who think in the same way – or in biological terms, as a consequence of too much testosterone. The more likely cause of lack of communication skills or indeed common sense displayed by those at the top of the banks has gone unchallenged. Instead of addressing the failure of men and how their behaviors could change, it has been suggested that an increase in the number of women might act as a brake on this 'male' recklessness.

In terms of different styles at board level, Susan Rice comments,

It is hard to stereotype. I think that both women and men adapt and change to some extent the higher up the organization we go. I think, and this is a generalization, women are probably better at looking ahead and imagining the future – and asking about the consequences of a particular strategy. Men look backward to the past more but then they have a collective experience to draw on which women do not yet. We need both perspectives.[92]

STATUS

Incensed by some of the claims that men and women are innately different in the way they communicate, Deborah Cameron, professor of language and communication at Oxford University, wrote a scholarly but eminently readable rebuttal of them. She reminds us that the relationship between the sexes is not only about difference, it is about power.[93] The long-standing expectation that women will serve and care for others is not unrelated to their position as the 'second sex.' But in the universe of Mars and Venus, the fact that we (still) live in a male-dominated society – a society in which the sexes are unequal as well as different – is, she says, like the elephant in the room.

Women's use of deferential speech and its role in undermining their status as leaders features highly in the popularist Mars/Venus literature. In her study on gendered talk in the workplace, Janet Holmes notes that communication involves more than one person. The way I speak to you is affected by the way you speak to me. There are expectations and assumptions. She concludes that different styles have 'nothing to do with the way women "are" and everything to do with the position women are put in.'[94]

Gherardi describes this symbolic order of gender, and notes that now women are no longer excluded from the public world of work, the order is broken. She sees women's behavior when they enter the public world as a way of repairing this break, 'through remedial work which makes their presence "discreet" women enter organizations but "take their place" in segregated jobs; in their work roles they express their femininity.'[95] She suggests that women's lack of assertive style can be interpreted as a ritual which repairs the offence caused by the infringement of the symbolic order of gender when they speak.

Sylvia Shaw refers to the women members of Parliament (MPs) she observed for her research on women's voices in parliamentary debates as 'interlopers.' She argues that women's response to be entering male territory is to 'observe the rules meticulously as a symbolic way of showing that you are worthy to belong.[96]

Insiders themselves can often break the rules. Women as outsiders do everything by the book, and frequently work harder than many of their male peer group to justify their position. The *Breaking the Barriers* research (2000)[97] found that women attributed their success to 'exceeding expectations.' They had to do better than the men to achieve the same level of recognition. Shaw's conclusion was that rule breaking or not was the only difference in style between men and women in the House. She concluded that women might behave in different ways at work not because they have a different style but because they have a different status and need to compensate for it.[98]

Some writers assume that women only encounter difficulty because they are under-represented in organizations. It is their minority status that makes them the interlopers, not their status as the second sex. Kanter, in her classic *Men and Women of the Corporation* (1977), referred frequently to the problems of tokenism, which would disappear once a certain 30 percent tipping point had been achieved. This line of thought would indicate that men who are under-represented in organizations would meet the same problems and need to adapt their management style too. However, the dominant group is not necessarily the one that has the most numbers, its identity is bound up with wider issues of power.

Do men feel the need to adapt to an organization numerically dominated by women? In her study on men working in non-traditional roles, Ruth Simpson found that the men felt comfortable working with the women while at the same time making efforts to reassert their masculinity.[99] She found that men benefited from their minority status through:

assumptions of enhanced leadership (the assumed authority effect), by being given differential treatment (the special consideration effect) and being associated with a more careerist attitude to work (the career effect). At the same time, they feel comfortable working with women (the zone of comfort effect). Despite this comfort, men adopt a variety of strategies to re-establish a masculinity that has been undermined by the 'feminine' nature of their work. These include re-labeling, status enhancement and distancing from the feminine.[100]

BRAIN AND HORMONES – REINFORCING STEREOTYPES

The cultural determinism of the Mars and Venus philosophy has been taken a stage further by a stream of scientific thought arguing that gender differences can be explained by brain and hormone differences – a biological determinism. The consequence of this 'discovery' is not hard to work out. Any efforts to change the ways of men and women are pointless. We are all hardwired (this term is now cropping up in corporate literature on diversity with alarming alacrity). Popular books on management and training have drawn on the 'scientific' theories of neuropsychology and neuroscience, a growing area of science,[101] and are citing immutable biological differences, either brain shape and size or hormones or both, between the male and the female brain as explanations of different communication styles and behaviors. This has been greeted by many with a sigh of relief.

The impact of this new strand of biological determinism can only be negative. In arguing that it is impossible to change what is fixed in the brain, this approach legitimizes stereotypes and explains away behaviors that may have no place in the modern-day workplace. And once the brain is involved we can invoke difference in skills as well as communication and behaviors we may have learned.

One diversity head told me that he had invited in a cognitive neuroscientist (a woman, so even better) to talk about how differences in male and female brains affected their behaviors and that the talk had been a huge success! 'The men can accept a scientific explanation for behavior much more than they can a touchy feely kind of seminar,' he said.[102] 'Scientific' evidence of hardwiring lets us all off the hook. Simon Baron-Cohen, perhaps the best-known and most influential proponent of gender brain difference, outlines his theory.

My theory is that the female brain is predominantly hard-wired for empathy, and that the male brain is predominantly hard-wired for understanding and building systems. I call it the empathising-systemising (E-S) theory.[103]

He has suggested that certain careers are better for those with the 'female brain': 'People with the female brain make the most wonderful counselors, primary school teachers, nurses, carers, therapists, social workers, mediators, group facilitators or personnel staff'.[104]

Given what we know about female segregation in the workplace, where women are bunched in the lowest-paid jobs in caring and serving occupations, what kind of change can possibly be envisaged from this literature? It reinforces stereotypes and the conditions that are preventing women taking their proper place in the workplace.

Deborah Cameron has argued that the complex scientific studies detailing men and women's brain differences are being taken out of context, picked up in an irresponsible way in the media, and feeding the commonsense notions of difference that are so often trotted out as soon as inequality is discussed. She says these create stories that feed into already existing stereotypes and discrimination.[105] Consultants and trainers have found the hitherto undiscovered (but very simple) solution to both discrimination and increased profitability! In their book *Using Gender Science to Create Success in Business,* gender 'experts' Michael Gurian and Barbara Annis explore what the latest scientific studies reveal about male/female brain differences, and explain how these impact the ways men and women negotiate, communicate, lead and run meetings. Then they teach you how to use this scientific gender intelligence for business success.[106]

It is worrying when popularist writers and consultants dip into a highly specialized and, as it transpires, highly controversial set of studies, and use them for the purpose of explaining gender difference in the workplace:

> Gender Intelligence, or Gender IQ, is not the same as gender equality. We base our evidence on work with scientists, psychologists, political leaders and board level executives, and we argue that there are real physical and chemical differences that affect the way that men and women think. Rather than regarding these differences as areas of conflict, we want to use them to maximize commercial performance and personal success.[107]

This strand of biological determinism should ring alarm bells with all supporters of gender equality. Ruth Bleier noted some time ago that 'the brain has frequently been the battle site in controversies over sex or race differences.'[108]

Fortunately, the emergence of this new biological determinism to explain gender differences has come under critical attack.[109] Cordelia Fine, herself a cognitive neuroscientist, sets out to demolish what she calls the neurosexism of Baron-Cohen and his colleagues, which has emerged to add fuel to the fire of difference theory. Fine says that as barriers of sexism fall away, there are fewer and fewer reasons to explain the continuation of traditional gender roles, so we return to the internal and biological explanations – like Baron-Cohen's theory that women are wired differently from men.[110]

Historically, biological differences have been relied on to maintain the status quo of gender relations. Many of the arguments used in the debates against women's suffrage prior to 1923 focused on the physical differences of women's bodies and their brains. Education was deemed harmful for women's reproductive health, and unfeminine. A leading Victorian psychiatrist said in an influential article in 1874 that a woman 'does not easily regain the vital energy that was recklessly spent on learning ... if a woman attempts to achieve the educational standards of men ... she will lack the energy necessary for childbearing and rearing.'[111]

Gina Rippon, professor of cognitive neuroimaging at Aston University, describes the idea that men are hard wired for analyzing and women's brains are better at empathizing as 'patronizing nonsense': 'There may be some small differences between the genders but the similarities are far, far greater.'[112]

That women's difference can always be turned to their disadvantage was illustrated only too well in the now famous Sears Roebuck case in which women's 'difference' was deemed to justify excluding them from highly paid commission sales jobs.[113] Asking why women are not in more senior positions can be met with 'Men and women are different' and/or 'It's biology' with even more confidence than is shown already.

Research shows that subjecting an individual to stereotyping results in psychological disengagement from behavior that is perceived as non-stereotypical. When women and men were told ahead of taking a maths test that in the past women had not performed well in maths tests, the women performed badly. When they were told that there had been no difference in men's and women's performances, there was no difference.[114]

Cordelia Fine delivers a much more nuanced explanation of our differences in behavior and communication, showing how social and cultural elements impact the mind, hormones, and sense of self-identity. The bombardment of gender-specific imagery that divides our society into pink and blue results in gendered behaviors being encouraged, rewarded, and in turn becoming 'natural':

it is all much more complex than a simplistic brain difference explanation can give us. Cultural beliefs are in the mind. They are in a messy tangle of mental associations that interact with the social context. The fluidity of the self and the mind is impressive and is in continual cahoots with the environment.[115]

And it may take many more than one or two generations to eradicate internalized patterns of behaviour.[116]

Our propensity to embrace tired old stereotypes may seem puzzling, but it is comfortable for both men and women. The kind of discussion that refers to hard wiring and essential gender differences is often appealing to managers and indeed trainers, because it diverts attention from power differentials in communication patterns, avoids hostilities, and offers simple solutions – 'Let's just all think a bit more and accept our inevitable differences.'

> Culture change is hard: it causes anxiety, conflict and, in some quarters, resistance. That is why the myth of Mars and Venus has had such a warm reception from the educated western middle classes.[117]

CONCLUDING POINTS

There is an ongoing change in our gendered landscape, and an accompanying shift in gender relations. This is a dynamic, albeit a slow one. We can hope that the impact and influence of a growing number of female leaders will change concepts of leadership and shift old stereotypes. Meanwhile we should resist the temptation to fall back on either cultural or biological-determinist explanations of gender difference.

The differences between men and women's management styles are too often being taken as fixed rather than responses to social and cultural situations. The difference approach, encouraged by the new 'neurosexism' as Cordelia Fine called it,[118] can be seen as a resistance to equality. The exaggeration of difference acts to strengthen boundaries which are being crossed all the time by women.

Rather than seeing women's difference as the reason for lack of progress, might we see men's indifference to or reluctance or refusal to acknowledge the value that women bring in the ways in which they manage, and/or the insistence that particular characteristics are a requirement for successful leadership as a means of resistance?

But as men embrace aspects of femininity deemed to be appropriate for management, it becomes all the more important to acknowledge that power inequalities are not changed through discourses of masculinity and femininity.[119] It is still predominantly men in positions of power in organizations. Bacchi argues that the sameness/difference debate stops short, and fails to criticize the system that encourages men to be a particular way – detached, competitive, and abstracted from personal needs.[120]

The work on masculinity goes some way to responding to this criticism. There is not one type of masculinity, there are many. As historically and socially constructed categories they define legitimate behaviors and identities for men. Although not yet discussed in organizations, masculinity is being introduced by the back door through the work on unconscious bias, because the bias is predominantly a male bias, since historically men have developed cultures and structures and processes that suit them.

In the end it is not about difference, it is about what is valued. Instead of merely asking whether men and women manage differently, it is perhaps more interesting to ask what constitutes variations in management style, with any difference between men and women being one such variation. It may be useful to ask whether the dominant style of management in your organization is the best for the business. Posturing and bravado, dominating meetings, and other types of managerial masculine behavior have no obvious business benefit. A thorough analysis of your management style will catch some of the gendered aspects of management communication and styles. A well-executed audit will include questions about decision making, meetings, leadership, communication, and emotions, and can be cut by gender. This will show up differences in division, function, and level of management.

5

THE PUBLIC/PRIVATE DIVIDE

INTRODUCTION

One of the hallmarks of UK Prime Minister David Cameron's leadership in his first year of government was his seemingly easy ability to show us the public and private side of his life. As a nation we saw the face of the grieving father of a much-loved disabled son who died without warning, the joyful face of a father of a new-born baby girl, and again the grieving face following the death of his own father – and all in one year. It was not just the media photographs, he was also able to articulate his emotions to the world. Putting aside the inevitable cynicism that sees a sympathy vote in every picture, his conduct as a leader cannot help but influence our national culture. Importantly he took his full two weeks paternity leave following the birth of his child.

The amount of personal life you can bring into work will differ according to the culture of your country as well as your organization, in fact from one division to another. In one global financial services company with a strong meritocratic ethos, a male manager told me, 'Our differences are left at the front door. We don't actually bring our private lives into the office at all.'[1] Chapter 3 highlighted the fact that women very often find this separation of home and work a strain.

David Cameron's public image of a caring family man is not evidence that he carries an equal share of the domestic workload, but we do know he places huge importance on his presence at home, and that Samantha Cameron has her own career in business. Similarly in the United States, President Obama refers to and includes his wife Michelle and their two daughters in many of his speeches and appearances to the nation in a respectful way, acknowledging Michelle frequently as his intellectual equal. We require our male and female leaders to be more accommodating and inclusive of lives lived outside the workplace than they have been historically. Women are new to the realms of power, and still suffer from the need to hide their private lives away. It is noteworthy that the public support Hillary Clinton gave as wife of a politician and president is not matched by her husband's public presence in her own political life. He is rarely seen at her side.

In many organizations those with caring responsibilities or any other issues outside work are obliged to manage their domestic responsibilities privately so as to be able to present themselves as the 'disembodied and universal' worker revealed by Joan Acker in 1990 as a man.[2] The second shift done mostly by women often goes unacknowledged by the company.[3]

The separation of home (private) and work (public) may pervade an organizational culture and have an impact on men and women in different ways, both in a material sense and through the gendered representations that this dualism brings about: for example woman as mother, man as breadwinner. An organization's culture indicates whether this divide is marked or being challenged, and whether it is being challenged on behalf of women only, or for both women and men. The divide holds many representations of gender and ideologies, which have repercussions in the workplace.[4]

HOME

The idea that home remains separate from work retains popular appeal, and carries with it particularly gendered notions of being. Home is where the heart is, the place of refuge when work is over, and a place of privacy. This image is a male-defined one because for most women, and those with children particularly, it is a place of hard work, done for love not money, and while it may hold emotional fulfillment for many, as was seen in Chapter 1, for others its privacy may hide abuse. Work is where a public face is put on, where people socialize and make history, where progress occurs, and what people are paid for. Until very recently the public world, was male. Women entering the workforce in greater numbers, combined with the increase in divorce and single-parent families, are challenging these boundaries, and in particular breaking down the 'private patriarchy' referred to by Walby.[5] Yet neither the erosion of the boundaries nor feminist critiques of this dualism of home/work, as illustrated by Acker,[6] detract from its power as a 'connotational system.'[7]

The dualism of home/work and the woman's role as comforter, facilitator, cleaner, cook, caretaker, and emotional support can be seen played out in organizations. Barbara Gutek called this a spillover of roles into the workplace, whereby women are found in greater numbers in support roles, human resources (HR), receptionists, secretaries and the caring professions, in many cases facilitating the important process of men's work.[8]

This dualism also has very real practical problems for women who may carry a dual burden, but even the prospect of motherhood can dent a woman's career prospects. Although it can be illegal I have come across directors who still ask whether a candidate is engaged, or thinking of having children. Biological reproductive capacity is a reference point that is constantly drawn upon to restrict or throw doubts on women's ability to be organizationally effective. Some of the younger women I have interviewed felt that the men were just waiting for them to marry, have children, and leave. They felt it was almost as though that would remove the competition. They are right, it would. A female broker I interviewed during my research at Investco commented:

I'm in an interesting situation right now because I got married six months ago and I'm nearly 37. There are lots of comments about having a family. I say 'No, we are not planning a family yet' and they reply, 'Oh you must be' or they say 'Oh you'd make a lovely mum.'[9]

This woman was uncomfortable that her marriage and decision to have a family had become such a focus for her colleagues. For men marriage meant settling down, and was taken as a positive move for their careers. For women it may signify potential disruption, and have a destabilizing effect on career prospects.

Another woman in the finance division of Airco who had just got married did not want to change her name because she didn't want the organization to know, as the managers would presume she would want children soon, and she felt it would hold up her promotion. References to women's sexuality may be one way to detract from the seriousness of their intent, and in a similar way, reference to their reproductive capacity is another more acceptable one. Young women today who are equal to their male peers are aware of the layout of the landscape that lies ahead. The young women with whom I have spoken shared the prevailing view that a successful career and motherhood were still two separate worlds which it was hard to reconcile, and that along the way a hard choice had to be made – their choice. A professional media analyst, aged 25, said:

I have always thought about career versus having children. I think it's one of the most difficult choices women who work face, especially ambitious women who would like to make a stamp on their industry as a man with their qualifications/experience would. The older I get (I am only 25), but still!) the more I think I do want to have children, and the more I realize that I will be forced to sacrifice some elements of that ambition to look after them.[10]

There has been much more acknowledgement of family life in organizations since the arrival of women in the workplace, and fathers now can display photographs of their children, and attend school sports days and other occasions without fear of reprisal. Indeed it may enhance their standing at work. There is another less ceremonious side of parenting which people are not encouraged to display in the workplace. A child's sickness is a nuisance, and is often never revealed, with mothers (or those with prime responsibility) preferring to take a day sick themselves, or at a push pretend that they need to stay at home to wait for a repair man. One mother I spoke to did not feel the same freedom as men might feel to attend her children's school events, but she went anyway and lied, telling people in the office that she was going to a meeting.

Organizations to a greater or lesser degree still try to mark off private concerns from the workplace. Personal difficulties are the realm of HR or, in large organizations, counselors. In recent years, health (expressed in organizational discourse as 'wellbeing' or the popular word 'wellness') and increasingly happiness are being brought under the organizational umbrella, influencing employee productivity as they undoubtedly do. It was noted in Chapter 1 that some companies are now actively engaging with issues of domestic violence, in recognition that this phenomenon more than any other health issue affects their employees in the workplace. Sick leave and maternity leave allow for out of the ordinary bodily needs to be dealt with away from the office. In practice, however, there can be no such neat separation. Try as people might to keep home life in a box at home, life experiences are not that tidy. On many occasions special situations need to be dealt with at work with sensitivity and care – bereavements, serious illnesses, adoptions – and these concerns cannot be left at the front door. These artificial boundaries were constructed according to male-centered assumptions about the extent to which the private can be marked off from the public, and can prove to be highly problematic for women.

In my research, women in Airco talked without prompting of their home life, husbands, partners, and children as being an important element of their work life. With the men I had to ask about their private lives, although one young man spoke voluntarily of his divorce. In the Investco case study the women were less keen on discussing their home life, and looked faintly surprised if I asked any questions about it. The boundaries there were firmly in place. Other researchers have had a similar experience. Elizabeth Kelan reported in her research on gender and technology workers in Switzerland that they were taken off guard when she asked them questions about their personal life.[11]

The popularity of working mothers' accounts in newspapers, and books like Alison Pearson's *I Don't Know How She Does It* (2002), attest to the numbers of women and increasingly men who struggle to maintain a professional front while dealing with the domestic side of life.

The two worlds of work and home have been spatially and temporally dislocated since the Industrial Revolution. The spatial separation brought about the concept of the working day, the timeframe for which we have never challenged despite huge changes in our economic activities. These boundaries are now being eroded. Home has become porous as work seeps into it, both physically and in terms of time. This is particularly so for professional and managerial groups. In the late 1980s there was an assumption that technology would free people up to spend more time at home with their families or in leisure, as work became more efficient. That just did not happen. Technology is the means by which organizations have been able to extract many more hours of work from their employees. People take work home in the evenings and at weekends, they are contactable all the time via mobile phones, they have communication links at home, computers, faxes, and emails. Nor is this just at home: people often make themselves available on holiday, carrying work mobiles and laptops along with their suitcases. The old presenteeism whereby visibility in the office was rewarded has to some extent been replaced by being available for work anytime, anywhere. This has both positive and negative repercussions for working mothers. A lawyer with two children said, 'I've been able to work four-day weeks but I'm always available on that fifth day so I have to have childcare five days a week. The office and clients know they can reach me on my mobile.'[12] This is the reality of much of the new flexible working for professionals – not necessarily in the office, not paid for that fifth day, but still always available.

Inroads from the private side of life have been slow to pervade the workplace. In the 1980s some organizations established workplace nurseries, but many were closed down, as they did not prove to be economically viable. Childcare in the United Kingdom has generally been left as the responsibility of the individual – not the state or the organization.

Babies, children, as well as old people, many disabled people, and sickness both physical and mental, are absent from the workplace. The publicity surrounding the 'Take Your Daughter to Work' day, which started in 1998 and is now named the 'Take Your Child to Work' day, illustrates how unusual it is for children to enter the workplace. I heard someone once describe the world of work as moving at the pace of the unencumbered physically fit man and woman, and anyone else is at a disadvantage. I went for an interview at a small consultancy some years ago, and my childcare arrangements fell through at the last minute. Rather than cancel I took my 10-year-old with me and left him playing a computer game in the reception area. Frowns of disapproval from the receptionist on arrival told me immediately I had made a mistake. This was considered unprofessional.

During my time at Airco, I was present at a meeting about a highly secret venture in one of the divisions. This project was planned on the assumption that the key managers who were being brought in – rather, ordered in – were available to give over their work lives exclusively to this project. Two of them were living abroad and had just been asked to fly over, little knowing that they were going to be asked to stay for several months. Both these men had families, but leaving them behind was not an issue that merited discussion. One man, who was a single parent, was mentioned by one of the senior managers in this secret meeting: 'We mustn't forget that H has some babysitting responsibilities.' This was greeted with awkwardness and embarrassment – by this stage the meeting resembled a briefing for a military strategy – but all men present were aware enough of the airline's equal opportunity culture not to say anything disrespectful. Also, I was there. There followed some talk about how putting effort in was all that mattered, and then a joke about a crèche in the project site, with some awkward laughter. This male single parent was unusual, and in unusual circumstances allowances may be made, but the rest of the team would give all the time the project needed, the managing director assured those present.

I suggest that the ideal worker for most organizations is still one who is prepared to be committed to full-time work, prepared to give it 'his' all, and that any external needs will be dealt with by a wife, partner, or other resources. Anyone who has ever seen a contract for work at investment banks like Goldmans Sachs knows that by signing it employees are giving their allegiance to work for the company above everything else. There is still the lingering assumption that work is somehow separated from the rest of life, and that it has first claim on the worker. Those with other responsibilities do not fit with the abstract 'job.'[13] Many women feel that to succeed on male terrain, they need to rid themselves of all vestiges of home. For some this is easy; for others it requires enormous psychic effort.

The divide of work/leisure is another inappropriate dualism when applied to women. The notion is culturally built into our concept of work, and again is gendered, because the assumption is that when a male worker is not 'at work' he is at play: that is, on the golf course, in the pub, or spending time with their family. However the reality may be different now that more women are working and the numbers of divorced fathers have increased. The City gyms are full of men and single women, and a glance at the local tennis courts on a Saturday morning shows most players are men. Many at-home mothers feel that their husbands deserve time off at weekends because they work so hard (and earn the money). For mothers in paid work there is little leisure time, because there is work to do as soon as they get home. The mothers that I interviewed spent all free time they had with their children and on household chores. A female senior marketing manager said, 'I used to play a lot of sport, go to the gym but that's out now. I shop on Saturdays and spend time with my children for the rest.'[14]

Although the private work of home has not been carried into the public workplace, there has been a trend whereby work incorporates leisure.[15] Apart from people enjoying their jobs, large corporations offer on-site facilities for all kinds of leisure activities. Modern offices for large corporations now usually include coffee bars, restaurants, gymnasiums, and swimming pools, as well as being concerned with design features such as artworks, atriums, and potted plants. These features are, however, geared towards the young and single, who spend so long at work that most of their friends are there, and they end up spending leisure time with them too. This also provides an attractive work environment where people are comfortable spending most of their time. In an interview with the author a 25-year-old banker said, 'The facilities here are great – there's a shop, gym, doctor, dentist, physio, manicurist, coffee shop, cafeteria etc on site so you never need leave the mother ship.'[16]

Technology which allows workers to tune into work wherever they are has also enabled more people to work at home, either full time or for one or two days a week. As we shall see when we look at organizational responses to employing parents, some organiza-tions encourage this, while others are still reluctant to accept that physical presence may not always be a requirement of the job. But while working at home means flexibility to juggle workloads and time to some extent, there is still work of a domestic nature that has to be done.

UNPAID WORK AT HOME – THE SECOND SHIFT

An inclusive culture should recognize the work that is done at home. The managing director of one of the divisions of Airco told me that he had had to take responsibility for his 12-year-old son for six months while his wife completed a degree course in France: 'It really made me appreciate how much she actually did that I hadn't noticed before.'[17] What he was not able to do, though, was appreciate that many of the women who worked for him probably had also to do what his wife did when they got home.

The uncritical acceptance by organizations and society, and women themselves, that a working woman carries a dual burden may be evidence enough that no real change in domestic responsibilities is expected. The dual burden, or 'second shift,' as Arlie Hochschild deftly phrased it,[18] acts as a major obstacle to women achieving positions of seniority in organizations.[19] For a shift of power away from men to be the inevitable outcome of women succeeding in organizations, a shift in the domestic arena is required, with men taking on more responsibility at home. As Doreen Massey puts it, 'if an employee works fourteen hours a day, someone else has to carry the other side of life.'[20] Even top consultancy firm McKinsey, renowned for the hours its own consultants have to put in, has recently come to the conclusion that 'Men have greater freedom. In seeking to create a balance in the work environment, should we not also encourage and enable a different, more equal balance at home?'[21]

We know that most women with families do two jobs, one at work and one at home. This is not a balance. The moment a mother gets through the front door she will have already psychologically switched hats and be ready for the emotional and often physical demands of one or more children, tired at the end of the day and eager for some attention from mummy. Working mothers like Allison Pearson have written amusingly in books and newspaper columns of their struggle to 'have it all,' which in reality means 'doing it all.'[22] The endless chores, responding to children's demands, and placating husbands, all get told with good humor and make entertaining reading. Many working women have read the tales of sunken cupcakes or tears in the early hours when trying to finish off a child's project, with the relief that recognition of one's own personal situation can bring. However, I have interviewed hundreds of working mothers over the years, and witnessed the stress and the pressure of keeping it all going in ways that frankly would not make an amusing column. The stories of the majority of working mothers just do not get told.

It doesn't help that an escalation of time demands has happened in the family as well as in the workplace. In the 1940s and 1950s mothering meant feeding and caring physically for a child; in the 1960s and 1970s care for their emotional wellbeing was included; and since then mothering now includes, in addition, enrichment of social life and building networks. Supervision of homework, participation in all kinds of extracurricular activities from judo to football to music lessons, all sports, and so on, is incredibly demanding of parents' time, and makes combining paid work with family life even harder.

Motherhood does not have a fixed meaning, it changes over time, place, and culture. The ideology of an all-encompassing hands-on middle-class mothering is quite new. A century ago when work was not an option for middle and upper-class women, surrogates, usually nannies, looked after their children. This freed mothers up for shopping, charitable causes and running the house, which included dealing with domestic staff. Working-class women who did work relied on their relatives much as they do today. Yet today all women can, and the majority do, work but are still held largely responsible for running the home and childcare, with little in the way of help.

Ideologies of motherhood vary from culture to culture and are often informed by economic and social needs of the time. In *kibbutzim* in Israel, children did not live with their parents but with the other children of the *kibbutz*, thus freeing up adults for important labor. Parenting and childhood as we know them in the West are the outcomes of a well-developed economy. The ideology of parenting in poorer countries is more likely to mean feeding, clothing, and keeping children healthy. It may mean parents not living with their children in order to work to keep them and provide them with an education. In the West, many professional families employ women from South-East Asia, particularly the Philippines, to look after their children and homes. These women themselves very often have children in the Philippines, whom they see perhaps once a year. They are being good mothers by earning money and sending it home to their families.[23]

In parts of Europe (for example, Scandinavia and France) the provision of state childcare has been instrumental in enabling women to return to work, and in developing countries like India and Brazil, the availability of relatively cheap private childcare and domestic labor, plus the extended family, makes life a lot easier for the working mother. In the 2010 *Financial Times* 'Top 50 Women in Business,' six were from India, and in Brazil 11 percent of chief executives are women.[24] In India, almost a third of the working population live with parents or in-laws. In the United States the figure is 3 percent, and in Britain it is 1 percent. A study carried out in 2010 by the US-based Center for Work–Life Policy (CWLP), argued that the social and cultural traits of BRIC countries play a large part in their women's ability to run both companies and families successfully. The authors also found evidence to suggest western women are vilified for trying to balance a high-powered career with family life. In Germany they came across a term to describe them, '*Rabenmutter*', meaning 'raven mother' after the bird's reputation for being neglectful of its young.[25]

In 1995 Susan de Vere, editor of *Top Sante* magazine, commented on a research study on gender roles:

> Women are exhausted as men still do not want to share the responsibilities at home. Men have made a token gesture of being 'new' men, perhaps by changing a few nappies but they would still rather sneak off for a pint after work and hope that by the time they get home the children and housework have been dealt with.

The report revealed that 76 percent of women felt they had too many roles to perform, 25 percent were stressed most of the time, and 54 percent felt exhausted at least once a week.[26]

In 2007 a large study conducted by researchers at Cambridge University reported that women who go out to work still do the bulk of household chores, so that while men may spend longer at the office, it is women who work more each week if domestic and paid employment is added together. The European Union-funded report, which examined working practices across member states, says that the average man in full-time employment works about 55 hours a week. In the United Kingdom that figure includes about 3.6 hours commuting, and eight hours of domestic work such as cleaning, cooking, and childcare. By contrast, the average working week for a woman in full-time employment in the European Union is 68 hours. For women in the United Kingdom that comprises 40 hours in the office, 3.3 hours commuting, and 23 hours a week spent doing domestic work.[27]

Even women who work part time put in longer hours overall than men in full-time work, because they do so many household chores. Women with part-time jobs work on average 57 hours a week. That is made up of 21.3 hours in paid work, 2.4 hours commuting, and 32.7 hours of domestic work. The domestic workload also prevents millions of women from working the long office hours typically required to break into top management and get a job with a high salary, the report said. A 2007 London Business School study on innovation in teams found that women team members were six times more likely than men to perform the domestic duties at home.[28]

There is no doubt that men today are more involved in family life. My father rarely came to sports days or school plays, but then he finished work at a civilized time and was always home by 7 pm – and that was after a commute. He didn't do household chores not because he wasn't there, but because it was not considered by either of my parents that that was his role. After supper we had a rota for washing and drying up, but it was accepted that my father was exempt because he went out to work. He was physically present but did not do much round the house. The garden was his domain.

Today fathers are more hands-on but because of long working hours they are probably less present in the family home than their own fathers were. A study showed that 54 percent of fathers with children under 1 year old feel they are not devoting enough time to them, while 42 percent of fathers feel they are not able to spend enough time with their children. Additionally, 62 percent of fathers think that, in general, fathers should spend more time caring for their children: fathers are working long hours, too, with six out of ten working more than 40 hours a week.[29]

Interim findings from research being undertaken for Working Families by Lancaster University Management School are positive on the future sharing of household responsibilities. A majority of fathers want to spend more time looking after their children, and are less stressed when sharing childcare and domestic chores with a partner who is in full time employment.[30] This study focuses on middle-earning men, which might have influenced the findings.

MATERNITY RETURNERS

How an organization handles pregnancy and return to work is a good signifier of its attitudes to its female employees, and its acknowledgement and integration of the private side of life. Until relatively recently pregnancy, lactation, and motherhood (reproduction) belonged to the private sphere. The entry of women into the terrain of male management and professions has meant that this private activity with its associated sexuality has now become an organizational issue too. It would seem that many organizations are dragging their heels in the accommodation of reproduction in their space – let alone a valuation of the skills it brings. Although they are the most common and natural thing in the world, and are increasingly experienced (vicariously in the case of pregnancy) by fathers, pregnancy and parenthood are still treated as aberrations from 'normal' working life. It is estimated that 30,000 women are sacked every year because of pregnancy, and a further 200,000 suffer discrimination.[31] Stories abound in most organizations of jobs being changed and clients handed elsewhere. The law provides protection for returning mothers, but how many women and men are familiar with it?

A female analyst at Investco told me:

> I took four months off although I was entitled to 29 weeks but I think that four months was too much for them. I had told them I was coming back but when I arrived they sort of looked surprised. My clients had been told that no one knew if I was coming back but I had made it clear I was. Even so, they insisted on employing another analyst and he only arrived one month before my return. It's really awkward as there is no need for two of us. I feel I'm being pushed out.[32]

In August 2010 Oksana Denysenko, an investment banker, won her case for sex discrimination after she was made redundant following her maternity leave. When she returned to her job at Credit Suisse the person who had covered her maternity leave was given her job permanently. At first, Ms Denysenko and her temporary replacement shared the work, but seven months later Ms Denysenko was made redundant when her employer said two people were not needed in the role. A London tribunal has now found that Ms Denysenko was discriminated against and unfairly dismissed. The tribunal judge said, 'The fact that the claimant had taken maternity leave and had ongoing responsibilities as a mother contributed to her selection for redundancy.' It was alleged that during her redundancy consultancy, her bosses said she would be unable 'to put in the hours.'[33]

No wonder then that senior women felt under pressure to return quickly for both financial and career reasons, so minimizing the inconvenience of their absence. A female director in corporate finance for Investco commented:

> I was back in my office for meetings three days after the birth of my last child. I regret that. I felt I had to come back for my clients and it was a stupid decision to have made. I blame myself, no one asked me to, I should have said to hell with my clients, I've had a baby, but I didn't.[34]

When I asked her whether the bank would have minded if she had taken three or four months off, she replied, 'Debatable. I think they probably would have minded but we never got that far. It is my clients who are the key, and all I thought about was that they did not suffer in any way.'

This woman was extremely successful in a very male-dominated part of the bank. She appreciated that it was a tough environment for a woman, but by engineering her work such that she won good clients and delivered consistently to them, she bypassed much of the potential criticism about leaving early or lacking commitment. She accepted that she received no particular support from her male colleagues. 'I operate as a one-man show. It doesn't mean that I can't have good working relationships with some of them but I don't ask for anything. Special favors? Oh God, you are dead in the water if you do that.'

Another role model, a female director in the fund management division, acted very differently:

> I took full maternity leave, and cut off from work completely. I did feel the first time, that if I didn't come back, there would be all the men saying, 'I knew she wouldn't come back,' so in a way I had something to prove. This was before I was promoted to head of the department. The second time, I had already been offered promotion, and I thought it's something I have to do, but I still took off my full entitlement. There is always the worry though, that they've managed without you for seven months – do they really need you?[35]

And in a private interview a female banker told me, 'Oh with the first baby, they're on the lookout for lack of commitment, or emotional instability or other things they think they can expect.'[36]

In some ways the increase in maternity provision in the United Kingdom to one year (broken into six months of Ordinary Maternity Leave with six weeks at 90 percent pay and a further 33 weeks at statutory maternity benefit of £125 per week, then Additional Maternity Leave of 26 weeks with no statutory pay) has exacerbated the 'potential risk' employers see in recruiting women of childbearing age. It has certainly been met with irritation and hostility from both men and women who feel it may result in a backlash against women. In one small financial services company, women felt that on return to work from maternity leave the company was reluctant to invest in them further as they might disappear again. Nichola Pease, deputy chairman of J.O. Hambro, an investment company, gave voice to that concern when she gave evidence to the Treasury Select Committee on Women in the City.

What I really worry about is that legislation and protection is turning us (women) into a nightmare ... how easy is it if they have three children over five years and they have three years out? ... I think we have too long a maternity leave.[37]

Plans to extend paid maternity leave from four months to nine months were shelved by former business secretary Lord Mandelson in the last government, bowing to the pressure of the recession and complaints from businesses.

Certainly since the decision to give 12 months maternity leave while giving paid paternity leave of only two weeks resulted in the biggest gap between maternity and paternity leave in Europe, reinforcing the polarization in the roles of mothers and fathers rather than challenging it. However more recently, following Scandinavian countries such as Sweden and Norway, there have been measures to allow fathers to share some of the mother's maternity leave. The changes in April 2010 mean that if a mother returns to work without taking a full year's maternity leave, the father will be able to take the remaining time, up to a maximum of six months, at a statutory rate of pay. The paid leave entitlement can be shared if the father takes his leave within the first six months.

The reality is that few fathers can afford to take time off on statutory pay of £124.88 per week, and only 4 percent of fathers are estimated to take up the entitlement, but this is a step in the right direction. This is born out by research in Norway, where there have been provisions for generous paternity leave for some years. The take-up of paternity leave increased when the government reserved part of parental leave for fathers only – from 3 percent in 1993 to 90 percent in 2003. However despite the provision of generous parental leave and childcare, only 25 percent of couples who are parents are both working full time.[38] Research shows that the demands of long hours when parents return to work and the ensuing construction of a business masculinity of 'anytime, anywhere' is at odds with political attempts to encourage men to do more parenting.[39]

To encourage greater paternal leave take-up some European countries are designating part of the leave as being solely for fathers, and if they do not take it, it is lost. In Sweden all working parents are entitled to 16 months paid leave per child, the cost being shared between employer and the state. To encourage greater paternal involvement in childrearing, a minimum of two months out of the 16 is required to be used by the 'minority' parent, usually the father. Denmark allows 52 weeks maternity leave, 18 of which must be taken by the mother, two weeks by the father and the rest, as the couple see fit.

The UK government also announced plans for increasing flexibility for parents, launching a consultation in January 2011, with the aim of introducing a more flexible system of shared parental leave in 2015. Announcing the April changes in a speech in January 2011, deputy prime minister Nick Clegg said, 'But we want to go further. We know that men need to be actively encouraged to take time off. And often parents want more flexibility than these arrangements will allow.'[40]

In other parts of world the provisions are less generous, with the average worldwide maternity leave being 16 weeks according to the World Economic Forum Gender Gap Report 2010.[41] However there are marked contrasts between individual companies, with many global companies providing above the legal minimum in parental leave. It is notable that the United States, where many corporate gender policies are far more advanced than in Europe, is the only developed country in the world not to give any state provision for paid maternity leave. US companies vary hugely in the amount of maternity leave they offer, and under the Family and Medical Leave Act 1993 are only obliged to give pregnant women (as well as those with serious illnesses) 12 months unpaid leave and protection of their jobs. The United States with its free-market philosophy and dislike of state interventions has always favored private-sector initiatives.

Previously the United Kingdom had stood out internationally for its long leave reserved for mothers, mostly at a low rate of pay, and its relatively weak parental leave. Cross-national research indicates that the more leave policies favor mothers, the more they damage mothers' employment prospects. The United Kingdom is now following the European lead and focusing on increasing the role of fathers in the domestic sphere. It will be interesting to see whether this is embraced by men and organizations or resisted, as competing constructions of masculinity in the workplace hold sway.

Such is the difficulty organizations have in handling maternity leave well and enabling the integration of new mothers back at work that a new industry has grown up to help them. Ernst & Young and Barclays Wealth are among an increasing number of organizations introducing maternity coaching. Women taking maternity leave are provided with an external coach prior to their leave, during the leave, and on return. This tends to be reserved for the most senior women as it is expensive. Probably more importantly there is often mandatory coaching for line managers, who are often male. In my own consulting experience I have seen increasing numbers of potential legal cases arise as a result of mismanagement of maternity, particularly following the numerous changes in law. Suzanne Bottrill, head of diversity and inclusion, UK and Republic of Ireland at Ernst & Young, explains, 'Before this the parents' network had provided informal support for keeping in touch and returning mothers. This is to kick start a broader change in culture towards working mothers and line managers.'[42]

Is this initiative evidence of culture change or the delegation of a marginal element of organizational life to external consultants? Finding support in other working mothers is important, but what is really required is a shift in the whole mainstream culture to integrate the other side of life into work life. And the reality of having responsibility for children and being at work should be understood by all employees. It is not hard to learn, but until recently it has just not been considered relevant to the world of work. Today it is.

As well as acknowledging the enormous change that having a baby means to women returning to the workplace, organizations would do well to recognize the new skills they bring. Such is the invisibility of the skills required to run a home and family that they are rarely recognized by women themselves, let alone organizations. In Chapter 4 on management style I discussed the fact that women's work is so little valued that the skills they bring into the workplace are also devalued or go unacknowledged, as they are expected, and seen as being natural – part of being a woman rather than acquired.

Dr Ros Altmann, giving evidence to the Treasury Select Committee on Women in the City, said:

> One of the big issues is if women do take time out to have children. Then they come back and it is very hard to make that catch up. The work that they are doing, the experience that they have achieved while having children, is not something that is valued at all in the workforce. I believe it should but it certainly is not in the City as far as I can see.[43]

I have yet to see the skills learned in the home valued openly in the workplace. If women have been slow to advertise these skills, fathers may not be. Tom Bradshaw of Fathers Direct has said, 'Dads who are actively involved in their children's lives will bring the same benefits to work as mothers do – that's why Volvo encourages fathers to take time off; they are better managers when they come back.'[44]

Women's mothering side is seen to detract from their professionalism, but somehow men's fathering side adds to theirs. Unless these paradoxes are acknowledged and addressed, no amount of work–life balance will help advance women's progress.

MANAGING IT ALL

As well as knowing people's relationship status, does the organization know which partner takes the main responsibility for domestic matters? Because of the public/private divide this is not something that an organization generally thinks it relevant to know about its employees. But if it is to take gender seriously, perhaps it should.

In Airco, 72 percent of male senior managers were married compared with 48 percent of female senior managers, but the real difference was that nearly three times as many male senior managers had children as female senior managers. This contrasted with middle management, where 40 percent of men had children compared with 35 percent of women. Only one married man took the main responsibility for the home, and he had no children. There is a double effect here: the married men are more likely to be taken care of, and have their domestic lives organized by their wives, thereby giving them an advantage in time and energy over even a single woman.[45]

We already know from the figures above how the dual burden affects women far more than men, particularly at senior levels. The senior men I spoke to in interviews were all married and had wives who took responsibility at home. Some of their wives worked part time. They all said that they did not see enough of their families, and they paid tribute to the amount of work their wives had to do alone because they were never there. Generally the men were aware enough to praise what their wives did and not take it for granted. One single mother in her early 50s said that the office all laughed when she went out to the bank at lunchtime or had to do other 'household chores.' A female manager in Airco's Cargo division said, 'It's all right for them, they have wives to do it for them. I'm on my own.'[46]

In some organizations things are changing more slowly than in others. In one law firm in which only two partners out of 23 were women, only two of the male partners had working wives and many men lived in the countryside – either commuting daily or living in London during the week. The only frame of reference they had was their experience of their non-working wives. So, as a woman lawyer explained in a private interview with me, 'they have no idea whatsoever of female challenges – caring/domestic duties and working careers. Perhaps when their daughters face challenges their views/understanding might change.[47]

A study jointly conducted by McKinsey and Amazone Euro Fund X, reported in *Women Matter,* selected the 89 European listed companies with the highest level of gender diversity in top management posts to assess the impact of having women at high levels on the financial success of companies. Two significant differences between the men and the women emerged during the research. First, many more women felt they had been discriminated against, and second, the research revealed a great disparity in family situations – 33 percent of the women were unmarried and 54 percent were childless. Only 18 percent of the men were unmarried and 29 percent of them were childless.[48] And in the London Business School study on innovation, again 96 percent of the male team leaders who responded had children against 48 percent of the female team leaders.[49] A *Harvard Business Review* survey found that in the 41–55 age range nearly half of the best-paid women (49 percent) were childless compared with 19 percent of men.[50] These statistics show that women are still paying a high price for career success.

The luxury of having a wife to take on all the domestic side of life leaves senior men free to invest all their energy in their work, which gives them an immediate advantage over a similarly married woman. We can see here how the material demands of family life disadvantage women in management in as much as they use up their resources of time and energy. This fact is illustrated by my findings, which showed that women experience a much greater conflict between home and work than men do (see the section 'Conflict' below).

Children are still unwelcome in most workplaces, and women, as primary carers, often have to go to great lengths to distance their concerns from those at work. Childcare problems are considered a nuisance and intrude on work time. Looking after the welfare of dependent children should be considered evidence of responsibility, not (as it so often is) a lack of commitment to the job. Picking up a child on time is rarely considered a good enough reason for leaving the office.

One very senior woman told me that most people in the airline would be surprised if they knew she had children, which she took as a compliment, meaning that she managed her home life so well that it never infringed on work life. Yet work life continually infringes on home life. The boundaries of home/work are being crossed only one way.[51] This particular woman took work home every evening and worked for an hour and a half after her children were in bed.[52]

One company where family life is valued and praised is consulting firm Sysdoc Group. It recognizes that there is another side of life besides working for money, and that at times this other side may need to take priority. This is perceived as a sign of responsibility rather than a lack of commitment to the firm, and in no way hinders promotion prospects. Katherine Corish, founder and chairman said:

We allow people to set their own timeframe. If you want to work two days a week, fine but you set your own performance targets for that. If in a year's time you want to work more then that's fine too. Life is a series of changes. Many of the women have husbands and partners who take care of family life if they are working full time.[53]

Corish is clear – it is not just about women: 'We have many men who have chosen to work for us because they want to be present in their children's lives.'

Women's burden at home is being eased, not by necessarily by their partners, but by the proliferation of home services to do the household chores. Now, in the United States, dinners can be bought at some childcare centers so that no one has to cook when they get home.[54] In the United Kingdom, supermarkets are offering more delivery services, more ready meals, children's parties can be organized by specialists, and dogs can be walked by professional dog walkers. However all this help has to be managed, and that is another domestic responsibility for a working parent.

CONFLICT

In the Airco study, a much higher percentage of women (62 percent) than of men (39 percent) felt there was a conflict between work and home. All of the mothers I interviewed, apart from one whose husband had taken early retirement, carried the dual burden of home and work. Many would work at home in the evenings or early in the mornings so that they could see their children for some of the day. The actual job of mothering is rarely analyzed, it is usually described succinctly as childcare, but in reality it is much more than being a mere presence 'minding' children. Apart from the enormous amount of emotional work involved, the organizational skills required to plan for your children's lives, regardless of whether you are at home full time, are considerable. Shopping for food and their clothes, laundry, preparation of meals, seeing to their hobbies, friends' visits, birthdays to remember, presents to buy, after-school activities, school matches, communication with teachers, let alone organizing activities in the holidays, cannot all be delegated to a paid help. 'Managing the nanny' was a phrase I heard several times from working mothers. The nanny is an employee, and as such brings with her a whole set of responsibilities: her pay, tax, insurance, and most importantly her wellbeing, all fall on the working mother. When I asked one senior woman whether her home skills helped her at work, she replied that it was her work skills that helped her organize her home. Nicola Horlick said in her book *Can You Have It All?* that her whole life depended on her nanny, who had been with her for eight years and without whom she could not cope.[55]

All the women I spoke to said that without their outside support network – good nannies, husbands, and families to back them up they would be lost. A female senior manager in Marketing, Airco said, 'I have a brilliant nanny who has been with us for four years. I totally trust her and work hard to make sure she is happy. If she asks for a pay rise she gets it, I need her.'[56]

Most of the married women managers I interviewed had husbands who worked as long or even longer hours than them. The exceptions were two women whose husbands had taken early retirement, and one of these took responsibility for the home. Both women were mindful of the fact that there was tension around their being out at work leaving their husbands at home. A female manager in Airco said, 'He hates it when I'm too late, especially if I haven't told him, so I try to keep sensible hours.'[57]

This is a good illustration of what happens when the gender order is broken, and roles are reversed. It causes discomfort to both men and women, and women have to do repair work to re-establish the status quo.[58] A sense of guilt as well as a reluctance to relinquish control in the domestic arena can sometimes mean that women who work long hours return home and often insist on doing the housework as well. This correlates with another study on the division of housework, which found that in households where both partners work, the woman generally does twice as much childcare and housework as the man, but as a woman's financial contribution approaches that of her husband's, her housework decreases. Then when she earns more than her husband, and even if he is not working, her housework increases.[59] Again, one interpretation, following Gherardi's thinking, is that spouses work together to counteract the discomfort created by breaking their conventional roles.

DISCOURSE OF CHOICE

The language with which we in organizations refer to these issues is important. If we do not challenge the artificial dualism of work/life or work/home, or indeed reinforce it, any decisions around maternity and working hours can be viewed as a woman or a man's individual choice. This discourse of maternity, and its unavoidable inconvenience, can run concurrently with the discourse (even a progressive one) of diversity without the contradictions being apparent.

114

The following conversation with a senior male director in the corporate finance department of a bank illustrates this contradiction. First he said that the company employed a lot of women (which it didn't), and that he had nothing against women working there.

Director: We are aware of people's family obligations but they have to realize that the client always comes first.
Me: That's asking a lot of any mother.
Director: Yes, it is, but then it's a voluntary thing. If she wants the same bonus as the others, she must do the same work.

The language of free choice means that it is the mother's problem and responsibility. She has to continue as if 'nothing has happened' as far as she can. If she can't, she has the choice of leaving. Her departure is viewed as an unfortunate but inevitable consequence of employing women. The conversation above took place ten years ago. In 2010 as I write, the issue is still framed in terms of choice, as the earlier quote from the media analyst (page 97) shows. Even the support shown towards men is put in the language of choice: 'We also want to allow men to make the choice of a professional career integrating a family dimension.'[60]

The assumption that work is what happens in the office, and private life is managed somehow, without effort, pervades most working cultures today. What constitutes work and who does it are often accepted cultural values that are embedded in society and organizational life. In the past male workers could arrive for work without the burden of worrying about the organization of domestic matters and children. Most of them still do so today. But this is changing. Organizations can play their part by recognizing that work is something that also goes on elsewhere, in the home, and that when their employees are not at work in their organizations, more than half of them will be at work at home. As part of an organization's culture, the public/private divide can perpetuate the reality of the dual burden for women, and continue to act as a rationale that makes it more fitting that men dominate senior organizational life. As men become more responsible for other aspects of their lives, like children in situations of shared care, single parenthood, and increasingly care of parents, organizations will be readier to acknowledge and value the rest of life.

One way in which some organizations are recognizing the conflicts of home and work is through employee parenting networks that provide support and networking for parents in the same firm. This constituent of culture encompasses the materiality of parental leave provisions that an organization decides to offer and additionally the prevailing corporate ideology of notions of work and the relatedness of home and work. With the domestic sphere becoming harder and harder to separate from the workplace, organizations can assess their own cultural attitudes to the divide. Does the organization know which of their employees are parents? One organization I was consulting in was making every effort to promote more women to senior positions, yet it did not know which of the few senior women had children. Does your organization value skills learned in the home? Do your employees think that these skills are valued? How easily can home life be discussed in the workplace? Do employees feel a conflict between home and work, and is there a gender split in this? Are home responsibilities automatically considered by managers in planning meetings and events? These are questions to be asked.

Leaders can themselves acknowledge the 'other' side of their life, and help make 'domestic' issues that affect everyone an integral part of work lives. I believe that this is what most women want, and that maintaining a strict separation between home and work can add to feelings of alienation from our mainstream work cultures. It will encourage an authentic style of leadership which takes as its reference point the assumption that all employees have responsibilities of one type or another, or calls on their time that are outside their paid work. The slow pace with which organizations demonstrate their ability and encouragement to integrate parents and carers in the workplace can be seen as a sign of resistance to women's equality in organizations.

6

ARE YOU GOING HOME ALREADY? THE LONG-HOURS CULTURE

TIME AS A MEANS OF CULTURAL RESISTANCE

In a law case several years ago, investment banker Aisling Sykes, 39, was sacked as vice president for spending too much time with her children, and won her claim for unfair dismissal from US bank, JP Morgan but lost her claim that 14-hour days amounted to sex discrimination. The tribunal ruled that because she was so highly paid her employers were entitled to 'make certain demands in respect of hours and place of work.'[1] The case was important at the time because it was an attempt to use the law to construe a requirement to work long hours as a means of indirect discrimination. However it appeared that the high financial gain exempted the bank from any responsibility to ensure a working environment conducive to working mothers.

This ruling reveals the gendered subtext to the apparently neutral phenomenon of long hours, which is still prevalent today. The fault is seen as the woman's – how can she expect to work those hours with four children? It (that is, she) is unnatural. Fathers can but mothers shouldn't. The long-hours culture often goes unchallenged, being justified on the grounds of high salaries or client demand. Hence any 'normal' mother is automatically disqualified from these high-salaried jobs.

This is a form of cultural resistance that like other seemingly gender-neutral competencies makes gender (and inequalities) disappear. Men and women are held to the same criteria to be successful bankers (and lawyers, traders, and so on) even when outcomes may be very different depending on gender. It is difficult to contest or challenge gender in this mode because it is tantamount to challenging the structure of the job itself. But this is what is required if we want to see women and men working together at the top of organizations.

The concept of long hours is now widely accepted as being part of an organization's culture, hence the use of the term 'long-hours culture'. At first glance, a long-hours culture might seem to be gender-neutral. There are no innate talents and skills in men that cannot be matched by women – stamina and energy are equally shared out. But, as shown above, it has an indirect effect on women in the workplace in as much as women still take primary responsibility for childcare and household management, and so the burden of working long hours adds to the pressure they already have of managing both family and career. Time is now a primary differentiating feature between men and women workers. Put simply, on the whole men can give more time to paid work than women, both because they are often exempt fom domestic responsibilities, and because their time is often made available by women's unpaid work. Time is a precious resource which is recognized in the recently coined phrase 'time poor.'

Buswell and Jenkins show how equal opportunities policies allowed men to deny that inequality exists while simultaneously redefining the 'good worker' as the one who gives most time to the organization.[2] They also see 'time' as a resource that is more available to men, who use it to segregate and disadvantage women within the labor market and labor process.

Men can only spend more time at work if they do less domestic work at home, and as their pay increases so does their exemption from the domestic sphere. My research, like others, showed that as job level and income bracket go up, so do the hours, thereby making that step to the top harder for women with families. Indeed in my research senior women were three times more likely to be childless than men (see Chapter 5 on the public/private divide).

Hochschild's study of a US company, *The Time Bind*, shows clearly how time is used in a competitive way among aspiring managers. A senior executive was quoted as saying:

> Time has a way of sorting people out in this company. A lot of people that don't make it to the top work long hours. But all the people I know who do make it work long hours. By the time people get to within three or four levels of the Management Committee, they're all very good, or else they wouldn't be there. So from that point on what counts is work and commitment.[3]

Senior managers may put in more hours but they also need help to organize their lives, and a partner at home is invaluable.

HOW MANY HOURS?

According to the Office for National Statistics, full-time workers in the United Kingdom average around 37.0 hours per week, part-time workers average around 15.5 hours per week, and just over a fifth of people in employment work more than 45 hours a week.[4] By EU standards this is a high proportion of 'long-hours' workers, though other developed countries such as Australia, Japan, and the United States have more than the United Kingdom. An independent study of long-hours working in 2003 found that those working the longest hours in the United Kingdom were men aged 30–49 with children and employed in the private sector (primarily manufacturing).[5] Although the United Kingdom has working time regulations, organizations in the United Kingdom actively implement the opt-out clause to the 48-hour limit which allows for companies to ask employees to agree to work more than 48 hours a week in a four-month period. But employers cannot force employees to sign an opt-out: it must be agreed to, and employees cannot be fairly dismissed for refusing to sign one. The United Kingdom has fiercely resisted European Parliament's attempts to restrict its use of the opt-out clause.

William Hague, then UK shadow foreign secretary, said,

> The Working Time Directive is doing enough damage as it is to British businesses and public services. Protecting the opt-out is crucial to both and there must be no concession to those who do not care what damage EU red tape is doing to them.[6]

National data shows that over a quarter of UK full-time employees work in excess of 48 hours per week: that is, longer than the Working Time Directive weekly working hours limit.[7]

Perceptions about the number of hours that constitute long hours vary according to the type of work and what is considered the norm at the particular place of work. In some organizations, where there is no such thing as overtime pay (as is true in management and many professions), employees are reportedly working 100 hours per week or more. Furthermore, many employers do not know how many hours their employees are working. Arguably this is an important and easy statistic to collect. However, research in general suggests that consistently working an extra ten or more hours per week, over and above contracted hours, is considered to be long hours in most organizations. Men are more likely to work longer hours than women, but this overall trend disguises differences in specific occupations. Women's hours are increasing as more women are entering more senior positions. A further point highlighted by research by the Institute for Employment Studies (IES) is that women with dependants are much less likely to work long hours than men living with children or a dependent adult.[8]

REASONS FOR WORKING LONG HOURS

Long hours may be thought of as a material aspect of a job, yet very rarely is a long working day a formal requirement of a job. Certainly in the businesses I studied, there was nothing written in the employment contracts for managers about hours. Most people's formal working day was 9 am–5 pm or 9.30 am–5.30 pm. The opt-out clause of the EU Working Time Regulations is now included in most managerial contracts. There is no formal overtime for managers; conversely there is the unspoken expectation that they will work as hard and for as long as is required to do their job adequately. This leads to a kind of self-imposed overtime. Workload pressure, company expectations, peer group pressure, and ambition have resulted in what is now a widely accepted concept – the long-hours culture. Many management tasks cannot be measured in tangible productivity terms, and this itself leads to the importance of visibility.

In the 1980s the advent of technology was greeted with the certainty that the higher productivity would result in more leisure time for workers and managers alike. The opposite has happened. In Chapter 5 on the public/private divide it is shown that technology has enabled our time to be made even more available for paid work. The long-hours culture has been encouraged by organizations.

An Institute for Employment Studies report showed that people were working long hours from sheer pressure of work, arising from heavier workloads, increasingly demanding customers (in particular increased expectation of 24 hours a day service), greater competition, fewer staff, and tighter budgets.[9]

In my research at Airco there was evidence of organizational pressure, with some people feeling that the long-hours culture was introduced deliberately in the early 1980s as part of a fear culture to fire up the management. The former chief executive himself worked punishing hours, and there were stories that in the early days of his appointment, managers were expected to be prepared to do anything at a few hours' notice. One manager who had been there at that time said, 'This may mean being given a brief at 5 pm to present the next morning – it kept management on its toes.'[10] The long hours became an embedded practice in the whole organization and became part of the culture. As a male manager in Marketing put it, 'The culture of this company is work. If I am honest there is an expectation that people, particularly if you have got to manager level, that people will work a 12-hour day.'[11]

In another study, *The Power of Time,* the authors chart the development of a long-hours culture in a large UK insurance company, which had been through several episodes of restructuring and reorganization resulting in large-scale redundancies.[12] Surviving managers were left with much heavier workloads, and senior management put pressure on them to work long hours. 'The CEO made it abundantly clear that he did not expect any managers to arrive home in time to bathe the baby.'[13] This was a key statement in defining a new culture of working long hours.

The authors note that although some junior managers questioned the need for longer hours, many responded with enthusiasm, with middle managers became increasingly competitive with one another. One said, 'People are beginning to compete with one another on how long they work in the evenings.'[14] They indulged in a good deal of impression management, such as leaving their jacket on the back of their chair.

The encouragement from organizations to work long hours quickly leads to employees competing with one another over the number of hours, they work, as the following conversation, overheard in the finance division of Airco, illustrates:

'What time are you in tomorrow, John?'
'Oh, about seven.'
'You, Peter?'
'Oh yes, perhaps a bit before.'[15]

Because everyone at Airco – apart from some working mothers and older men – stayed late in the office, the only way of marking oneself out was by coming in very early. So both ends of the day were being stretched, and the fear of missing out or being thought lazy meant that the majority worked increasingly long hours. Doreen Massey also found an element of individual competitiveness in explaining the long hours worked by scientists in her study on high-technology workers in Cambridge (England).[16]

Within workplaces the interaction between employees can produce a culture that glorifies long hours of work. This may derive partly from competition between individuals, but it may also result from various peer-group pressures – the need 'not to let the team down,' for instance, can become a form of social compulsion.[17] Organizations may exploit this competitiveness and indeed harness it to extract maximum work output from employees.

In a 2004 study on the gendered impact of organizational change and the implications for workloads and working hours, Ruth Simpson found that restructuring was associated with 'presenteeism' (the tendency to stay at work beyond the time needed for effective performance of the job) as fear of redundancy and uncertainty over promotion opportunities led to a need to demonstrate visible commitment.[18] She also found that this presenteeism was found to be gendered: it was associated with a competitive masculine culture, and was seen by women as a form of 'male resistance' to their presence as managers. The men were playing on their freedom to work long hours against women's inability to do so because of home demands.

As well as workload pressure, the other acceptable reason for working long hours is client demand. This is the reason many women who return to work flexibly in professional services firms drop out of client-facing areas of work. Client service is often viewed as a reason to resist flexible working. Some research into UK law firms found that these perceptions are not reflected in reality. The clients themselves are often parents, and work in organizations that may be addressing work–life issues.[19]

However, the 'necessity' to give clients a round-the-clock vigil is still accepted as inevitable by many of the young graduates entering professional services firms, as this young female lawyer confirmed:

> The firm offers flexible working etc. but to be honest, it's about the business needs of the firm, which means being number one for clients, usually globally and always at great expense. However nicely it's phrased, only people who commit to the firm make it – which is probably fair enough. There are women partners, and they try the flexible hours thing, but there is no such thing as 'hours' here really – you're expected to be fully available all the time.[20]

Katherine Corish, founder and chairman of Sysdoc Group (a consulting services firm), gives this 'client rationale' short shrift:

> We are totally committed to delivering the best for our clients and set out the expected outcomes at the beginning of the project. The idea that you have to be available 14 hours a day for a client is ridiculous. In some situations the client's own staff get put in positions of having to work on a project with consultants who are working these hours and they have to work those hours too. We have a duty of care to our clients' staff too. We lead by example and show that high levels of productivity come from motivated focused teams, not incessantly long hours that burn good people out.[21]

Another business reason given for long hours is that many organizations are now operating in a global culture and across different time zones. This may involve early-morning starts to catch the end of the day in Asia as well as late evenings to catch the US day. Certainly in the City the globalization of trading has resulted in a longer and longer working day.

Before embarking on a flexible work policy route, organizations would do well to examine the rationale for their long-hours cultures if it exists. It will vary from department to department. For example in Investco the pressure to work long hours was more intense in the Corporate Finance division than in any other part of the bank. Respondents routinely worked 12-hour days. The long and anti-social hours were deemed necessary because of the arbitrary nature of the business. When a deal had to be completed, there was always a deadline. This often meant that when a person was working on a transaction (that is, a merger or acquisition, take-over or privatization issue), they would be up all night on several occasions, as well as possibly working weekends. Presentations to pitch for new business had to be prepared, and as this was not core work, it was often done in the evenings and weekends. These time-dependent tasks explained some of the ludicrously long hours put in periodically, but they did not explain why people routinely stayed in their office late in the evening. This is when the culture came into play – working long hours was seen as evidence of commitment in a division where there was a higher element of competition than elsewhere in the bank.[22]

Corporate finance has always been an elitist area of the investment world, and was virtually closed to women 25 years ago. There are plenty of young people more than happy to put their social lives on hold to work long hours and work their way up the ladder. The financial rewards are substantial. In a case like this, the discourse of time has been used by the organization to qualify certain members and disqualify others.

One senior male corporate finance director told me, 'It is ludicrous for the young to work these hours and be sitting here at 10 o'clock at night. On the other hand if I saw someone regularly going home at 6.30, then I'd think that he can't have much work to do and I'd better give him some more!' (He laughed.)[23] A female assistant director in corporate finance told me, 'My day starts at 8.30 am and, with about one half hour for lunch, I leave at around 8 o'clock – that's when I'm not busy. Otherwise I am here till midnight at least.'[24]

Again, as in Airco, there was an element of macho competition over the number of hours worked. 'We had to do a presentation with only one week's notice recently and one chap worked 115 hours that week,' said a senior ECFD director, with a certain amount of pride in his voice. Senior directors were unconcerned about the length of the day, and indeed it seemed to be useful as a way of sorting out the 'men' from the 'boys,' testing their stamina and commitment.

Doreen Massey has described the working of long hours by high-technology scientists as being bound up with a specific form of masculinity.[25] Her case study respondents were not only forced to work long hours by the specific demands of their kind of work, they actually wanted to because they loved their work. Hence the particular form of masculinity to which she refers is bound up with the attachment to their jobs, which require abstract and rational thought traits that are associated with masculinity. She suggests that the long hours reinforce the separation between 'other possible sides of life' from the abstract conceptual 'pure' mode of being, emphasizing the dualism of home and work.

The other important factor in the Corporate Finance division at Investco was the extremely high salaries that could be earned there, which might have explained why people were willing to put their home lives on continual hold to spend more time in the office. Desire for wealth can also be one of the explanations for people working such long hours. There is a lot at stake, the rewards are high, and plenty of others want them, and will sacrifice any leisure time to have them. In business life, the salaries of senior management in both private and public sectors in the United Kingdom have rocketed in the past five years. If we analyze this trend in gendered terms, we can see that the higher the salaries, the more the informal barriers will act to protect this very elite group. It was revealed in 2010 that of the 172 highest-paid civil servants in the United Kingdom, only 32 were women.[26] One of these informal barriers is the long-hours culture. Opportunity Now researchers repeated in 2010 a survey conducted in 2005 on perceptions of barriers to women's progress, and found that work and family seemed to have become a more significant barrier over those five years.[27]

In Airco senior managers worked one hour longer on average than middle management. A female senior manager said, 'There is a feeling here that the more senior you are, the more available you have to be to the organization.'[28]

Like any expression of culture, leadership influences it. If the boss works very long hours, the message is clear. In some organizations even though senior management work long hours, they are more likely to have control over their time. In the broking division of Investco, the leader was new and had a reputation for being a hard taskmaster. He had married and had children relatively late in life, and had recently introduced a new regime of early starts, although he left himself at 5.30 pm most evenings. A female analyst in his division described her working day:

I get in at around 7 am, which is about one hour earlier than in my last job, which means leaving the house at 6.15 am. I typically leave at around 6.30/7 pm although if I have a set of results coming through or I am writing up notes after a trip I will be here until 8, 9, 10, even 11 pm. It's all part of the new regime – the burden is on us analysts to produce more, market more.[29]

Asked about her boss's early departure, she said that he could do so because he was the boss, but the department couldn't, and he expected them to work later.

The Institute for Employment Studies report[30] drew attention to time management issues. Although a few respondents in my study felt they would be able to reduce their working hours if they were better at managing their time, in some organizations there are clearly issues with prioritization, individual inefficiencies, and work organization. An Airco female finance manager said, 'I suppose that knowing that I am here from 8 am to 6.30 pm I plan to fill that time, taking that bit extra at meetings, on telephone calls, and so on.'[31]

Certainly employees working in organizations that have a meetings culture often find that huge chunks of their day are taken up in meetings, leaving little time to do their actual work. Some organizations have called for a time limit to be put on meetings. As one of its gender initiatives ten years ago Procter & Gamble introduced a policy whereby no meetings could be held outside standard business hours – that is, 9 am–5 pm – unless everyone was happy with the time.

Many women complained that there was far too much emphasis on hours spent in the office rather than what is done while they are there. A woman working in Investco Corporate Finance told me, 'I can do this job in fewer hours. But it will be seen as not giving the commitment. Being visible is a way of drawing attention to yourself. You are noticed more by being here at 10 at night than by consistently producing a good product.'[32] Women's productivity and efficiency can often be obscured when it is the giving of time that symbolizes productivity, commitment. and personal value.[33]

Some companies have also issued best practice guidelines on time management, including how to manage meetings, or challenge the need for meetings.[34]

Robin Schneider, MD of Schneider-Ross, consultants in diversity and equality, sees a trend of micro management by leaders at the top of organizations often leading to inefficient use of time:

This is a downside of globalization – time zones etc. The pressure for CEOs to produce short term results have dragged CEOs into micro-management which then drives that leadership style down through the organization. This not only takes a huge amount of time (and therefore adds to their own working hours) but also means senior leaders are not developing their people. There is a danger that the only people who get on are those who are prepared to put in the same ridiculous hours and the pattern repeats itself. The question is whether we will start to see higher performing CEOs who take a more balanced approach to their working lives.[35]

WOMEN AND LONG HOURS

Judi Marshall found that many women managers moved out of male-dominated cultures to build a life that was more balanced between home and work.[36] Contrary to the popular belief that women leave professional roles after 15 years to go home, the majority take their skills and experience and apply them elsewhere, often setting up their own businesses or working for a smaller company with more regular hours. The big corporates are losing a wealth of talent by not addressing their working practices.

My research showed that the shorter hours are worked by two groups of people – older men and working mothers. The former were nearing retirement and were under less pressure to work long hours. Many women in the airline and the bank adapted their routines to fit in with the long-hours culture. My findings corresponded with an Institute for Employment Studies survey[37] which showed that women with dependants were much less likely to work long hours than men living with children.

Many women in Airco adapted their working day to fit in with the long-hours culture of the airline. A female manager (cargo) said, 'I start at 9.30 am, which is late but I wanted one part of the day with my daughter, and I think I knew in my heart that once you get into Airco it is difficult to get away at a reasonable time.'[38]

Taking work home was one way working mothers found they coped with the workload, although they lost points for not being visible. A female senior manager in Marketing remarked, 'I try to leave at 6 pm but my boss on the main board has an infuriating habit of fixing meetings for 6 pm and I have to attend.'[39] This woman squeezed in one and half hours of work every evening at home when the children had gone to bed. A female manager in Finance said, 'I work from 4–6 am most mornings at home so that I can get home in the evening at a decent time and spend time with my son and husband.'[40]

However, working shorter hours – or in reality working a normal working day – was not popular with other managers. A male manager in Cargo talked of a colleague, who had just returned from maternity leave and was leaving work every evening at 5.30 pm: 'It'll be all right if it's now and again but if it happens consistently people will get pissed off.'[41]

One female analyst in the broking division of Investco had a small baby, and said:

I leave the house at 6.45 am and try to get home by 7 pm. I see her for five minutes in the morning and then half an hour at night but then she has to go to bed. Even if I leave at 6 pm no one says anything but I know the work is there, the pressure is there, it's very subtle. Sometimes I come in at 5 am to finish a report.[42]

The message being sent down to young men and women as they enter some of the professions is clear, even today. One young female lawyer interviewed for this book told me:

So you can make 'good' progress, but will probably make more sacrifices than progress. You just have to decide if you think it's worth it – and whilst the money at the top is substantial, it isn't astronomical for the hours you are expected to put in (i.e. invest-ment banking might become more civilized with seniority, law doesn't), so you have to LOVE the job, more than your marriage, and as much as your children. I can't see any other way of doing it.[43]

Lucy (27) works in a fund management firm, and deliberately chose an area of work where the hours are not too crazy. 'I had done some work experience in a US investment bank and knew it wasn't for me. I wouldn't have asked in the interview but I knew enough about the job to know that the hours are manageable even with a family. I get in at 7–7.30 am for the market opening at 8 am but can leave at 5–5.30 pm which is great.'[44]

More recently in discussing flexible working, an HR professional of an accountancy firm said in an interview with the author, 'Well yes we are trying to do a lot on flexible working. But it's up to women themselves. They cannot expect to gain promotion if they are not putting in the same hours as men.'[45]

Common sense tells us that there is a limit to brain productivity after a number of hours, and that endless 12-hour days cannot be sustained without burnout or some other form of ill-health. A London Business School study on innovation found that male team leaders were more likely to work significantly longer hours than their female counterparts, and as a result more likely to suffer from exhaustion.[46] If any company has advertised flexible working without addressing how long the majority of their managers and senior managers work, there will be little change in the numbers at the top.

The research findings suggest, then, that in areas of prestige and high status, for example the senior levels of all organizations and in corporate finance in banks, the long-hours culture may act as a form of closure to exclude women. At a time when women can offer almost everything that men can in terms of ability, skills, and experience, time becomes an important differentiating feature which makes men appear more suitable than women.

There will be little change in the numbers at the top for organizations that introduce flexible working policies without addressing the many hours the majority of their managers and senior managers currently work.

ORGANIZATIONAL RESPONSE TO THE LONG-HOURS CULTURE

We have seen how organizations can and do develop and encourage long hours both to improve productivity and to foster competition between managers. The dilemma now for organizations that are increasingly becoming dependent on women's labor is how to accommodate women without losing the perceived benefits of an overall long-hours culture.

There have always been organizations that have constructed jobs around women's time demands, and therefore have been able to bring them in as a valuable source of cheap labor. Between 1971 and 1993, 93 percent of the increase in women's employment was in part-time work, where women make up 85 percent of the work force and pay for part time workers is 37 percent below the average full-time male worker.[47] Large employers of women such as retailers and factories have had many different forms of flexible working in place for years. These include nine-day fortnights, school hours times, and term-time-only working. Business has been able to benefit from the desire and need for mothers to work and earn money. Currently 42 percent of working women and 12 percent of working men are in part-time employment, with 57 percent of women in manual jobs working part time compared with only 24 percent of women in management and professional jobs.[48]

When women began entering management and professions 25 years ago, there was little part-time work available, as these jobs had been structured around the lives of men who had wives to look after their children and home. Following the equality legislation, employers with large numbers of women employees introduced family-friendly policies for management. But the low status of part-time work meant that few women with serious career intentions made use of these. In the United States those that took advantage of time out, or went part time, signaled to their workplace that they were stepping off the career ladder and moving down a notch to the 'mommy track,' and much the same happened in the United Kingdom. Women with children were being given a stark 'choice': work the same hours as a full-time worker, which were becoming increasingly long, or leave.

The impact of long hours combined with the increase in mothers working also has social consequences, and work–life balance has increasingly become a government issue too, particularly in some parts of Europe. Many welfare states in Europe are founded on the basis of social citizenship or entitlements, with rights to education, health, and social security traditionally justified as necessary for social and economic well-being. Europeans generally enjoy more employment protection than US workers. Employment protection varies within Europe, with Norway for example having a widespread welfare state including provision of childcare and a history of supporting female labor market participation. The Netherlands have been more conservative in their support of 'traditional' gender roles for men and women. The family is emphasized and external care provisions are limited. The United Kingdom has been somewhere between the two. Female participation is encouraged but there has been little provision of state childcare. However all European countries are being heavily influenced by the European Union. The combination of slowing and in some cases falling, birth rates and increased longevity means we are facing a declining working-age population. In this context it is vital for future economic growth that women (and for the same reasons older people) work, and the Union continues to introduce employment measures in legislation and regulations to facilitate this (part-time working rights, increased maternity leave, and the right to ask for flexible working). All member governments have had to follow with their own country-specific measures.

The extent to which women work in different countries is also determined by the prevailing cultural norms and values. Japan has always emphasized women's role in the home, and has been very slow in promoting women's advancement in the workplace. It is only the extremely low birth rate and concern over the ensuing shrinking workforce that is making the Japanese corporate world pay attention to the under-utilization of women in the economy.

The right to ask for flexible working was extended in April 2009 in the United Kingdom to include all parents with children up to the age of 16 (and disabled children up to 18), and many believe that the Coalition will increase this to 18 for all children. The long-term goal for campaigners is to introduce a right to flexible working for all employees, although there is a lot of resistance from employers.

Organizations have been nudged by EU law and by a spate of governmental and lobby group endorsements of the business case for flexible working. Losing qualified women at certain stages of the management pyramid has in the past sometimes suited businesses by lessening the competition for promotion at a key time in men's and women's careers. The business case is not always cut and dried. Several years ago, one senior property director told me that he got a good ten years from the female graduates in his firm and then expected the majority to go, leaving the path to partnership clear for their male colleagues. However, as more companies take on a higher percentage of female graduates they cannot afford such an attitude.

The numbers alone should frighten companies into taking action. A recent OECD report shows that women are more likely to get places in the top universities, and once there they go on to get better grades than men. They were also shown to outnumber men in high-status subjects such as law and medicine. Women have been entering university in greater numbers than men in recent years, with the participation rate for young women standing at 49 percent compared with 38 percent of young men. The prediction is for women to represent 65 percent of all graduates by 2015 (they currently comprise 58 percent).[49]

There is also a desire on the part of women to return to work after having children, but not necessarily working in a long-hours culture. Many women now endure long training and are reluctant to give up their careers. There is evidence that those who reduce their working hours often have to accept reduced status, pay, and career prospects – in other words to change jobs. Research shows that downgrading when moving to part time affects as many as 29 percent of women from professional and corporate management jobs and up to 40 percent in intermediate jobs.[50] Lawyers are becoming teachers, and bankers becoming classroom assistants in order to keep working but to work hours that are compatible with family life. An Equal Opportunities Commission investigation showed that for many women, working part time had been a compromise, and that 51 percent of women aged 25–54 were working below their potential because it was the only work they could get which they could combine with caring for children.[51] Some years ago a position for part-time assistant in a bookshop in a small commuter belt town received over 500 replies. The bookshop owner was astonished at the quality of these CVs – they were mostly professional women who had left their careers but wanted to work. It is a waste to the economy as well as to the wellbeing of these women if their expertise, skills, and potential are not being used. The increasing demands of modern motherhood combined with long working hours in paid work are making it increasingly hard for women to combine the two.

WORK–LIFE BALANCE

Despite the pressures from government and lobby groups, many UK companies have dragged their feet in adapting to a workforce that have responsibilities outside paid work. The family-friendly policies introduced by companies with many female employees in the 1980s and 1990s were not adopted in other more male-dominated industries. During the late 1990s and early 2000s there was concern that family-friendly policies introduced for the benefit of parents (predominantly mothers) might be resented by childless workers and men.[52] Added to this, women knew that taking up these arrangements in many cases meant instant career death. The response of organizations and interest groups to this potential backlash by childless workers and some men, and the reluctance of women to take up their entitlements, has been to shift the emphasis from family, women, and children to the more neutrally intended concept of work–life balance and flexible working.

Work–life balance seems to have struck a harmonious chord with organizations. Although responsibility is often given to the diversity and equality function, the work–life discourse aims to be gender neutral, reason perhaps for its appeal, as well as its promise of win–win – for business for the employee. Work–life has become the official discourse in both Europe and the United States, although in Asia and the emerging markets it is considered a luxury for developed economies. Government think tanks, academic departments, consultancies, and conferences have produced literally thousands of papers, research, and reviews on the topic. The UK lobby group Working Families launched the first ever national Work–life week at the end of September 2010.

The emphasis of work–life is that each individual has other calls on their time besides their work, and that these should be facilitated. Following the language and philosophy of the diversity movement, this is about individuals, not groups. While work–life balance is seen as a lifestyle choice and a limited issue for individuals (particularly women), the introduction of flexible policies will make few discernible changes to organizations' structure or culture.

THE TERMINOLOGY/LANGUAGE

The paradox is that the very term 'work–life' itself perpetuates one common part of all organization cultures, which is the assumption that work is somehow separate from life. In Chapter 5 on the public/private divide the cultural dualism of work/home was challenged. What work–life implicitly suggests is that there is only one sort of work – paid work – and that what happens when we are not in paid work is not work. However what women and men – but still mostly women – do at home is also work. Is life not work too – or only something we live when we are not at work? The dualism is founded on the gendered concept of work, which means that men work for money and go home for leisure and rest. Not only is this no longer the case for many men, it was never the case for working mothers. Researchers Suzan Lewis, Rhona Rapoport, and Richard Gambles use the term 'integration of paid work with the rest of life,' which doesn't have quite the zing that work–life balance has, but is a more accurate and realistic description.[53] Work–life balance conjures up a harmonious picture of hard work at the office, clocking off at 5.30 pm to enjoy a game of tennis, then a long walk followed by supper with friends. However the fantasy that equates time at home with so-called free time is a strictly masculine delusion. This is a more realistic account of life for a working mother:

> One common scenario sees him scoring major brownie points for working from eight to six – during which time he manages to read the paper, take several coffee breaks, eat lunch at a café and catch up on the latest office gossip. Her 'part-time' hours of paid work from ten to four sound like a comparative doddle – and they would be, too, if she didn't have sole responsibility for almost everything else that keeps the household running: getting the kids off to school, picking them up again, planning and shopping for dinner (which she does during her lunch break), cooking it, supervising homework, organizing baths, folding the laundry etc. etc. The opportunities for 'concealed leisure' in such a schedule are few indeed.[54]

The change in terminology has not done much to challenge the mindset that the topic is primarily a women's issue. The efforts to make work–life a gender-neutral policy and to create policies which

132

treat a game of golf and looking after a sick child as the same in terms of individual choice leave too many assumptions and values about the role of women unchallenged. The interrelationship between the acceptance and availability of different ways of working and gender representation in an organization is obvious, even if people wish to refer to them as two discrete issues. While women continue to take on the primary role for childcare, it will be a women's issue. If and when men take an equal share of responsibility for childcare and home care, it will be a parenting issue. Until the very way in which we organize our work lives is challenged, then organizations can continue business as usual.

In their analysis of discourses of work–life balance, Janet Smithson and Elizabeth H. Stokoe concluded that language change without culture change is bound to fail.[55] They found that while the language of the policies has changed to try to shift the emphasis away from 'mothers' and 'families' in an effort to de-gender the issues and obtain a better buy in from organizations, their study participants were still operating in a highly gendered context. They continued to associate work–life balance and flexible working with women and mothers. When the authors framed questions in gender-neutral language the participants (men and women) always responded in a way that associated flexible working with women. The authors argue that the use of gender-neutral language in corporate discourse in these policies also perpetuates the myth of a gender-neutral organization.

It has also been suggested that the age-old assumptions around gender relations are reinforced through flexible working. In her study of new media work, Diane Perrons noted that employees frequently worked very long hours. The use of home working, she suggests, allows mothers to fulfill the script of good mothers and good workers without altering the status quo at home.[56]

Lawyers are renowned for working very long hours, particularly in the City of London. So it is noteworthy that Allen and Overy, one of the largest City law firms, is now allowing its senior partners to work flexibly.[57] This is inextricably linked to its efforts to address the gender imbalance at the top of the firm. Currently 15 percent of its partners are women, but 62 percent of its graduate intake is female. There is an option of working four days a week or taking additional leave of up to 52 days, for up to eight years. Flexible working is already available to its junior partners and support staff.[58]

However, such was the concern from women about wanting to go part time that when I arrived at one professional services company to hold some focus groups on the issue, some women would not attend in case others heard about their interest and penalized them for it.

The names have changed but in many organizations flexible working, which does not necessarily mean part-time working, still carries with it a loss of status and power. An organization that professes to 'have' flexible working options does not necessarily have a truly flexible working culture. Truly flexible organizations do not need to follow the legal regulations and 'add on' flexible working policies. Look at an entrepreneur who does deals on a beach, from an airplane, from home, or in an office. This is flexible working. Most people in control of their time will work when and where they work best. Unfortunately in most organizations this form of 'smart working' is usually only reserved for those at the top who are not accountable to a line manager.

The senior partner of one professional services firm I know of has a large house in the north to which he flies most weekends, leaving the office on a Friday afternoon and returning to the office in London on Monday mid-morning. This is flexible working – but he didn't ask HR for it. A female lawyer in the same firm is formally part time, working four days a week, but in reality does five days work in four days, and has to be available on the fifth day in case of meetings, but earns one fifth less than she was earning before she started this arrangement. Her frustration is understandable.

While different ways of working inevitably help many individuals, they rarely impact on the organizational culture or challenge embedded practices. In my research and practice women were still worried about the loss of status they would suffer if they cut their hours. If they could have retained their job and their status (many were not so worried about money), many would have worked a shorter week. But they did not want to take a step down on the career ladder or do a less interesting job.

A female manager in Investco's Corporate Finance department had requested shorter hours in lieu of a promotion so that she could at least see her small son in the evenings. By this she meant that she wanted to be able to leave at 6.30 pm. Permission had still not been granted. Another mother working as an analyst in the broking division had a small baby and also wanted to leave at 6 pm, but only did so a couple of times a week. These women did not want to work part time, just a regular eight-hour working day.[59]

THE BUSINESS CASE

The work–life balance debates have been gathering pace for over 20 years now and arguments to promote balance are increasingly framed in the 'business case' discourse.

The stated aim of the first National Work–Life Balance week (October 2010) was to highlight why UK plc must tackle the way it works in order to increase productivity, loyalty, and wellbeing. It was announced that 'Work–Life Week would show that work–life balance was a win for everyone and was as vital as ever during tough economic times and that it was possible to combine work and care or outside interests and still be successful at work and home.' Ahead of its launch Sarah Jackson OBE, chief executive of Working Families, explained:

National Work–Life Week will highlight the importance of promoting a healthier work–life balance and tackling the way we work. Britain has the longest working hours in the EU and this is resulting in stress, ill health and less productive employees. In fact, stress has become the number one reason employees take time off at a huge cost to UK plc. Offering better work–life balance makes good business sense: Working Families research has shown a positive link between flexible working and employee performance.[60]

Children and mothers are missing words in this endorsement of work–life balance. Organizations emerge as those with most to gain and the health of employees has been stressed. Gains for businesses are spelled out in the Flexible Working Task Force paper as falling absenteeism and higher retention, leading to a reduction in costs; increased productivity; increased ability to recruit from a wider talent pool; and greater loyalty among staff.[61]

Sarah Jackson acknowledges Working Families want to have their cake and eat it. The evidence shows that work–life works better when it is part of the DNA of the company and not solely for mothers of young children. She told me in an interview:

We don't want flexible working to be just for women or there will be no real cultural change. We need to promote it for everyone and yet also reclaim the family friendly element. We want people to combine paid work with family life. To do this we have to show businesses that it is better for them too.[62]

For some this is a hard sell. For others the numbers have spoken for themselves. BT's wide ranging offer of flexible working arrangements, which is not aimed specifically at women, has nonetheless resulted in improved retention of female staff, as 96–99 percent return to work after maternity leave.[63]

Famously Dame Stephanie 'Steve' Shirley built up her highly successful software company – formerly F International, it was renamed Xansa in 2001 – in the 1960s and 1970s by employing highly qualified mothers who worked part time. 'I founded the organization by recruiting professionally qualified women who had left the industry on marriage or when their first child was expected. And structured them into a homeworking organization which I then went out and marketed.'[64]

Making the link between ways of working and trust explicit, Katherine Corish, founder and chairman of management consultancy Sysdoc Group, explains that flexibility and trust was deliberately built into the organizational work design:

> I set out to deliberately build a flexibility and trust into our work design. It is not a written policy, it is how we work. People have all sorts of calls on their time and we honor this. If I need to take some time off someone will help. No one person is indispensable.[65]

Sysdoc, described as a family-centric consultancy, is successful in competing against the big UK consultancies, where consultants often work a 60-hour week, and won the Opportunity Now Award in 2010 for the most agile UK organization.

FATHERS' RIGHTS

There has been a discernible shift back to family care in the debates on work–life, which now include elder care as well as childcare, but this time there is much more emphasis on fathers. Working Families is the UK's leading work–life balance organization, and its chief executive Sarah Jackson believes the way forward is for men and fathers to push for flexible working:

> We can't really go any further with women pushing for it alone. At the moment though men look at what happens to women who opt for flexible working in terms of career prospects and make the perfectly rational decision not to ask for it even though by law they are [entitled to do so].[66]

There are many men who would wish for shorter hours and more time with their families, and Working Families is conducting research with Lancaster University on this topic.[67] In a 2010 briefing paper it concluded:

Employers who manage to become gender-blind in their work–life balance implementation and culture (not just in policy) will develop a business advantage over those who seek to recruit from a dwindling pool of men who do not want or are able to forgo a better work–life balance. However, the gains should be large; the demand for better flexibility for men will not only come from them but from employed women too. *Men hold the key to greater flexibility for all, and through this, to better business performance.* [emphasis my own].[68]

The interim report findings (November 2010) show that there are positive signs of fathers wanting more involvement in childcare and domestic responsibility, and urge organizations to engage more with fathers on the subject of flexible work and childcare.[69]

BT, one of the leading companies in the equality and diversity field, was early in attempting to engage men in the debates on work–life. Its decision to sponsor the April 2004 Father's Direct conference came after it recognized the need for fathers to be involved in the debate on work–life balance. Richard Reeves argued the case for organizations to change culturally to allow more fathers to do more childcare without penalizing their career chances.[70] This is what women have been asking for over many years, but perhaps it will only really happen when men ask for it too.

The focus on fathers is gathering pace. The Family Friendly Working Hours Taskforce has argued that both men and women want to find a balance between work, family, and caring responsibilities.[71] It has cited evidence from a EHRC working paper that 62 percent of fathers surveyed thought fathers should spend more time caring for their children.[72] Another study from the Government Equalities Office reports that 33 percent of fathers said they miss out on and would like to be there for breakfast with their children, and 19 percent would like to be there at bedtime – that's less than one in five![73] There are many men who work at home one or two times a day or month at home, but there are few who do so because they are solely responsible for the children. Some research on fathers at home found that although these fathers were able to build new relationships with their kids, they commonly did not contribute a great deal to household tasks.[74]

In her study of IT workers, Elisabeth Kelan notes how the common discourse of working at home to enable parents to combine paid and care work was not used by men in discussions of working at home. Her interviewees commented that children might interrupt and disturb them if they worked at home. The assumption was that someone else cared for them. In fact, 'Children were used as an indicator of why one should not work from home.'[75]

One of the hopes that different ways of working will become a norm of many organizational cultures has been that young men coming into work take a look at the long-hours culture and reject it – as seen in the quote above. However there are signs that young men are prepared to put up with the long hours for the end financial gain. Graduates in the big four accountancy firms and lawyers and investment banks are put through grueling schedules as soon as they join. What is the purpose of this? It cannot be productivity. Has it become a ritual filtering-out of those who cannot take the hours? However good the maternity provisions and offers of flexible working are later on, the formative early experience of many graduates is hard, involving their working all hours, and sets the cultural tone for their careers there.

A study into work–life balance early on in careers found that although initially graduates seek work–life balance, their concern for career success draws them into a situation where they work increasingly long hours and experience an increasingly unsatisfactory relationship between home and work.[76]

In the recent Opportunity Now research on barriers to women's progress, there was almost no difference in the perception of barriers, including women's family responsibilities between older and younger men, undermining the commonly held belief that a younger generation of men in the workplace are more sensitive to equality issues. The most cited barrier to women progressing at work, according to men, was that women had to balance work and family responsibilities.[77]

RECESSION GIVES FLEXIBLE WORKING A BOOST

Flexible working has been given an unexpected boost not from parents' demands but from the recession of 2008–9. Economic necessity, not social progress, has resulted in an increase in flexible working. The CIPD reported that the recession caused a shift from full-time employment (down by a net 580,000 – 2 percent – in the two years to spring 2010) to part-time employment (which increased by 910,000 – 4.1 percent), with the shift caused by people working shorter hours to help employers cut costs and minimize redundancies.[78]

The car industry as an example responded to the dramatic fall in demand for cars through a combination of shorter hours, pay freezes and pay cuts, increased leave, and suspended production.

Toyota reduced all working hours for one year from April 2009 and suspended production for two weeks in February and two weeks in April, whilst Nissan introduced a four-day working week for all. Some seized the opportunity to impose a more lasting change.

Paul Lee, senior partner at UK law firm Addleshaw Goddard, pointed out that 'the qualities required to achieve a work–life balance – flexibility and nimbleness – are also essential during these uncertain times. There has never been a better time to embrace change.'[79] In February 2009 KPMG introduced a new scheme, 'flexible futures,' designed to minimize the prospect of large-scale redundancies in the current recession and enable the firm to retain its talented people. Under the scheme, staff were invited to sign up to indicate their willingness to reduce their working week by a day, with that day going unpaid, and/or take sabbatical leave of 4 to 12 weeks at 30 percent of pay, and 85 percent of staff signed up for the scheme. The flexible futures initiative ended in September 2010. However the firm is confident that it has had a lasting impact on attitudes to flexible working, and that managers (and employees) are now more comfortable discussing it.

'Whilst it was an agile response to a particular set of circumstances, flexible futures permanently changed the understanding of flexible working in the business,' a partner at KPMG explained, 'For the first time large-scale adoption of flexible working was seen as a business solution not just a means of accommodating individual needs.'[80]

Women Like Us is a social enterprise set up to help women with children find flexible work at an appropriate skill level. It recorded a surge in demand in 2008 from employers regarding part-time positions, since 'taking on high caliber part time workers was a less risky strategy than employing experienced hires full time.'[81] Karen Mattison MBE of Women Like Us noted that:

> We are experiencing greater demand than ever from companies who want to recruit people with talent and experience but at less cost. The idea that you can get more for less is one that is understood in particular by SMEs who are brilliant at being creative with resources. In this way part-time recruitment has been a silver lining for women, who have been looking for mid to senior level roles, in the recession.[82]

Flexible working has always been a useful option for employers in specific industries – shift work for mining, factories, and call center work, part-time working for working mothers, and now more recently as a way of reducing fixed costs at times of economic uncertainty.

What is still not clear is whether this has been to the particular benefit of working parents. As one senior executive in a large engineering firm told me, 'the people we want to go part time are not necessarily the people who are asking to go part time.'[83]

Nor do we know at this stage whether the increase of flexible working will result in a culture shift that will endure with the return of the better times. Organizations like CIPD and Working Families have shouted loud and clear that a good work–life balance is important for the health and wellbeing of workers and the economy alike. The association of flexible working with recession and less pay may not enhance its status, and there is already evidence of a return to long hours. The CIPD research 'Working hours in the recession' found that the proportion of people who work more than 45 hours per week (one in five) fell by 1.1 percent in the two years of recession.[84] However there are now signs of an increase in long hours working since the trough in 2009, following the loss of nearly 1 million jobs and a shift to part-time working since the start of the downturn. This suggests that the fall was a forced 'detox' for the UK's workaholics, most of whom will be eager to start putting in the hours once the economy gathers steam.

Sarah Jackson says it is not yet clear if there are any lasting changes:

> Most of the professional services firms are now out of recession and have ended their compulsory flexibility schemes. Some people have been left feeling vulnerable and sore. Now their hours have increased we could see an increase in presenteeism as those who were forced to cut their hours strive to regain their status and standing at work.[85]

In the latest research from Opportunity Now on barriers in the workplace (which was a repeat of some research done in 2005), the struggle to balance work and family life was the biggest barrier, cited by 82 percent of respondents, with 57 percent saying that the perception that working mothers were less committed was also a barrier.[86] These figures are higher than in the original research. In times of recession, competition for jobs increases, and behaviors associated with job insecurity like visibility and presenteeism also increase.

CONCLUSIONS

Women and men are renegotiating their roles at home. Organizations are a part of that. Their employees' family situation is no longer something that companies can ignore. Working mothers will have a real work–life balance when their husbands/partners do half the total housework and childcare and women are paid on a par with men. Young women are entering the world of work and have high expectations for their careers and how they share family responsibilities with their partners.

While patterns of work at senior levels are determined by the lives of men who have wives and partners taking care of the domestic side of their life, there will be little change to the numbers of women at the top.

Of all diversity policies, work–life balance is the most popular. Perhaps it is the easiest to relate to, and in some ways it is less challenging than other barriers to gender equality in the workplace. Their introduction and increasing popularity of flexible working initiatives are testament that the 'other side of life' is being acknowledged. However they also enable organizations to carry on business as usual whilst adding on policies to help out parents.

What we really need is a radical rethink about the way we work, a move away from the timeframe that suited families and economies 50 years ago, so that the many talented women who are currently not working to their potential can take their rightful place at work, for their own good and for that of society.

Finding out how many hours a day employees work is easy. Ask them. Subsequent questioning can focus on the reasons for the hours they work, including the leadership example. Other steps that organizations can take include assessing meeting times and banning after-hours meetings unless they suit all attendees, like Procter & Gamble did some years ago. A breakdown by division function and seniority can be revealing, and provide plenty of data from which to begin rethinking the ways in which people work. Focusing on the work outcome and not the process can ensure that presenteeism is minimized, and challenge the client expectation rationale that drives so much of the long-hours culture.

7

LET'S HAVE A DRINK! INFORMAL NETWORKING AND SOCIALIZING

INTRODUCTION

> Somewhere behind the formal organization chart at Indsco, lay another shadow structure in which dramas of power were played out.[1]

Work groups bond and develop their mutual ties in many ways, but one important way is through informal networking and socializing. Kanter's epic tale of Indsco in her book *Men and Women of the Corporation* charts the terrain of the informal side of organizational life where alliances are built, reputations managed, and organizational resources traded. Another aspect of an organization's culture that may appear gender neutral, informal socializing and networking, has been shown to be a barrier to women's progress in organizations. In their research on women retail managers, Tomlinson, Brockbank, and Traves found that their interviewees highlighted the significant, subjective and political processes at work.[2] They (women managers) stressed the need to engage in 'political maneuvers and game playing.'[3] The authors said that, despite their equal numbers at entry points, women remained poorly represented at senior levels, suggesting that 'subjective and informal processes were important determinants of women and men's progress.'[4]

The formal structures of authority, described by Max Weber, have long been recognized as an incomplete picture of power in organizations since they were not able to:

> reveal the cross weaving of the structure by less formal relations of power, the values and patterns of behavior which are independent of these formal rules and which develop out of the interaction of persons in groups in the organisations.[5]

It is now widely acknowledged that these informal rules, which supplement and may even undermine official rules, are an important part of organizational life.[6]

Exclusion from the informal side of work may mean being left in the dark about imminent promotions, not being given frank performance appraisals, or not understanding the significance of particular meetings. More importantly, friendships are forged through the informal network, often crossing barriers of official seniority. Whatever the formal rules of bureaucracy, in business it is friends and contacts that give you the final edge. The importance of informal rules is particularly relevant when it comes to promotion and selection. As soon as people reach general management, companies start looking for someone who can oil the wheels, who can bring in other business and contacts, someone who will socialize with the right people, who is pleasant to go drinking with or to introduce to others. It is not hard to see why men may score higher here than women. In most organizations men have set the stage for many years, and the actors know their parts well. Newcomers have to learn their lines if they want to take part, and pay attention to how the lead actors interact. Collinson, Knights, and Collinson discovered the importance of informal relationships in their research on discrimination in recruitment.[7] The high degree of informality in the use of selection channels and criteria was supplemented in several insurance companies by the use of job interviews conducted in the pub. A recent recruit told the researchers:

> The idea is to see how you shaped up informally, in a social situation, to see how you handle yourself over a couple of drinks and an informal chat. If you can operate on a sporting level and have a good chat that's the sort of thing they're looking for.[8]

While some men may find informal activities difficult, particularly if they are from a different culture, or for example are teetotal in an environment where after-hours drinking is an important 'work' activity, the informal side of organizational life is far more problematic for women. Failure to be included in the informal networks of an organization means exclusion from a wealth of potential business information and client contact, and can have severe consequences on career progression, as well as leading to isolation and personal distress.

Informal exclusion is powerful, and hard for women to complain about because each example sounds trivial, but added up, the whole picture is one of most women being excluded from a primary organization communication system. The importance of informal life at work is often not really felt until a person reaches a senior position. A senior person is required to be a representative of the organization, reflecting its character. Hilary Williams, an ex-director of British Gas, commented after successfully suing the company for sex discrimination) that 'When entertainment of business customers took place I was never invited. Looking back, I can see how many things I was excluded from – the golf days, the dinner parties, the after-work socializing, clay pigeon shooting.'[9]

Lorber sees women's exclusion by men from these informal networks as being from lack of trust, due to the fact that men and women are brought up in different cultural worlds.[10] Other management writers have attributed the informal network as functioning to reduce uncertainty within the organization.[11] Kanter has argued that the uncertainty of management resulted in the need for informal processes to secure 'trusted' people. She says that:

> It is the uncertainty quotient in managerial work, as it has come to be defined in the large modern corporation, that causes management to become so socially restricting: to develop tight inner circles excluding social strangers; to keep control in the hands of socially homogeneous peers; to stress conformity and insist upon a diffuse, unbounded loyalty; and to prefer ease of communication and thus social certainty over the strains of dealing with people who are 'different,'[12]

The group preference for homophily (the tendency for individuals to associate and bond with similar others), hampers attempts to promote a culture of inclusion and diversity, but is hard to break down.

Kanter noted that many of the women were not included in the networks by which informal socialization occurred and politics behind the formal system were exposed. She explained her findings with the concept of numerical (proportional) gender imbalance. She says that women are excluded because they are 'tokens': that is, outside the dominant group, not because they are women, and that it would be the same for any token group. It is their rarity and scarcity rather than their femaleness that counts. She captures the exclusionary tactics of these dominants in her study.

> In some cases dominants did not wish to have tokens around all the time. They had secrets – they moved the locus of some activities and expressions from public settings to which tokens had access to more private settings from which they could be excluded.[13]

She defines tokens as a subgroup composing less than 15 percent of the whole group. In her theory an increase in numbers of tokens would reduce the negative effects.[14] It has since been argued that Kanter's emphasis on number balancing as a social change strategy failed to anticipate the backlash from the dominant group. In attributing negative consequences to token members to tokenism, Kanter diverted attention from their root cause, sexism, and its manifestation in higher-status men's attempts to preserve their advantage in the workplace.[15]

Kanter's explanation ignores the wider social fact that until about 40 years ago women had on the whole been confined to the private world of home, leaving much of the public world of work (professional and managerial) a male-dominated zone. Men have always had access to men-only establishments, and have fought hard to preserve them, displaying a desire to exclude women from many areas of their life. There are many dining clubs in London that still exclude women members. Their importance as meeting places for men may be declining, but they are testimony to the existence of something other than mere fear of uncertainty, which leads men to exclude women. As an example, Whites is an exclusive men-only club in London. I cannot think that this prohibition is because its male members would be reduced to a state of anxiety and uncertainty if women joined. In some men-only clubs women are allowed in for certain activities like playing bridge, but have to enter by another door. The members do not want women there, and that is reason enough. Pubs have until relatively recently been another male zone, serving as public meeting places for a many different groups of men. It wasn't until 1982 that the Court of Appeal ruled that bars and pubs could no longer refuse to serve women, as it constituted sex discrimination.

Male bonding, which often involves specifically excluding women, occurs both within and outside organizations.[16] Looking at how and why men exclude women in wider social settings gives us more insight into what happens informally within organizations.

The specific exclusion of women in informal work relations is implicit in the expression 'old boys' network.' Ethnic minority men may experience many of the same barriers to inclusion as white women, but ethnic minority women will experience even more. Twenty years ago in her study of women managers, Trudy Coe found that the greatest barrier to women in management was the existence of a 'men's club': 'the old boy's network is viewed as the major obstacle at every level of management'.[17]

In the 2004 Demos research *Girlfriends in High Place,* author Helen

Wilkinson noted that the old boy network came up time and again as a career obstacle.[18] In the same year research[19] revealed that almost two-thirds (64 per cent) of non-executive directors found their most recent position informally through friends and business associates, despite the fact that the previous year the Higgs Review (2003) had called for the pool of candidates to be widened.[20] Today headhunters are used more by public companies conscious of the corporate governance code, but they too have been taken to task for depending too much on informal routes for recruitment.[21]

Binna Kandola asks, in his excellent book *The Value of Difference*,[22] what is the old boys' network? Having established that if you are not in it, you aren't going to be able to respond, and if you are in it, you won't have any reason to respond or even awareness that you are a part of the network, he suggests using social network analysis which traces informal connections between people within an organization. It is not clear how this is done methodologically, but I assume it is not an exact science. In what ways could this information be used by an organization? Human relationships cannot be reduced to models or diagrams. It would not give the rich data and nuances of the interactions of people in their personal networks. Only good qualitative research can do this, and some academics are doing so.

A female researcher finds it hard to gain entry to men's networks. When Barbara Rogers researched her book *Men Only* she had to use male moles to get through the doors and explore the informal networks.[23] There is a problem with attempts to describe or reduce a network to several key relationships – its power lies in its fluidity and intangibility. It defies a structured analysis because it is unstructured. Understanding and acknowledging the importance and influence of informal networks may be all that and organization can, or realistically should, do.[24]

Although the old boys' network usually refers to the informal relationships of senior managers within and outside their organizations, the boys start young. A female trainee accountant, 26, commented:

> I joined my accounting firm on a large grad scheme that was hugely male dominated in my department, corporate finance. I have found this to be both an advantage and a disadvantage. It is an advantage in the sense that as one of the only girls it is easier to stand out, have people remember you and also to network. However I feel restricted from certain social activities such as the evenings in the pub watching the football, golf holidays and the occasional trip to gentlemen's' clubs on a night out! My male peers are able

to do all these things with our male seniors, which is something I feel I miss out on.[25]

Organizations will value informal networking differently. In large bureaucratic organizations where employees remain for a long time, internal networks are usually important for maneuvering one's way through and up the organization. In organizations with a high turn-over, people will invest less time in establishing strong networks, and are more likely to build networks externally. Ibarra has done interesting work on networks, and showed that senior women are more likely to network outside their immediate place of work than men.[26] This may be down to the paucity of available women at a high level in any one organization.

Women are aware of the need for networking. A manager in Corporate Finance at Investco told me, 'Networking is very important but I don't do enough. I find it hard to do it with a load of blokes, and in a way they don't expect us [women] to do it.'[27]

In a discussion on promotion, one female assistant director in Corporate Finance at Investco at commented that managers needed to network, and that thinking that it was enough to be good at your job was a 'very female perception.' However she found it hard to know how to network: 'Good question, I'm still trying to work that out. It's very subtle. For example you get championed in this organization. It just doesn't happen. Men choose in their own likeness.'[28]

Ibarra considers networking vital in today's business world but does not think that women are any worse at it than men.

> Women aren't either more or less capable of networking, but since it's easier for people to make connections with people who are similar, the fact that there are fewer women in senior positions in business can be a barrier.[29]

WOMEN'S NETWORKS

In response to their exclusion women began their own professional networks in the early 1980s. These networks, both internal and external, have been formed out of a need to end feelings of isolation and exclusion from the mainstream. They are formal as opposed to informal.

One of the first, the City Women's Network, was formed by four women in 1978. Now extended to professions outside the City, it offers senior women the opportunity to network with other senior women. Industry-wide groups like Women in Banking, and broader-based ones like European Professional Women's Network (EPWN), have enabled women to network with women from other organizations. The networks act as a social and business meeting place. London president of the EPWN, Michelle Brailsford, said that, according to member's feedback:

> The advantages of being a member of the European Professional Womens Network include having a forum for talking business with like-minded women; having a forum for sharing issues and opportunities across cultures, functions, generations, and industries; and making contacts; finding coaches, mentors.[30]

British Telecom started a women's network in 1986, and they are now a common feature in many large organizations. These have been followed or accompanied by other employee networks for parents, ethnic minorities, disabled people, and gay, lesbian, bisexual, and transexual (GLBT) groups.

Employee networks have proved very popular. They vary from business to business, from being purely a meeting place for women who may be under-represented to being the center for all gender diversity initiatives in the organization. They function in a very different way from the informal networks of men, and cannot be compared. The act of setting up a network makes it formal and visible. Informal networks are invisible. However the provision of a forum in which women can form relationships is important in the absence of other types of forums, which men have developed over many years.

Although initially some senior women seemed reluctant to help other women on their way up the career ladder, endorsement now by leadership of women's networks has encouraged women to participate without fear of being attached in any way to a 'feminist' cause. Networks can be an acceptable vehicle for channeling criticisms or voicing concern, although there are ongoing efforts to prevent them being accused of being 'whine and wine' clubs.[31] They are nearly always supported by key male leadership, which gives them legitimacy. Indeed sometimes the position of chair of a women's network is sought after just because of the opportunity it gives to mix with senior male leadership, who will often take an active interest in the activities. It raises visibility and is therefore seen as a promotion route, but the price is high, as women run these networks in a voluntary capacity on top of their day job. Within a large organization meeting other women from different divisions may also provide career-moving opportunities.

Other senior women have commented to me that there is little point in having a women's network when it is men on the whole who can help you get on. This correlates with Ibarra's work on networks, because she found that minority members are likely to do better when they have relationships with a diverse group than if they limit themselves to relationships with people like themselves. What was of benefit from belonging to an employee network was learning from the experience of other minority members.[32]

It was not long, though, before some organizations experienced something of a backlash with complaints from men about positive discrimination. Because of this many of the networks make a point of inviting men to certain events, and some have now included men completely (for example, UBS's women's network is called All Bar None).

The initial rationale for networks was to provide role models, support, and networking opportunities for women. A women's network can be a good way of drawing women's attention to the female role models in a company, or even in an industry. Being together with a group of women can be inspiring as well as supportive. However for senior women it was different. They were able to be the role models and mentor younger women, but did not find the support they needed themselves, because of the inadequate numbers of women above them. This is where the external professional networks have met a need.

In recent years there has been much more of a focus on the organization drawing on the expertise of the employees in the women's networks. Companies will usually provide some funding for networks, but in return they have to demonstrate the business benefits any network would bring. According to a report women's networks regularly provide insight and input on recruitment, retention, and reputation issues, as well as increasingly providing input on PR, product development, and marketing.[33]

Funding is usually tight and has to be bid for, and women organizers have to run the networks in their own time and on a voluntary basis. It does seem that the organization is getting the best end of the deal. Having a women's network permits an organization to support a gender initiative without too much challenge to the status quo. Some organizations are now giving their networks power not only to develop strategy, but also to implement internal diversity initiatives. It all sounds a far cry from a male network, which entails less work and more play – socializing in clubs, pubs, or golf courses, usually on company expenses.

In some organizations women's networks have been very

influential. In Shell, the networks are used as a way of engaging men and exposing them to issues facing women in the company. Holding conferences, seminars, and informal talks to which men are invited is a non-controversial way for men to hear about what it is like for women with whom they work.

Elizabeth Kelan noted in *Performing Gender at Work* that many younger women are not interested in joining networks seeing them as irrelevant and for the older women.[34] Sarah Bond, diversity head of KPMG, thinks that teaching women networking skills in general is what is now needed rather than providing a separate forum for networking.[35]

MENTORING

Another route to relationships that are outside the formal hierarchy is through sponsorship and mentoring. Sponsors provide introductions through which an individual becomes established in their profession, and socialize their protégés to the values and behavior that are appropriate to the work culture.[36]

> Boy wonders rise under certain power structures. They're recognized by a powerful person because they are very much like him. He sees himself, a younger version in that person. Who can look at a woman and see themselves?[37]

There was concern when women first entered the management domain that men might hesitate to take on women protégés for fear of adverse reactions from their wives and colleagues.[38] In some industries men may indeed 'champion' a woman. The successful media personality and editor Janet Street Porter has said she has had a number of male sponsors in the media world, on whom she has depended heavily for support.[39]

At Airco, a common feature among many of the senior women was their close relationship with the male chief executive. Whilst it is still mostly men at the top of organizations, it is important that younger women form mentoring relationships with them to further their careers. Companies introducing mentoring schemes quickly found that the senior male mentors gained as much from their more junior female mentees as the mentees gained from them, as their thinking was challenged in a constructive way. Indeed this was the intention at Procter & Gamble a few years ago when a reverse mentoring scheme was introduced, which had the added advantage of the senior men learning from the young women. And as part of a training scheme at Swedish car company AB Volvo, senior male managers are given a female mentor who watches their progress on learning about gender (see Chapter 9).

Mentoring is directly linked in with the informal networking and the bonds that men may form together to the unconscious exclusion of women. This is another aspect of informal life in organizations that has now been formalized to provide opportunities not only for men, but also for women, to participate and benefit. The tendency to select and recruit in one's own likeness is widely acknowledged, which has meant that women and ethnic minorities are often excluded from the informal sponsorship that goes on in organizations.

A female senior manager in Airco Finance remarked, 'There is an affinity between men around mentoring – they feel comfortable. Perhaps they recognize themselves in others and want to do well. So it reinforces the old image.'[40] Mentoring is part of the process through which gender hierarchies in management are reproduced. It exploits the particular emotional complexion of relations between men, rather than being simply an important training and development tool.[41] Mentoring schemes for women, like women's networks, have been a popular initiative for companies to take. They are uncontroversial, and purport to level the playing field for women and minorities without challenging the status quo, the everyday workplace culture.

Many organizations, particularly large ones, have been using formal mentoring schemes for graduates for many years. At Airco there was an official mentoring scheme for the airline graduate intake every year, but employees told me that what mattered more was what was happening unofficially. The formal mentoring system was praised, but as one senior manager said, ultimately it does depend on personalities, and whether you get on with each other has a bearing on how much time you spend with a person. Matching personalities cannot be done formally.[42] Ibarra and her colleagues have shown that women are not mentored in the same way as men; she maintains that women's mentors have less organizational clout and do not sponsor them as often as mentors of men do.[43]

Sponsorship is arguably more important than mentoring. It implies a more immediate work-related relationship rather than someone who may impart advice but will not be actively involved in the furtherance of a career. This is the blue-eyed boy syndrome, whereby a senior executive ensures that their protegé travels up the company fast. Sylvia Hewlett suggests that it is the lack of sponsorship that is really holding women back from the final frontier of business – the boardroom. She says that one-to-one relationships between a senior man and more junior woman just do not happen because of lack of trust and fear of being suspected of an illicit sexual liaison, so 'the promise of sponsorship is probably the most important missing piece of the jigsaw for high performing women within sight of the very top of their professions.'[44]

The glacial pace at which women are arriving to take their seats on FTSE 100 boards prompted the launch of the FTSE 100 Cross-Company Mentoring Programme in 2004. Its primary purpose is for women to again advice from and access to well networked senior business leaders, but a side-effect is that top men begin to see gender in an informal way. Co-founder of the programme Jacey Graham is delighted with the impact it has had in the United Kingdom. 'Not only are chairmen and CEO mentors learning more about the issues aspiring women directors face, many of them have become real champions for change and many of their "mentees" have joined Boards of private sector companies as well as public and voluntary sector organizations,' she says. The programme has been replicated in other countries too, which is a real testament to its impact. 'This isn't the whole answer,' said Jacey, 'but its success highlights the critical part senior male business leaders play in leading this change.'[45]

A BUREAUCRATIC LONG-TERM CAREER CULTURE – AIRCO

During my research at Airco, I found that the airline, despite its 30,000 employees, was like a very large family, and as such, it was important for employees to fit in. Like all families there was a good deal of squabbling, but when faced with an external threat, people showed enormous loyalty. Getting approval from 'parents' (that is, the leadership) was the driver for much of the behaviors.

Airco's size and the many different elements of business within it meant that recruits came from a wide spectrum of society, although the low numbers of ethnic minorities entering management were a cause for concern. One senior director said that he always recognized an airline employee. 'They are a type,' he said, and then went on to describe in vague terms what he thought they were – not very stylish yet very confident. I quickly saw what he meant, and came to recognize the 'type' without being able to describe it very accurately myself.

People moved around the airline quickly, both vertically and horizontally, into different areas, and there was an awareness that knowledge of what was going on in other parts of the airline and having contacts was crucial to career progress. When a job became vacant it was advertised internally, but very often a name would be suggested, so both personal contact and reputation were important. Airline staff tend to stay a long time, and the need to build up contacts within the organization was more important than making contacts outside.

While Airco seemed a very friendly place in which to work, there was a lot of behind-the-scenes planning and maneuvering, with some people being in the know and others not. Who you knew and who you knew well was important for your career development. This is hard to avoid in large, bureaucratic organizations where visibility is important. It results in resentment in employees who lack these networking skills, as well as fears that hard work alone is not sufficient to succeed. It was clear at Airco that many of the women were not as interested in office politics as men (see Chapter 4).

A male manager in Finance told me, 'Airco is very political – merit is not sufficient, more sometimes primary in succeeding, and women need to be able to infiltrate and be very political themselves,'[46] and a female senior manager in Marketing said, 'It is a very political place. It is a very difficult company to join from the outside because there is such an entrenched network.'[47] Good relations with senior employees were highly rated in Airco – over 40 percent of respondents to my survey thought that a good relationship with a senior person and politically aware risk taking were the most rewarded work attributes.

AFTER-HOURS SOCIALIZING, INCLUDING CORPORATE ENTERTAINMENT

Informal relationships are often developed through after-hours socializing. Going out for a drink after work on a Friday night is a common event for many office workers, both men and women. But like working long hours, after-hours socializing is harder for those with caring responsibilities. When I worked as a journalist in the late 1980s and early 1990s, drinking was almost part of the job, but following the birth of my first child, the after-work drinks lost their luster. I wanted to get home, and hangovers and babies do not mix well. When it comes to team drinks, not taking part means missing out on the gossip, and importantly bonding with colleagues.

Time spent together out of the office is often what creates close working relationships and friendships. Organizations recognize this, which is why some plan away days and other corporate social events, often including families.

One woman in the City commented, 'There will be equality in the City when the pubs have as many women in them as men in the evenings.'[48] Knights and Morgan's study of an insurance company showed the construction of a male culture 'around the job' which included socializing after work. There was, the authors noted:

> No formal bar to women selling, but the way the culture developed, the expectations of the work, what the tasks involved, the social networks through which support was mobilized all ensured that women were unlikely to be employed except in isolated cases.[49]

Women in Cynthia Cockburn's study of male resistance to equal opportunities told her that their absence from all-male gatherings after work impeded their progress, cutting them out from important sources of information. One man said, 'We have a phrase "You'll learn more in the pub than you will in the store."'[50]

Pubs matter, too, in terms of more regular kinds of activity: office gossip, what promotions are going, buying a useful colleague or boss a drink, deciding what we all think about so and so, or finding out useful bits of information about the job when it's very competitive and there is no formal training.[51] Until the last 20 years, they were public meeting places totally dominated by men. The growth in wine bars during the 1980s, however, made it easier for the inclusion of women in drinking after work, and pubs now are much more inclusive of women in both their décor and their wine lists. Making inroads into men's public domain has not been without some resistance. The Fleet Street wine bar El Vino fought and lost a legal battle to keep women away from the bar, and private men's clubs offer a different kind of after-hours venue.

The drinking culture is such now that young women as well as young men can and do go out and drink copious amounts of alcohol. This can be a useful skill in a hard-drinking industry, but because of double standards women who match the men drink for drink may also suffer criticism. One property firm with a hard-drinking masculine culture found it was recruiting a certain type of female graduate – those that could drink with the boys and swear with the best of them. However an older senior director told me, 'Some of them try too hard to be like men.'[52] Indeed some of the young women's behavior was becoming a problem. When one had to be carried out of a pub after downing too many shorts, the HR director was asked to have a word. There were other industry people in the pub and it did not look good for the firm's image. Drunken men are acceptable but drunken women – NO! A woman cannot operate by men's rules and get away with it.

CORPORATE ENTERTAINING

Informal socializing and networking has been a part of City life since its beginnings. Business was transacted in coffee bars, with not a lawyer in sight, so trust and certainty of a person's integrity was vital. Introductions were made between friends, and very often a business deal was born. The old Stock Exchange motto 'dictum meum pactum' ('my word is my bond') underlines the role that trust played in the transactions of the City.

In this sense the informal processes were a vehicle for reducing uncertainty in the way that Kanter has described.[53] Although the world of finance is a very different place now, the emphasis on informal meetings and building up relationships remains an important part of City life. City socializing is mostly about making a client feel special, offering them something that the next company cannot match, or making them a friend, so that loyalty and business ensue. Business and leisure often intermingle in the City. All manner of entertainments and treats are at a brokers' or bankers' disposal, to woo a potential client or reward a generous client. While corporate entertaining is on the formal agenda, in reality many clients become friends and attend private dinner parties and events. 'I'm just about to go skiing with a bunch of clients who I've got very friendly with over the years,' a female manager in broking told me.[54]

In Investco, the percentage of men (82 percent) who took part in corporate entertaining was nearly double the percentage of women (44 percent) regardless of the division. There were also big differences in gender when it came to how important they considered mixing socially with clients to be. Only 8 percent of women respondents said that socializing with clients was very important, compared with 32 percent of men. Only 9 percent of men thought that it was unimportant, compared with 36 percent of women. Mixing with colleagues was considered important by 28 percent of women and 36 percent of men. Over half the respondents said that domestic responsibilities limited the amount of after-hours socializing they did, but there was a marked difference by sex – 36 percent of men said that domestic responsibilities constrained their informal socializing compared with 63 percent of women. The most senior woman in the bank, who had five children (a Superwoman – see Chapter 3 on the gender agenda) recognized the part corporate entertaining played, but said:

No. I won't do any entertaining and my clients accept that. At the end of the day what they come to me for is advice not entertainment, someone else can do that. But they keep coming to me for advice and they don't complain.[55]

A late-night walk around the City of London or even parts of the West End will reveal large numbers of dinner-suited men going to and leaving dinners at the big hotels, at the livery companies, or the Chiswell Street Brewery, followed often by going to clubs. Although many of the gentleman's clubs now permit women members, they still maintain men-only bars, and are known for cigar-smoking men of a certain age.

In some parts of the bank, entertaining clients was considered to be crucial. There were several men in the Corporate Finance division, who for one reason or another were more available than most – one was divorced and the others lived in London during the week while their wives were in the country. They all enjoyed socializing and took on a lot of the client entertaining. One of the heads of the division said he was out four nights every week.

The fact that nearly twice as many men took part in corporate entertaining as women, and it was considered more important by men, may have had career implications, as socializing with clients is an important aspect in the present career structure of the City. Women's exclusion from these activities may impede their progress in the organization, even though they themselves may have felt they are unimportant.

As the numbers of female clients in the City have grown, particularly in fund management, the usual offers of shooting and fishing have been replaced with other types of entertainment like spa days, or cookery weekends in Italy.

SPORT AS MEANS OF ENTERTAINING AND INFORMAL NETWORKING

Sport is an integral part of business life. Doing it, watching it, and most importantly talking about it, sport also acts as a bonding mechanism for men. Boys start to take part in team sports from as young as 3 years old. Look out on a Saturday morning in any park and there will be toddlers almost being taught how to kick a ball. Girls will probably be inside a hall somewhere wearing a pink tutu and learning ballet, which has no lasting advantages in the workplace apart from good posture. Many men have learned to communicate through sport, and men who have recently met often talk about sport as a bridge into conversation. 'It's an icebreaker and anyone can join in, no matter what education or class they're from,' a male manager in Airco said.[56]

This may sound trite but its importance should not be underestimated. A sound knowledge of football, rugby, cricket, or preferably all three (in the United Kingdom: of course, other sports play the same role in other countries) can be vital for forming relationships in business. Boys learn these sports from an early age, and often their relationships are formed around a shared love of a sport. The prolific use of sports metaphors in business language, such as 'playing a fast ball' and 'under starters' orders', shows how much sport pervades the business workplace.

Research in the Netherlands on how the sports history of account managers informed their work revealed two clear themes: team and leadership skills, and perseverance and toughness, skills that they strongly associated with success in their jobs.[57] Many successful sportsmen go on to do after-dinner speaking and start motivational training or coaching businesses. The relationship of sports and business is strong. In Val Singh's excellent study on boardroom cultures, she notes that sport was an important topic in the social time of two of the four company boardrooms she researched, and this was commented on by the few female board members: 'One of the female directors said that she made efforts to introduce conversation topics such as theatre and art, when she had enough of the men's sport-related chat.'[58]

Rogers views sport as a kind of shared fantasy.[59] Although some men play sports, the real point of sport for men in groups is watching it and talking about it. As Michael Korda observed some years ago, most men are more concerned with knowing and reading about sport than doing it, and it is a woman's ignorance of sport that attracts their ridicule, rather than her inability to play.[60] As I write this morning in January 2011 the headlines are full of the dismissal of a veteran Sky sports presenter for being caught off air ridiculing a young female assistant referee, claiming that women know nothing about the offside rule. The male identification with sport has its effects in the confining of women, their sense of being limited, even though sports presenters are increasingly glamorous young women. And the younger generation is finding the same pattern. A 28 year-old female fund manager told me:

> We go out together occasionally after work, not much during the credit crisis though, so we got out of the habit. But the boys are all golf mad, playing with each other and with clients. It is difficult as a woman because we just don't have the same kind of activities to do

157

together on a casual basis. The girls don't play anyway but I don't think they would want us to. They like being boys together.[61]

Airco had its own sports clubs and teams, in which some of the young men I interviewed took part. Conversations around sport are used as a communicating mechanism for men that women rarely share. Discussing Saturday's big match on a Monday morning is not usually how two women bond at work. This may not matter if the numbers of men and women are equal, but a woman who particularly dislikes sports chat might perhaps be working as the lone woman in a group of men. While they are not ostensibly offensive to women, conversations centered on male sports exclude women from participation. As one woman told me, 'You are just left standing there, not being able to contribute and feeling stupid.'[62] As the numbers of women football fans grow it will be interesting to see whether the younger generation do have more mixed-gender discussions of sport. Golf in particular was a feature of airline senior managers' lives. 'Oh yes, there are still golf days that women don't get invited to,' a female senior manager in Marketing said.[63]

And women were quite clear that sport acted as a conduit to sponsorship and career promotion. A female senior manager in Cargo said, 'It still appears a boy's club with younger men being more readily accepted into the network of more successful older men by a shared interest of sport – football, golf etc. and therefore they are nurtured and chosen for promotion.'[64]

A lot of business has traditionally been conducted on golf courses, and it is often for business reasons, as well as social, that people want to join prestigious golf clubs. Although this game is enjoyed by many women, it is usually on a non-business level, as ladies golf. Apart from anything else the length of a game makes golf prohibitive for working women who have family commitments. Even when there are mixed games it seems that women may miss out. Some research in the United States was conducted on the impact of mixed golf. Women teed off from a different position from men, and so they missed out on the opportunities for talking and bonding.[65]

The importance of sport as an integral part of selling was confirmed by Collinson and her colleagues' study on recruitment. One respondent told them:

The biggest thing is the sport actually. I play cricket and football. There's a broker in town, who I've played football with for years so I now do business with him. At our sports club it's all solicitors and accountants, all the sorts of contacts you need .... you see it's a lot easier to 'do things' on a Saturday, after the match, over a few pints in an informal situation.[66]

One professional woman, new to a male-dominated broking office, signed up for a golfing weekend on an email that was going round the office. She was the only woman to do so, and received an embarrassed phone call to say that it was a bit awkward because the players would be sharing rooms. She told me in interview, 'He then said we've never had a girl sign up before. I got the message and pulled out. It's a shame because I'm a good golfer.'[67]

The enormous growth in corporate entertaining and the corporate takeover of events like Wimbledon, the Henley Regatta, and international rugby are evidence of the close relationship between sport and business. Attending sports events is a big part of corporate entertaining. Some of these events are just as accessible to women as men, like race meetings at Ascot or Cheltenham, or going to Wimbledon tennis, or attending Henley Regatta. However, there are not so many women rushing for tickets to Test matches, rugby internationals, and football matches, and more importantly, not so many would be invited. Someone said to me that the more elite the sporting activity, either watching or participating, the less likely women would be there. High on the elite stakes are a day's shooting and a day's fishing on a sought-after river. One American broker, Merrill Lynch, flew out a number of clients to Iceland for three days' fishing. Others take clients to the Hong Kong Sevens, Football World Cup, and the Ashes. Substantial amounts of money are spent on corporate entertaining, something I once pointed out to a chairman of a company who was complaining about the cost of women going on maternity leave.

An organization can assess how important sport is in the working lives of its employees, whether it is used as a bonding mechanism for men, and whether women feel excluded by it.

Sport's apparently neutral characteristics make it appear a harmless interest for men. Its exclusion of women is rarely commented on, instead being taken as the natural order of things, and of course no one wants to be a spoilsport.

A paper by Jill Radford and Eve Hudson given at a conference in 1998 discussed the links between the success of a local football team and the increased violence in the area – another unpalatable connection.[68] There are numerous examples of top footballers who have committed violence against women in their private lives, further evidence of football's harnessing of some harmful characteristics of masculinity. Some of these exclusionary aspects of sport need to be held in mind when discussing the role of sport, whether playing it, watching it, or talking about it in organizational life.

SEXUAL ENTERTAINMENT

The next chapter on sexuality will note that the sexualization of our culture is having an impact on organizational life. One of the more obvious ways is through sexual entertainment. Whether or not the individuals take part in any of the sexual entertainments on offer, they form a background to the whole City culture, and it is important to highlight this.

If sport offers one set of enticement to clients, sex is certainly on offer as another. Some clients may be taken to Stringfellows or Spearmint Rhino on a Monday night for lap dancing; there are more sophisticated arrangements to cater for different tastes. There are many clubs, both private and public, where hostesses look after customers, and overseas trips have been known to include the procurement of prostitutes for clients, particularly Far Eastern trips.

During her time as campaign officer for the Fawcett Society, Kat Banyard ran the two-year campaign Sexism in the City, and with Rowena Lewis published *Corporate Sexism* in 2009, which highlighted the discomfort many women felt about the use of pornography and sexual entertainment in and around their workplaces.[69] The campaign resulted in the launch of the Fawcett Charter in 2008. This represents a coalition of leading employers committed to promoting an inclusive work environment by challenging the objectification of women at work. So far only 11 organizations have signed up, two of them big corporates, BT and Barclays Wealth. Although some organizations will have policies expressly forbidding employees to use sex establishments for work purposes, these are hard to enforce.

Banyard and Lewis's *Corporate Sexism* report found that 41 percent of the UK's lap-dancing clubs specifically promote corporate entertainment, and 86 percent of the London clubs offer discreet receipts which enable the cost of the evening's activities to be claimed as a company expense.[70] One banker I spoke with said that he had to go to these clubs because he knew that certain clients, particularly some foreign ones, expected it, 'We do have a general policy but when it comes to clients, the company turns a blind eye. They bring in too much business.'[71]

Craig Jones, global head of diversity at Barclays Wealth, said that Barclays Wealth decided to support the Fawcett Charter because they saw the Fawcett Society as a thought leader and influential. He said, 'It is really important to address these issues. Companies should have a moral compass. Many men as well as women feel they have to participate in forms of entertainment when they would rather not. It is excluding and unacceptable.'[72]

Barclays Wealth was a sponsor of an event at Worcester Race-course. When the chief executive saw an advertising campaign poster featuring a horse with two half-naked women he withdrew the brand sponsorship, saying, 'We did not want to be associated with it. It alienates our female clients and half our workforce is female.'[73]

Lap-dancing clubs have proliferated in recent years, encouraged by a ham-fisted piece of legislation, the 2003 Licensing Act, which classed them as part of the leisure industry rather than sexual-encounter establishments. The result was that the number of clubs in the United Kingdom doubled to 310 in the four years to 2011. A national campaign fought jointly by Fawcett Society and Object has been successful, and clubs will now have to be licensed as sex estab-lishments. Some local councils have announced that they will not issue any further licences, something that has provoked some angry outbursts from club owners like Peter Stringfellow, who warns that it will result in the opening up of illegal clubs.[74]

Both in my research and consultancy, women viewed the boys' get-togethers with an amused or bemused acceptance, the 'let them get on with it, they are children really' sort of attitude. When you are immersed in a culture as male as the City, it is easier to accept a lot of it, particularly if it is not directed at you personally, than to make a fuss. But in the eyes of women outside the City, some of the entertainment leaves a lot to be desired.

In my research, divorced and single women were just as likely to rate the men's club as a barrier as their married counterparts. This is an area, then, when the 'rationale' based on the 'women have fami-lies' dries up, and exclusion is based solely on gender. I contend that this is a patriarchal exclusion which occurs right through society. Although the existence of a 'men's club' may be acknowledged by employees, my research shows how elusive that 'club' is. It operates through a number of informal processes, but it is, in effect, more than the sum total of these processes. Its elusiveness and subtlety make it adaptable and it may flourish even within an equal opportu-nities culture. A female senior manager in Human Resources at Airco said:

> There is still an unsaid, some sort of comfort that men have around each other that they don't have around women. There are still golf days, there are still boys' nights out, still a strong sense of male affinity that you sense rather than necessarily see.[75]

Apart from the obvious obstacles for women with families and the exclusion from informal socializing where sport and sex are used, I found evidence that women are not as keen on using the informal route at work. They showed a dislike of internal politics.

It doesn't help that many of the clubs that have been meeting places for business contacts and dining clubs in the evenings specifically exclude women. On top of that, domestic commitments obviously restrict some women's scope for after-hours socializing. The inclusion of 'wives' at dinner parties at a senior level makes it hard for a woman if she has a reluctant partner or is single. Add the fact that the extensive use of sport as a means of entertainment condones the frequent exclusion of women from these activities, because of the masculine nature of the sport, and lastly, the sexual nature of many forms of entertainment which exclude women or, if they are included, marginalize and embarrass them, and it is easy to see very clearly why, where informal socializing is central to business success or career progress, women find themselves at a disadvantage. From a business point of view, the large amounts spent on corporate entertaining are hard to justify when compared with the poor maternity benefits on offer (for example, in the case of Investco) and low diversity budgets (in other companies). Perhaps this in itself provides a hint of the priorities of an organization. Client entertainment is about favors as well as bonding, and while it remains a perk for senior men and an opportunity for them to bond together, it is likely to remain part of business life.

WOMEN IN THE BOARDROOM

Excluding women through informal networking and socializing is active resistance to their progression in the workplace, and its purpose is particularly to protect routes to power. The informal side of life really comes into play at senior levels of the organization, and is perhaps the biggest barrier of all to women, who by the time they reach these levels will usually have made their decision on the children issue, by either not having them or sorting out good childcare arrangements. One senior banker told me that she left her organization because she knew she could go no further. There were no women in the inner sanctum, and although there were no specific incidents of overt discrimination, she knew she had reached the limit.[76] This of course can occur for men too.

There is not much an individual organization can do apart from being aware of the power of these networks. Women's (external) networks and the Cross-Company Mentoring scheme have been set up as a means for women to progress without the informal male route. Although I disagree with Kanter on the reason for women being tokens, I agree with her conclusions – that until women arrive at senior levels in sufficient numbers, the shadow structure will continue to exclude them. Individual mentoring efforts will eventually enable some women to get on to the top table, but the only mechanism for real change at this point must be legislative.

There is nothing like impending legislation to concentrate the mind. It is legislation that has ensured that equality issues are on the corporate agenda, and it may well be that the stubborn under-representation of women on major corporate boards, at 12.5 percent, is no different.[77] Discussing the use of quotas during the evidence sessions of the Treasury Select Committee on Women in the City following the banking crisis, the sole female committee member, Sally Keeble, asked Professor Goodhart, 'Can you think of an instance where men have said in the interests of equality we are going to stand aside without there being a specific change which says there has to be equal representation?' Professor Goodhart could not.[78]

The Treasury Select Committee Report concluded that quotas were not an appropriate way forward.[79] The preferred approach in the United Kingdom has always been to urge voluntary change, and indeed many vocal proponents for more women to be represented on boards are not in favor of quotas.[80] The Kingsmill Review on Women's Pay and Employment (2001)[81] decided against compulsory gender pay audits for the private sector, relying instead on their voluntary efforts, and so far the only required action in the boardroom (from the Walker Review of 2010) is for diversity to be a consideration in the appointments of new directors.[82]

Other countries in Europe are going much further. The first to introduce quotas was Norway in 2002, where the law demands that public shareholder-owned corporations (called ASAs in Norway) must have an average of at least 40 percent women and 40 percent men on their boards or face dissolution. Female representation on boards has risen from around 6 percent in 2002 to more than 40 percent, and the number of women board members in Norway has more than doubled.[83]

Norway is not alone. Spain uses a similar approach, though there it is based on recommendation rather than legislation. Companies with more than 250 staff are required to develop a gender equality plan, and new laws recommend a proportionate number of women on boards. The number of female directors in the largest listed companies has risen by almost a third. Australia is putting in place a 'comply or explain' system, and France, the latest to propose gender quotas, wants to go even further than Norway, imposing 50 percent quotas on boards of companies listed on the Paris Stock Exchange by 2015.

The much-publicized Independent Review into Women on Boards,[84] chaired by Lord Davies was published in February 2010, and played safe by recommending voluntary targets for FTSE 350 companies rather than quotas, although it did not rule out the possibility of quotas in the future if targets are not met. It also recommended that all companies publish their targets as well as the overall numbers of women they employ.

The European Commission is also considering the issue of female representation on boards, and is perhaps more likely to recommend quotas, which the Davies Review said were not supported by the majority of contributors to the consultation process.

The Davies Review suggests that FTSE 100 companies should aim for a minimum 25 percent female board representation by 2015. Less well publicized but the number-crunching point of the report is that from March 2011 two-thirds of board appointments should be men and one-third should be women in order for these suggested targets to be met.

The *2010 Female FTSE* report published in November also urged a comply or explain model for organizations. It recommended that chairmen of all FTSE 350 companies be required to offer an explanation if there were fewer than 20 percent of women directors on the board, and that this should increase to a 30 percent after three years.[85]

There is growing support for quotas,[86] and while quotas for non-executives is not an answer to the lack of female executive directors on boards, which is where the real power lies, it could have a positive influence on the boardroom culture as well as on strategic decisions. Higher numbers at that level will also signal to women lower down the organization that there can reach the top even if they are not in the old boys' network.

8

SEX IN THE OFFICE

INTRODUCTION

All organizational cultures will express something about sex as well as gender. Emotions, personal relations, and sexuality are supposed to be left to the private sphere, yet all three, while they are repressed to different extents, are present in all organizations.

There is now acknowledgement of (some) emotions and personal relations in workplaces, but sexuality remains a controversial subject. Deleted out of the bureaucratic model, sex, like emotion cannot be deleted out of human beings. Most organizational discussions on sexuality focus on sexual harassment or in recent years on sexual orientation, as these two categories are specifically targeted by UK law. It has been illegal to discriminate on the grounds of sexual orientation since 2003, and there have been huge changes in the acceptance and inclusion of lesbians and gay men in some organizations.[1] Sexual harassment, meaning unwanted sexual conduct or creating an intimidating environment, is also illegal but sits uneasily within the diversity framework, carrying as it does more negative notions of power and inequality. Training on sexual harassment usually concentrates on concepts of dignity and respect, rather than questioning the dominance of a type of male heterosexuality that objectifies women. Arguably targeting women (harassment) and lesbians and gay men for scrutiny oversexualizes both groups, perpetuating the belief that it is only their presence in organizations that is sexual. Heterosexual men, who are by far the most dominant sexual group in most organizations, are not considered a problem.

Sexuality in organizations encompasses more than sexual harassment and the accommodation of a minority of non-heterosexual employees. It existed before women arrived to work with men as equals. Anyone who has watched the popular television series *Mad Men*, which is about people in an advertising agency in New York in the 1960s, has been reminded of that fact. Pinching bottoms, flirting, and sexual comments were an integral part of office life. Today much of that behavior has been forbidden, but a senior male director said to me, 'Basically underneath the surface, the men haven't changed that much.'[2]

Attractions, affairs, and marriages often begin at work, more so now that women are more likely to work with men than they were 20 years ago, and the long-hours culture means that there is precious little time for professionals to socialize after hours. Office banter can make the work environment enjoyable for employees. There can be a fine line between having fun and offensive behavior. I include sexuality as part of an organization's culture, and use the term sexualized culture. That sexuality may be embedded in an organization's culture in the same way as gender is recognized, for example by the researchers who pointed out that 'Male managers with female subordinates may use sexuality, harassment, joking and abuse as a routine means of maintaining authority. This may be thoroughly embedded in the taken for granted culture of the organization.'[3]

The ways in which sexuality may or may not be expressed and by whom in organizations, the ways it may be overt in an organization or actively utilized by those in it, and the ways it may promote or inhibit men's and women's progress in the organization, are areas of interest in the promotion of diversity and equality.

SEXUALIZED CULTURES

Feminists first brought to the public eye the issue of sexual harassment in organizations, and have been successful in bringing this concept into the margins of management theory, and certainly into mainstream thinking on the discrimination of women at work.[4] Sexual harassment is generally taken to mean many different types of unwanted sexual attention, and the focus of much feminist and feminist-inspired research into sexuality in organizations has been on the incidence of and reasons for sexual harassment.[5] Feminist accounts of sexual harassment have interpreted it as representing one of the means by which men retain power over women.[6]

A few years on from the first analysis of sexual harassment, some academics began to see sexuality, like emotion, as part and parcel of organizational life. Hearn and colleagues described it as being a fundamental, but neglected, structuring principle of organizational life,[7] and claimed that it could also be seen a subtext of organizational life. Sexuality, like other hitherto hidden gendered aspects of organizational life, was revealed like other taken for granted norms as privileging male experience and interpretation.

166

The feminist focus on women as victims of sexual harassment, with its overtones of unequal power relations, lost favor with some feminists who wished to see a more positive emphasis put on women's sexuality at work and explore the potential pleasure derived from it.[8] This may include attractions, flirtations, and the ability to express their own sexuality – and perhaps use it. Pringle chose the discourse of sexuality in her empirical study to show how bosses exercise power over their secretaries through pleasure. However much the secretary gains pleasure from the relationship she has with her boss, the imbalance of power remains. She has to operate within that. Pringle states, though, that, 'Gender and sexuality are central not only in the boss–secretary relation but in all workplace power relations.[9]

There has been much debate about the limits of construing sexuality as subversive for women, and whether the terms on which they may gain pleasure are ultimately set by men.

Gherardi, in her work on gender and symbolism in organizational cultures,[10] uses the term 'organizational sexuality,' which seems to have a life of its own. She rightly points out the multitude of sexual overtones in organizational life, but imbues these with an organizational identity. She sees organizational sexualities as strategies devised to cope with the demands of a dependence relationship: that is, between the employee and the employer. The entry of women into previously male-dominated organizations has turned them into arenas where gender relations between men and women have to be negotiated.

Most of Gherardi's material is taken from case studies of shop floors, where the role of sexual banter may well be to alleviate boredom and act as a device to cope with a subordinate employee position, but in management and the professions this is less likely to be the case. In the majority of organizations it is very much a male heterosexuality that dominates the workplace.[11]

Organizations frequently use women's and increasingly men's sexuality in the ordinary course of their business, as illustrated in Adkins' research in the tourist industry.[12] Certain types of work, like bar work, waiting at tables, and reception work, require workers to be attractive and in some cases dress in a uniform. Although the laws restricting wording in job advertisements act to discourage overt requirements for 'attractive' staff, firms still employ women and in some cases men for their looks. One professional services firm in the north was renowned for the attractiveness of its secretaries. I was told by an employee, 'It doesn't matter if they are short on skills, the men like good-looking secretaries. The more senior the director, the prettier the secretary.'[13] Many clothes retailers now demand a certain look from their store personnel, both male and female, which enhances their brand image.

Women and men both enjoy the attractions of working with the opposite sex; there can be a buzz in the atmosphere for heterosexual employees, which just isn't there in single-sex workplaces. It is important to remember that there is a difference between mutual attraction and sexual harassment. It would be impossible to censor out all attraction and affection between members of an organization. MacKinnon, whose work did much to promote public recognition of sexual harassment as a legal issue, was keen to emphasize that it was not her aim to repress all free expressions of sexuality: 'Objections to sexual harassment at work is not a neo puritanical moral protest, against signs of attraction, displays of affection, compliments, flirtation etc.'[14]

In an effort to keep their working environments harassment free, some organizations have introduced fairly draconian policies concerning communication between men and women. There are no-touch policies, no-flirt policies, and heavy policing of language. The most frequently voiced complaint from employees that I receive when I arrive as a diversity consultant is that all the fun will be taken out of the workplace.

The problem thrown up here is that if we understand sexuality to be patriarchally structured, women themselves often find it hard to know what stands for a compliment and what might be read by others as being disrespectful. If, as Pringle says, it is men who define women's pleasure,[15] then the difference between coercive and non-coercive heterosexuality is hard to pin down. This element of hegemonic acquiescence by women in the face of sometimes unpleasant aspects of male sexuality is highlighted in many of the studies of sexual harassment in which women find it difficult to name the behavior as such.[16]

Having established that every culture is sexualized, how do we identify in what ways and when it matters?

Indicators of a sexualized culture may be found in the dress of the workers and the physicality of the workplace. By this I do not just mean pin-ups of 'Page 3' girls, but other indicators that the organization may encourage an expression of sexuality, rather than aim to repress it. For example, consider the differences between the environment in a public library and a Soho advertising agency. This draws on Gagliardi's ideas about architectural symbols.[17] The visual layout, what people look like and wear, who is at reception, the art on the walls, the furniture and building, tell a story.

The next indicator is the communication, the language and humor used during the course of business. What do you hear when you walk in to an office? What are interactions between men and women like? Do both men and women feel comfortable with the language, and is there a gender difference?

Another indicator may be the existence or not of sexual harassment, a notoriously difficult area on which to gather data. As we shall see, later in this chapter, individual sexual harassment – one person harassing another – can occur in any type of culture. Studies have shown that it is more likely to occur in male-dominated cultures, but my research did not confirm this. However the reluctance of women to bring incidents to attention itself reveals an aspect of the culture which is excluding. The opposite type of culture brings its own problems. If banter and sexual talk is part of the everyday office language, when does it become offensive and therefore harassment? Research that I and my colleagues carried out for the UK Ministry of Defence (MoD)[18] clearly illustrates this dilemma. A line has to be drawn, and it is usually the women who draw it.

Different cultures will have different expressions of sexuality: some are strongly heterosexual and some are not. My research in Airco found that the dominance of heterosexuality has an influence on both gender relations and working style.[19] Some sexualized cultures may be intimidating and exclusionary to women (and this might constitute sexual harassment), and this can be construed as evident resistance to the presence of women as equals. Other cultures may not be harassing, but do not prevent some individual harassment from taking place. If there is evidence that victims of harassment do not feel able to report their experiences, then the culture condones the harassment. This is frequently the situation in workplaces today.

In Chapter 1, I wrote briefly about the increase in the sexual objectification of women in the United Kingdom (as in many other Western countries). There is now easier access to, and therefore more widespread use of, pornography; there are increasing displays of sexual violence of women in films, an increase in trafficking of women for sex, more focus on body image than ever, and an increase in forms of sexual entertainment such as pole dancing and lap dancing. Such is the proliferation of sexual images of women in print and web media that as a society we seem dangerously immune to their impact.

The Fawcett Society's campaign 'Sexism and the City'[20] joins the dots between women's experiences in the workplace and a wider culture in which women are subject to sexist stereotypes and are increasingly objectified. Its campaign to have lap-dancing club licences change from bar establishment to sex establishment was successful. Kat Banyard, author of *The Equality Illusion*,[21] led the campaign for Fawcett before going on to found UK Feminista, a campaign to end gender inequality. She thinks that this increasing sexualization of our culture has massive implications for the workplace.

A British survey of 11,000 adults carried out between 1990 and 2000 found that the number of men who admitted to paying for sex rose in that period from 1 in 20 to nearly 1 in 10. Dr Helen Ward, the author of the report, linked the phenomenon to the general mainstreaming of the sex industry.[22]

This is an uncomfortable subject for both men and women, and some might say it should not be discussed in a book about the workplace. However, in their report *Corporate Sexism*, the Fawcett Society found 20 percent of men admitted to accessing pornography at work.[23] The report said that exposure of employees to pornography at work is rife. An extensive body of research evidences that pornographic images are harmful to women, and promote sexist attitudes and behaviors.

The internet has given rise to the 'pornification' of our culture, according to US campaigner Gail Dines, whose book was written to banish any notion of porn being merely benign titillation.[24] Contemporary pornography is increasingly violent, with the abuse of women a regular feature of all porn. Dines explains men's enjoyment of this abuse and humiliation of women as to do with masculinity and gender inequality. By watching the domination of women, the men participate in it, shoring up their masculinity. Pornography and men's use of it is intrinsically linked to inequalities between women and men: 'it eroticizes the dominance of masculinity over femininity of men over women.'[25]

The use of pornography at work, whether through technology or other means, infringes the Sex Discrimination Act, creating a hostile and intimidating environment for women. The use of explicit sexual language also creates a hostile and intimidating work environment for women, and can be construed as sexual harassment. It is difficult to police the technology, but legal issues apart, the influence of increased sexual objectification of women must impact on gender relations in and out of work. Cultural meanings attached to gender follow women into organizations.

THE PROFESSIONAL WOMAN'S DILEMMA

Many years ago I was in a meeting with a fund manager in which I had to recommend potential investments to him. I was in mid flow of my presentation when he interrupted me, and asked me whether

I had changed something: my hair, or had I plucked my eyebrows in a different way perhaps? This totally threw me off my train of thought, and I stammered a response and struggled to return to my share recommendations. Afterwards I reflected on how I was feeling, which was surprised and somewhat irritated – instead of listening to what I was saying, he reminded me that what he noticed was how I looked.

At the time I was a very junior investment analyst and an easy target for such comments, but senior women are not immune to being reduced to their sexuality, as the transcripts of evidence in sexual harassment lawsuits show. However senior or powerful a woman may be in her organization, she is still vulnerable to punitive assaults on her sexuality. She can be cut down to size by a comment of a sexual nature. What do we call this practice? It doesn't fit with our everyday understanding of sexual harassment, it is an insult using the sexist discourse. A lot of male 'harassment' of women is just this: insults or bullying drawing on the resource of a sexuality discourse which denigrates women.

As a society we have become desensitized to the background of images of women, displayed in sexual positions for the pleasure of the male viewer/buyer. Whether it is an image of a woman in ecstasy while eating a chocolate bar or the vacant expression of a naked woman in a lads' magazine, every day at work women have to differentiate themselves from these images of sexually available women. As the story above demonstrates, women's organizational status can be overridden by their sexual identity in just one comment.

Women are acutely aware, often unconsciously, of this potentially disruptive aspect of their presence in the workplace, and will go to some lengths to minimize it. Most men will get up and put on their work clothes without too much thought. Dressing for work for a woman may involve thinking about not looking too sexy. Sexy is not serious. If you look too much like a woman, particularly a type of woman held up by the media to be sexually available to men, you will be derided in a business setting. There was a furore when it was announced that media presenter Mariella Frostrup might be given the job of fronting the serious news documentary television programme *Panaroma* in the United Kingdom because she was not considered to have enough gravitas – translated, this means she was too sexy. 'The BBC was again accused of dumbing down yesterday after it emerged that it was considering hiring glamorous presenter Mariella Frostrup to front *Panorama*' was a typical media comment.[26]

However women also need to retain some femininity or they will be labeled as too 'like a man' – another punitive assault. Women need to walk a tightrope of impression management.

Male managers in most organizations dress in a very similar way. Dark suits constitute a form of uniform to denote impersonality and uniformity, and of course this desexualizes them. Expressions of individuality are allowed in minor details such as the choice of color, provided it is gray, blue, or black, whether the jacket is double or single-breasted, whether the trousers have turn-ups or not, and the design and color of tie. More expression of self is allowed in the arts professions and industries such as advertising, and more recently in hedge funds where suits are not de rigueur and the clothes hint at independence of mind.

When women first entered the professions and the managerial strata of organizations they often emulated the managerial uniform, wearing dark suits and even, in the 1980s, floppy ties. Power dressing was in, with shoulder pads on jackets to give a more masculine shape and heels to increase height. This conservative style of dress stressed their 'sameness' to men, and expressed a desire to fit in with the environment. It is strange then that trousers were, and still are in some organizations, seen as 'unprofessional.' Trousers on a woman were not considered feminine. El Vino, a wine bar in London's Blackfriars, refused to serve women in trousers until the late 1980s, even though the Court of Appeal had decided in 1982 that bars and pubs were no longer able to refuse to serve women – but it didn't mention women in trousers.

The professional dress code for women not only presented a uniform, rational image acceptable to the male environment, it also disguised female sexuality. There are many ways in which women take responsibility to manage sexuality, and although it seems as though it is their own sexuality they are managing, what they are doing is actually managing men's sexuality.[27]

In my research at Airco, nearly 40 percent of women respondents said they dressed so as to avoid attracting sexual attention, but the differences in the different divisions were marked. A far smaller percentage of women in Cabin Services (28 percent) and Human Resources (25 percent) than in the other divisions dressed so as to avoid attracting sexual attention. In these divisions, which were not aggressively heterosexual, women were less self-conscious about their own sexuality and did not feel the need to hide it.[28]

There is a media obsession with the clothes worn by women in the public eye. Female politicians are used to getting as much media coverage for their shoes or bad dress sense as they are for their policies. Politician's wives get even more attention – Michelle Obama features regularly in magazines, usually being applauded for her style and choice of clothes, as if this was the most important aspect of her identity.

A few years ago, an image consultant was the guest speaker at a women's dinner held in the bank where I was a director. After dinner we were told how we should dress to progress. I learned at that particular women's dinner that make-up was a must, particularly lipstick, hair should be short to medium length or tied up, earrings should be worn, and a belt. One should never have bare legs and one should always wear a pair of heels, but they must not be too high. The aim was to look smart but not too sexy.

In 2009 there was media criticism of the Bank of England when it emerged that it had held a similar Dress for Success seminar for female staff, advising them on what clothing, shoes, and make-up to wear. The guidelines were the same as those given to me five years before. Lawrence Davies, of solicitors Equal Justice, said, 'It is indicative of an institutionally sexist environment. If women are being judged by what they wear then it suggests they are being treated differently to males.'[29] But the seminar was defended by a director of Naked Ambition Personal Branding Consultants, who said that how you looked was important for success. 'How you dress can make you have more authority and command more respect,' she said.[30] This reveals the fundamental belief that without the uniform of the right clothes, women lack authority and are not respected.

The advent of dress-down days in the 1990s brought a particular dilemma to women. While the men put on their other uniform of chinos and polo shirts, the women in Investco chose mostly to ignore it. 'I have enough trouble being taken seriously without coming in in a pair of cotton slacks and casual top. No way,' a female analyst in Broking told me.[31]

An unwritten rule for professional women is to dress differently from the secretaries and administrative staff. This is another code meaning they should not look too attractive, or available, and therefore distract men's attention. Secretaries can look sexy but bankers, lawyers, and managers cannot. While working in the City I received a note from personnel advising me not to change for the firm's Christmas party. When I asked about it, I was told that only the secretaries changed. The men didn't, and therefore the professional women didn't.

In December 2010 Swiss banking giant UBS issued its client-facing staff with a 44-page dress code, covering everything from the color and size of suits to dietary tips and the length of toenails. Women were advised not only to wear make-up but the type and amount was also given in detail. Staff were also advised on appropriate underwear and hair dyes![32]

Women are highly visible in male-dominated offices, and what they wear will be noticed. On a trading floor women receive comments all the time, about the color of their tights, their belts, their hairstyle, and it is considered part of the job to take these in good part, although men too are ribbed if they come in with a new hairstyle or new tie. Some women enjoy the relative freedom they have in what they wear compared with their male colleagues. A senior lawyer working in a bank told me how she liked to dress in unexpected ways. This was not to shock or look sexy but to express her own quirky dress sense and character.[33]

Comments about appearances are a minefield littered with potential grievances. A remark by a friend might be fine. At other times it is less straightforward. One professional woman said that the men in the office made constant remarks about women's looks, which she just ignored. However one of her colleagues in a different department, with whom she had to speak on the telephone every day, asked her what she was wearing – on a daily basis. She was young, only two years into the job, and she felt she had to accept this intrusion in order 'not to rock the boat.' 'I think he thinks he is being friendly and taking an interest,' she said.[34]

My research findings on dress accord with Collinson and Collinson's view that women take it upon themselves to manage their appearance to ward off unwanted attention.[35] While sexual attention can be welcome in the right circumstances, most women feel that it detracts from their professionalism in a work setting. And that is very often its intention.

THE SEXUAL CONTINUUM – FROM HAVING FUN TO SEXUAL HARASSMENT

There are so many types of harassment, from a hostile environment to personal comments and unwanted requests for sex, it may be more useful to think of sexualized behaviors on a continuum.

BANTER

A wisecrack about what a woman is wearing can be justified as being the same as a crack about a man's tie. Banter is now a catch-all word for all kinds of office talk, characterized usually by humor and an undercurrent of teasing in a good-natured way. It derives from a specific type of locker room repartee, and I suggest that, although women readily engage in banter, the practice is actually imbued with a type of masculinity not readily accessible to women.

Organizational language is full of sports and war metaphors which are not customarily used by women. Banter often includes the use of sexual language and humor, and is the more benign and acceptable side of sexualized talk in the workplace. The fact that it often includes female colleagues is frequently used as a defense against claims of a hostile environment.

In June 2010, PC Barbara Lynford was awarded £273,000 after the tribunal found that the Sussex police had discriminated against her and she had consequently become mentally ill and unable to work. At the time it was believed to be the highest award to a public sector worker, and she was in line to win a further £300,000 for the loss of her pension. The size of the award led to criticism, and claims that she had suffered just a bit of 'banter.' However her lawyer said, 'This case highlights the plight of many women working in male-dominated professions. Too often sexual harassment and bullying is passed off as acceptable "banter."'[36]

There is a body of work that explores the use of sexual language and sexual humor by men at work.[37] In industries where it occurs – usually male-dominated – there is reluctance to see all aspects of this banter stamped out, as it serves a number of purposes depending on the context. Common in industries where there is danger and risk, it can alleviate feelings of powerlessness, shore up a particular type of masculinity by emphasizing women's differ-ence, act as a male bonding mechanism, alleviate tension, and in certain manual jobs alleviate boredom.[38] It is also very common in areas of high tension and risk around money, such as trading floors. In our MoD research, a female officer in the Royal Navy described its purpose:

> banter between team members is teasing and jesting – it lightens up morale. Due to our working environment it is a way of loosening up and letting off steam. However it does need to be a two-way thing and have parameters.[39]

Sexual banter which is useful for stress breaking or bonding may be used as a justification for the continual use of sexual language that is sometimes derogatory to women. However it means that the only way for women to fit in and get on is to participate in a discourse that often denigrates their own sex. To object would mean being labeled a prude. A female army officer said:

Some women officers join in with it and tell stories against women themselves, or comments about other women's bodies. It's sad that they have to turn against their own sex to feel part of their work environment.[40]

The MOD research showed evidence of explicit talk about sex among men, which may be exaggerated when women enter the scene and they almost become an audience to it. Cockburn found similar behaviors in her study of printers, and explained it as men reminding women of the 'maleness' of the territory.[41]

Both the airline and the bank where I undertook research had divisions in them where swearing was commonplace. Newcomers into an environment where swearing is the norm can find it shocking. A female manager for Investco Capital Markets said:

I couldn't believe the language. I just sat there with my mouth open for the first few weeks, saying, 'I'm sorry, what did you say?' I'm sure it would count for sexual harassment in the United States. But here everyone swears, even the directors' language is peppered with expletives. The words lose their power when they are used so often. I hardly ever swear, so if I do they all know something is badly wrong.[42]

However even women interviewees who ignored the language or swore a bit themselves drew the line at certain words, particularly the 'c' word which still retains its offensiveness to women. In another department, Treasury Operations, there was little bad language used at all. A woman manager working here said,

Usually this kind of department is bad – generally for harassment and language but because of the boss here, he doesn't like that kind of thing, so no one dares do it. The behavior is excellent and it is a nice place to work even if there are very few women. People are polite.[43]

These examples illustrate the power of leadership in setting the tone of a division, department, or even organization. The boss disliked swearing on religious grounds and so there wasn't any. The by-product of his stance was that the women I spoke with there found the working environment pleasant.

Perhaps unsurprisingly in the MoD research nine out of ten respondents reported sexual humor and stories as a commonplace occurrence. However, it only caused offense to 30 percent of the servicewomen some of the time. This highlights the importance of context.[44]

On the whole, my experience is that women find some elements of sexual banter boring rather than offensive. A common irritation women interviewees complained of was being asked about their love life on a regular basis. Giving clients marks out of ten for looks, and asking whether any of the new graduates are 'shaggable,' are part and parcel of life in many workplaces in the United Kingdom. Those who work in large blue chip companies or in the public sector, which has a history of equality and diversity, are actually in fairly rarefied work environments where there are specific policies on sexual harassment and sanctions against those who transgress. This puts a lid on bad language and sexual banter.

Sexual humor can include women and at the same time marginalize them. Equally, offensive and malicious language and behavior can be sanitized and rendered 'harmless' by calling it a joke. And more often than not, if women don't find it funny they will be accused of not having a sense of humor. Women from a financial services company said in a focus group that 'they gave as good as they got' when it came to sexualized language and jokes, and that 'women can be pretty filthy too.' However despite the 'equality' of women behaving like men in terms of drinking, use of sexual talk, and even sexual activity, this itself attracts criticism. As the academic Cynthia Cockburn noted, 'What is funny coming from a man is obscene coming from a woman.'[45]

Indeed there was evidence in the MOD research that men disliked women joining in with them. A senior male non-commissioned officer (NCO) in the Royal Air Force (RAF) said, 'They try to overcompensate to fit in, so they swear more, fart more, drink more, open their legs as much, and try to behave like men but end up losing respect as you don't want to see girls behaving like that.'[46] So with banter of a sexual nature the choices for women are to join in but not too much, ignore it and risk being marginalized, or resist it and risk being labeled a spoilsport.

Much of the banter that goes on day in and day out could be constituted as sexual harassment. Harlow, Hearn, and Parkin have called it the noise and din of harassment.[47] Yet it is commonplace. In my experience in organizations – and this was born out by the research on sexual harassment in the armed services – it is younger and more junior women who are the most likely targets for this drip, drip type of harassment.[48] Senior women to some extent are protected by their seniority, particularly in a hierarchal environment like the armed services. This in itself points to a power explanation of sexual harassment, rather than its being behavior driven by sexual desire.

The MOD findings also showed that the more common the behaviors, the less likely they were to be considered sexual harassment. It is also clear from all the research to date that many women remain uncertain which behaviors properly qualify as sexual harassment, and are often unwilling to label male behavior in this way. Complaints about behavior, and particularly about environmental harassment, usually come to light when there are other grievances that it is more acceptable to express.

The confusion about the definition of harassment is exposed in a case reported in May 2010 in which a manager at HBOS bank, Haley Tansey, claimed she had faced a 'harassing and laddish culture' at the office in Halifax, West Yorkshire where she worked. Men produced a list 'grading' women colleagues according to their attractiveness. A number of incidents took place over the 17 years she worked there, including sexual advances and comments about her body. Her claim failed because she filed her complaints too long after the three-month deadline allowed for each incident, although the panel did accept her version of events. The HBOS legal representative defended the result of the trial, saying that Mrs Tansey was not a 'cowering wallflower,' but was assertive in the workplace, and that she 'did not actually believe these were acts of sexual harassment at the time.'[49]

In my time as a researcher and consultant, many, many women indicated to me that they disliked the sexual comments and the working environment they experienced, but would not have complained about them because they were unaware that this kind of treatment was illegal, or that there were remedies open to them. Very often women will attribute the behavior and language to the job rather than to the men themselves. For example a young female City trader told me, 'You go into this type of work and you have to expect it.'[50]

DRAWING A LINE

The MOD research was illuminating in identifying the ways in which senior managers and women themselves tried to control the boundaries of acceptability. Cockburn found that older women acted as bystanders and protected younger women.[51] One older woman in the financial services sector told me, 'I have to act as mother every so often and stop the boys going too far.'[52]

Women who work in a highly male heterosexualized environment develop strategies for coping. Most will have their own personal

178

boundaries. However, in an environment where sexual language is rife it can be quite hard for women to be clear about what they find offensive. Most of the interviewees in Airco and Investco identified certain swear words that they found unacceptable, and all disliked it when sexualized or bad language was focused on them. One invest-ment analyst in a broking firm said to me that she didn't mind the sexual banter and comments about women as long as they were not made about her.[53] In the MOD research there was general agreement that a woman put a limit on things, the men's language would get worse and worse. This left the responsibility on the women. A junior rank female in the RAF said:

> Sometimes in a group the banter gets going and one of them will say at the beginning, 'Just tell us when it gets too much.' But its hard to know when to suddenly come in with 'it's too much' as it just sort of accumulates. I wonder if they just say that to cover themselves – you know so that if there was a complaint they'd be able to say, we did say stop if got too much.[54]

It may be important here to distinguish the use of sexual language per se and the use of sexual language which denigrates women. Sex per se should not necessarily be seen to be a taboo subject because it offends women. It is only so when it is derogatory to women (and this is very often the case because of the social sexual objectification of women). Women may be just as likely to use sexual language as men in certain situations, particularly in an all-female group. It is the context and the intent behind the language that will distinguish what is harmless to a woman and what is offensive. Women all have their own limits and boundaries, and this makes it hard to iden-tify when this kind of language is harassing and when it isn't. The backdrop of an increasingly sexualized culture everywhere makes it harder to determine what is and is not sexual harassment.

Results from the MOD study made it clear that not all sexual comments, jokes, and talk are unwelcome, even if they are directed at an individual, but whether or not they are acceptable depends on the context.[55] Most women know the difference between a joke and a more unpleasant put-down. It is not just the words themselves, it is in the tone of the voice and the look on the face, and these may be accompanied by other kinds of behavior. The tone of voice, whether the speaker is angry or not, whether there is a pre-existing relation-ship with them, whether it is in a formal setting or in front of other people, are all relevant factors in turning acceptable comments into unacceptable ones.

REPORTING

In my research in both Airco and Investco no one complained about the sexual language and humor. Even though many of the working environments women work could be construed as intimidating under the law, there is a general resistance to labeling behaviors as sexual harassment, particularly if they are normative – as if the naming of them would expose the woman as being an outsider.[56]

It is clear from surveys which have allowed for more latitude in sexual harassment for women's own interpretations that many are reluctant to employ the term when talking about their own experience.[57]

Forty percent of women in Airco had been on the receiving end of unwanted sexual attention in the airline, yet not one woman had reported it. This percentage itself is breathtakingly high given the airline had been an equal opportunities employer for many years. Even in Marketing, a division in which nearly half the senior managers were women, the percentage was high. Sexual harassment does not only occur in highly heterosexualized cultures. In the MOD research only 5 percent of those women who said that they had had a particularly upsetting experience had reported it.[58]

It may not be possible to eradicate all unwanted sexual behavior in organizations, but it should be possible to create cultures in which women and men can have complaints dealt with quickly and fairly. A culture in which it is better to stay quiet than report sexual harassment is a culture that is exclusionary to women.

The media portrayal of women who make claims of sexual harassment perpetuates two myths: first, that those women are exaggerating or lying in order to make some money, and second, that sexual harassment is an unusual event. There is little in the way of accurate statistics on sexual harassment. It is a difficult topic to research because it is so subjective, and there is reluctance on the part of women to acknowledge it. As discussed, in order to take their place as professionals women have to play down their sexuality, and the last thing they want to do is to complain about behavior which may be construed as sexual harassment. A major study initiated by the European Commission in 1987 proved beyond doubt that millions of workers in the European Union are affected by sexual harassment.[59] The report, which led to the introduction of EEC guidelines on Sexual Harassment (1991), showed that, depending on the questions asked and in what sector of activity the survey was conducted, between 25 percent and 80 percent of women had been subject to sexual harassment in their working lives. The penalties for bringing about a complaint are high. Apart from the stress involved,

The legal definition of sexual harassment in the UK

Sexual harassment comprises 'unwanted verbal, non-verbal and physical conduct of a sexual nature'. The conduct in question must have the purpose or effect of violating the complainant's dignity or creating an intimidating, hostile, degrading, humiliating or offensive environment. Conduct will only be taken to have that effect if, taking all the circumstances into account, including in particular the perception of the complainant, it is reasonably considered as having that effect. The new provision does not define what constitutes 'conduct of a sexual nature,' which it is left to the tribunals to determine. Some examples of physical, verbal and non-verbal conduct of a sexual nature are found in the European Commission's guide:

- Physical conduct of a sexual nature – 'unwanted physical contact ranging from unnecessary touching, patting or pinching or brushing against another employee's body, to assault and coercing sexual intercourse.'
- Verbal conduct of a sexual nature – 'unwelcome sexual advances, propositions or pressure for sexual activity; continued suggestions for social activity outside the workplace after it has been made clear that such suggestions are unwelcome; offensive flirtations; suggestive remarks, innuendoes or lewd comments.'
- Non-verbal conduct of a sexual nature – 'the display of pornographic or sexually suggestive pictures, objects or written materials; leering, whistling, or making sexually suggestive gestures.'

Source: S.4A(1)(b) (Employment Equality (Sex Discrimination) Regulations 2005), now incorporated into the Equality Act, which came into force in October 2010.

any woman in the City knows that if she sues she will never work in the City again.

KEEPING QUIET

Nearly half (45 percent) of all respondents in the MOD research[60] who had had an upsetting experience chose not to tell anyone at work about it. Why? Regardless of the perceived outcome, telling someone requires a perception of a workplace environment in which colleagues and/or superiors will take the complaint seriously. Research shows that women often belittle the importance of experiences of sexual harassment,[61] and indeed in the MOD study 34 percent did not think it was important enough to tell anyone. Some 15 percent had worries over the consequences to the offenders, and our qualitative research showed that women are aware that sometimes there will be damaging effects on a man's career. Ultimately most did not want this, they just wanted the behaviors to stop.[62]

THE IMPACT OF A NON-HETEROSEXUAL CULTURE

Changing social mores and the introduction of a legal requirement not to discriminate on the grounds of sexual orientation have meant that the non-heterosexual aspect of sexuality is now being addressed by some organizations. However, in the largest-ever study on lesbian, gay and bisexual workers, the authors found that there was resistance to culture change through the ways in which heterosexual norms prevailed in everyday workplace interactions and organizational events such as Christmas socials.[63]

UK lobby group Stonewall has been very successful in engaging business in championing the rights of non-heterosexual employees in the workplace, and now has 400 corporate diversity champions.[64] Prompted by concern about the small number of openly gay women in the workplace and even smaller numbers involved in work initiatives such as networks, Stonewall conducted some recent research into the experience of gay women.[65] The research revealed that gay women thought their gender was more of a barrier to their success at work than their sexual orientation. In other words they had enough to contend with in being female, without further trouble from coming out as gay. The respondents attended women's networks more than the LGBT (lesbian, gay, bisexual, and transgender) networks, which were dominated by gay men. One woman said that the LGBT network ratio of men to women was 10 to 1. However the research showed that women's networks could be better at including and acknowledging the experience of lesbian and bisexual women.

It is important that no employee feels excluded because of their sexuality, and there is evidence that initiatives like setting up networks and support groups are helpful in ending isolation and in challenging any homophobia in the workplace.

Airco provided an unusual opportunity to analyze the impact of a large group of gay men on a divisional culture. Because it

them. As a young financial analyst I attended the notorious investment analysts dinner in the Grosvenor House Hotel in 1983. Before I left the office on the day of the dinner, my boss called me over and warned me not to get into a lift with men on my own after 10 pm in the evening. I was perplexed – these were middle-aged married men. There were very few women there that night, and as time went on and more drink was consumed, I began to see what my boss was talking about. The leering, lurching, and grabbing were quite shocking coming from rather posh blokes in the City. Twenty-five years later, the sexual subtext is if anything more visible.

Seeing male-defined heterosexuality acting as a resource on which men may draw is helpful. Making sexual comments to women may be accompanied by discrimination or marginalization in other ways – for example being left out of important meetings and social events. Sexuality is too often linked with women to be left without an agent or even in the hands of organization. Women arrive on the scene, which is immediately sexualized, yet it is male sexuality that pervades the workplace, with or without the presence of women.[69]

It is contended that men sometimes construct workplace cultures characterized by explicit and predatory sexual discourses that derogate and undermine women.[70] Where this is outlawed by the organization, harassment may take the more individualized form of targeting one woman at a time. From my research and practice sexual harassment takes place in varying forms regardless of the segregation or non-segregation of the women concerned.[71] It takes place in offices I would not describe as sexualized at all. A sexualized harassing culture may act as a means of closure to women because of the discomfort of working in that kind of environment. A culture that allows individualized harassment to go unreported is also excluding as it leads to the individual women often having to leave rather than speak up.

ORGANIZATIONAL ACTIONS

Determining to what extent an organizational culture is sexualized can be done through an employee survey and interviews, usually best conducted by an external consultant for confidentiality issues. Asking about sexual language, comments on appearance, unwanted sexual attention, and dressing to avoid sexual attention, together with qualitative data and observation, will provide an indication of the culture. The possibility of legal liability arising from the outcomes of such an audit has made many organizations leave the subject well alone, waiting for individual cases to rear their heads to be dealt with quietly. As a diversity consultant, I am often asked to avoid the topic of sexuality and sexual harassment in my audits.

Organizations have found it easier to impose a blanket ban on swearing and sexual imagery and unwanted sexual attention of any kind than to create the conditions for honest discussion about sexuality at work. One of the difficulties in gaining male cooperation in corporate initiatives on sexual harassment is the refusal on the part of most men to recognize that they possess any power. That is, they play down the power dynamic involved and avoid making links between the personal and the political. There is resistance in seeing that having a bit of fun at women's expense is actually an expression of male dominance over women.

Hard as it is, well-run mixed-group workshops on the expression of sexuality at work, including what could be construed as sexual harassment, with open discussion is the best way forward in creating a more aware culture. Although discussions alone are unlikely to solve the problems altogether, they will make it harder for men to employ the common excuse that they didn't know such behavior would be construed in this way. They can also improve both men and women's awareness so that they do not always presume heterosexuality in the workplace.

9

LEADERS AND MEN

LEADERSHIP

It is generally accepted that committed leadership is crucial to any successful culture change. There are, we know, some prominent leaders, committed to diversity, vocal in their support and active in their participation in mentoring and sponsorship of women. Schein says that the most powerful mechanism a leader has for communicating what they believe in or care about is what they systematically pay attention to. Schein lists signs of leadership's commitment to values as:

- inferences from what leaders do not pay attention to
- looking at inconsistent signals
- allocation of resources
- the leader as a deliberate role model, teacher or coach
- how rewards and status are allocated
- how a leader selects, promotes and excommunicates
- formal statements of philosophy, creed or charter.[1]

Some research on leaders and change warned of the consequences of inconsistent signals towards diversity from leaders.

> Leaders' behavior is under the microscope. Any gap between the organization's values and the leader's behavior will allow cynicism to creep in which can derail a change programme.[2]

Abu Bundu-Kamara is head of diversity and inclusion at Pearson plc. The publishing giant has had two female executives on the board for over six years – chief executive Dame Marjorie Scardino and chief executive, Financial Times Group, Rona Fairhead. This is a situation that many organizations aspire to, yet it was achieved in Pearson without any major initiatives or specific intent to diversify the board.

In a piece of Opportunity Now research[3] it was suggested that the men on the board at the time were more liberal and socially aware than most FTSE 100 directors, and were prepared to make room at the top for these women. These were men who were actively engaged in diversity issues outside the organization, and were not threatened by having female leadership (Sir David Bell, Pearson's director of people who retired last year, John Fallon, and John Makinson).

Despite having two female leaders, Pearson recognized it still had a glass ceiling. It undertook some work in 2004 to examine why, with a high intake of women at entry level, only 20 percent of the top 100 senior managers were women. Focus groups at the time showed that women had issues with aspects of their working environment, which the men had no idea about despite the fact that they worked side by side. Surfacing issues can itself be the catalyst for a change in culture. Today that figure is 27 percent, and as Bundu-Kamara says, the figures need to improve further.

According to Bundu-Kamara, the key to pushing through values and instilling cultural change is leadership:

> It is not only Marjorie; all of us in senior teams take responsibility and ownership of diversity. She takes the lead with her aspiration for Pearson to be a fair company in all aspects of employment and has undoubtedly influenced the working culture in her time here.[4]

But not all leaders doing enough. Too often responsibility for culture change falls on the shoulders of the diversity function, itself often marginalized and under resourced. Dr Gillian Shapiro, managing director of Shapiro Consulting, says, 'Diversity professionals need a mix of skills, the diversity knowledge but also core business experience and an understanding of strategy. They need to be senior to be influential, and often they are not.'[5]

When organizations want to reposition themselves in a market, or change their brand, they spend literally millions of pounds in their efforts to do this. Yet when it comes to changing their culture to become more accommodating of women and minorities, the millions of pounds often fall to thousands. And the task is usually left to a very small group of people, sometimes only one, who are not necessarily powerful in the organization. Almost always these professionals themselves are women, from an ethnic minority, and/or gay: that is, they are from an outsider group, yet they are expected to change a dominant group culture. Diversity budgets are notoriously small in business where money talks. Set up to fail?

It certainly looks like it. No wonder some diversity professionals are tired.

One of the most successful leaders in the area of diversity is Sir Nicholas Montagu, former chairman of the Inland Revenue, who believes that action is as important as words: 'The key is to make diversity a non-negotiable part of the business culture – like profitability. You want to be here then that is what we believe here. That means sacking a high earner if his behavior is sexist or disrespectful.' Sir Nicholas also thinks that it is necessary to send the signals that reinforce an inclusive culture, like ensuring that part- and full-timers are treated on an equal footing when it comes to promotion.[6]

Several years ago while he was vice president and managing director UK and Ireland at Procter & Gamble, Chris de Lapuente (who has now retired from P&G) made Helen Tucker HR director UK, bringing her over from Geneva when she was four months pregnant.

> I knew she would only be with me for a few months before going on maternity leave but she was the right person for the job. There may be short-term pain but we need to look longer term. It is up to the organization to take on this challenge.[7]

Barclays Wealth offers an example of inspirational leadership combined with a strong relationship with the diversity function – a powerful combination. Tom Kalaris, CEO of Barclays Wealth, is a model leader when it comes to promoting gender equality in the company, says global head of diversity Craig Jones. He continually supports the quest for gender progress, by firing off emails, requesting action, attending both internal and external gender events regularly, and actively trying to recruit and support the best women – banging the drum. This of course means that his executive team follow. This is the type of leadership commitment and involvement which diversity professionals need in order to do their job effectively. For Barclays Wealth, the business case is the driver. Women are getting richer and they need private banks. This clear link is what makes investment in promoting gender equality a no-brainer. Dr Gillian Shapiro and Melanie Allison's research into diversity professionals found that aligning diversity to overall business objectives was vital in order to engage leadership attention.[8]

SUSTAINABILITY

There are dangers though of having such a committed leader. What happens when they leave? Even if diversity has been embedded in processes and procedures and seems to be part of the DNA of the organization, if the new leader is not as committed, progress falters and indeed can reverse. This is an argument for ensuring that diversity is included in succession planning. It does not make sense to hope that the next leader will feel as strongly, because if they don't, years of work can go out of the window – and quickly. It is also an argument for ensuring that the whole board is engaged and committed to change – not just the chief executive.

Despite its early leadership on diversity ten years ago, and despite having had the City's first female senior partner in Janet Gaymer, law firm Simmons & Simmons has now been reported as having one of the worst records for female partnership of the top ten City firms. Its tally now stands at 12 percent, with equity partner representation even lower – women make up 8 percent of the equity partnership.[9] In an article in *The Lawyer*, senior partner David Dickinson agreed that Simmons simply did not consolidate its early position on the gender issue.

For 15 years through a number of leadership changes, BT has been at the forefront of most cutting-edge thinking and activity on diversity – ahead of the game in flexible working, in assessing systems and processes for bias, and in engaging in challenging issues like the equalization of culture. When a committed leader changes, the expertise and continuity of other key senior staff can ensure that the foot is not taken off the pedal. Pam Farmer has a long title – people and policy manager for global services, group functions and supplier diversity of British Telecom. She has been at BT for 20 years and working on diversity for 15 years. Her boss, Caroline Waters, director of people and policy, has been spearheading diversity at BT for ten years, and her colleague Dave Wilson has also been working in the diversity team for ten years plus. The knowledge, expertise, and contacts built up over that time is pretty unique to the diversity industry, which is renowned for its lack of career structure and high turnover of professionals.[10]

This continuity of expertise is central to BT's success in maintaining and sustaining a consistent leadership on diversity. Pam Farmer says it is in the DNA of BT and it is constantly reinforced:

> It is this reinforcement and consistency through good and bad times that has kept diversity a key BT value. Our strategy in bad times is to find friends in the business – this has proved an effective powerful and sustainable approach in good times too.[11]

Caroline Waters has been successful in keeping diversity on the corporate agenda by engaging the company's leadership, whoever they are, in support. As any diversity professional knows, this is a skill in itself. Thanks to the efforts of her and her highly skilled and experienced team, BT's brand is now associated with diversity, and it is called on from all quarters for advice. This external reputation of excellence feeds into and influences the internal approach. 'If you are known for being good at something, you better carry on being good at it,' says Pam Farmer:

> Once a key part of your business understands its importance and sells diversity as part of BT then it is mainstreamed. It was when our sales community understood that they could sell diversity as part of the BT brand that it really got into the business and mainstreamed. Not that here is not more to do. There is.[12]

The tendency for organizations to regress once the key change agent has taken their foot off the accelerator shows how resistant employees are to change. One way of embedding values in a more sustainable way is to ensure that those coming into your organization hold the values personally. This is often neglected during the recruitment process, with the emphasis being on understanding the diversity of the recruit rather than making sure that the values of the recruit are the same as the espoused company values.

To keep the strict values and trust that make her company function so effectively, Katherine Corish, founder and chairman of consultancy firm, Sysdoc Group, is particular about who she recruits, 'Number one is values. People must be smart. If they are smart we can train someone for fifty jobs. But we cannot change their values. We have a values based interview system. They must cherish children – they are more likely to be good with clients.'[13]

In order for leadership to walk the talk, they need to understand all the issues. Getting a leader to accept they do not know everything about diversity is the first and most difficult step. We hear talk of senior men 'getting it' usually as a result of having a personal experience. We could be waiting a long time if we are waiting for the personal conversion to diversity of all leaders. Acknowledging ignorance on any topic is hard for this intelligent and successful group of people, but it is particularly so for a topic where there are so many everyday commonsense explanations around. However, Robin Schneider, managing director of diversity consultancy Schneider~Ross, sees progress. 'I am guardedly but continuously optimistic. There are more signs that the people at the top are understanding diversity and inclusion and what that involves i.e. long term culture change, which takes sustained commitment effort and time.'[14]

He thinks that there are more engaged leaders today, and they have to be actively pushing the rest of their board and senior management, insisting upon accountability. 'Unfortunately, there aren't yet enough of them. Sometimes, I do wonder if there is something out there about the clubbiness of elite men that makes it hard for them to open up to different ways of being.'

Dr Gillian Shapiro also sees some leaders with a real understanding of difference and diversity, for whom it matters personally. They see that different perspectives have value. 'However they are still a minority both in and outside companies,' she says.[15]

When we talk about leadership in diversity, given that 95 percent of executive directors of publicly listed companies in the United Kingdom (and almost everywhere else overseas) are male, we are also talking about men. They are the dominant group, to whose interests furthering gender equality needs to appeal. It is often assumed that middle management is where things get sticky with diversity and there is most resistance. I would argue that it is at senior levels, where if the leadership are committed, change could be pushed through quite easily, that the real resistance lies.

CHALLENGING MEN

When Jeremy Isaacs, CEO of the former Lehman Brothers, launched a research center for women in business at the London Business School, he said, 'Business remains a world created by males for males.'[16] Both UK governments and organizations have so far shied away from implicating men too much in the equality process, although there has been an increasing focus on their role as fathers (see Chapter 6).

BT began focusing attention on the role of men at home in the early 2000s, and the consequences have been felt in the workplace. Internal research on fathers in BT, which employs more than 100,000 people, found that men felt restricted by stereotypes of them, which did not display all their differences. This provided an opportunity for images of men and masculinity to be promoted in the organization in a broader and perhaps more rounded way.

Caroline Waters explained:

We are encouraging activities like working with the disabled, which promote the more caring side of men and improve communication skills. It's broadening the range of leadership skills and encourages a more inclusive way of working. It is all about good communication. Encouraging men to bring their feminine side to the fore can be liberating for them and for the women who work with them.[17]

In the United States and Europe however, there has been recognition that further progress cannot be made without some fundamental shift from men. Catalyst undertook some work on *Engaging Men in Gender Initiatives* in 2009.[18] This identified the factors that make men more likely to engage with gender initiatives, and obstacles that prevent men from doing so. Eleanor Tabi Haller-Jorden, general manager of Catalyst Europe AG, sees that the greatest challenge now:

is to break the traditional link between gender and role, to see men and women as individuals and to enable them to pursue the career and personal goals they choose. We are in the midst of a critical period of transition but we cannot shift gears overnight. There are still questions to be answered. But the dynamics that have been put in motion by women are converging with the needs of men.[19]

These efforts to engage men rely on an appeal to their needs. For example their desire to be at home more will be met by having a more gender-equal workplace. This is not the same as an appraisal of the masculine cultures that continue to reward men and not women. However we have to start somewhere, and the engagement of men with diversity in this way is such a start.

Certainly, men as senior leaders are more engaged in the United States than in the United Kingdom. At the Catalyst awards dinner held every spring in New York, half of the 1,600 attendees are men and approximately 100 CEOs attend, the vast majority of whom are men. There are very few UK CEOs who think gender issues are important enough to go to an awards dinner. Some leaders in the United Kingdom, however, have acknowledged the key role men need to play. John Varley, outgoing chief executive of Barclays Bank, wrote in the preface to an Opportunity Now report:

Change is uncomfortable; sharing power, if you want to think about it that way, is uncomfortable. No wonder then that our heads of diversity often feel they are swimming up- stream. We have the duty and the power to make that journey much easier. Cultures can be changed but only if enough of us – white men – want that change. You could say this is a rallying cry.[20]

That rallying cry still has not been heard by enough leaders in business. This is about more than male leaders supporting women; it is about addressing their resistance to sharing power.

In Chapter 4 the ways in which masculinity and management are wrapped up in one another were discussed. Our concepts of leadership too are imbued with a certain masculinity, which we implicitly accept by using female in front of the word – female leadership, itself reinforcing the paradox of a women being a leader. This invisibility of masculinity allows certain characteristics to go unchallenged which we may associate with 'leading' rather than with aspects of masculinity. An example is the uncritical acceptance that senior levels of management require 'toughness' and the ability to work very long hours. Heroic imagery of leadership still dominates the management literature, and only this month I received an invitation to attend a leadership workshop taking place on the battlefield of Waterloo. The deconstruction of leadership as we see it to reveal the masculine bias is, I would argue, the next phase of the gender equality journey. Academics have been engaged in this for some time, but it is now time for all senior leadership serious about diversity to introduce some self-reflective and critical thinking into the nature of leadership and masculinity.

EUROPE

Europe has considered the involvement of men to be one of its strategic orientations since the early 2000s, and has been encouraging businesses to innovate and act accordingly. Indeed Europe has seen men as the key to change for a few years. The low birth rate and aging population mean that Europe needs its women to both work and have more children, and getting men to take up more domestic responsibility is seen as the only way of achieving both. The emphasis is on gender roles in the domestic sphere, rather than any comprehensive engagement with excluding behaviors and practices in the workplace.

The 2008 Equality Report from the Council of Europe concluded that there was a need for 'improving both the supply and quality of services helping to reconcile professional and private life for both men and women' as well as 'tackling stereotypes in education, employment and the media and emphasizing the role of men in promoting equality.[21]

A report from ORSE, the French study centre for corporate social responsibility, declared:

After 25 years of French public policies to promote professional equality between men and women, one thing is sure. Action centered specifically on women has shown its limits. Professional equality cannot be achieved without involving men and promoting the benefit equality holds for them.[22]

There is no mention of the business case, just as there is no mention of diversity. Instead the report acknowledges that a debate about 'the gender stereotypes, and the promotion of equality in private public and economic spheres' is required.[23]

Historically, attention on gender has been directed at women, and more recently cultures, as if cultures were autonomous subjects, separated from the people who make them. Oganizational cultures are now being linked to men and their behaviors and attitudes.

Men and masculinity have been debated extensively by male academics, and their nature has emerged as a key theme in this book.[24] The masculinity of most organizational cultures, the working day structured around men's lives, the dominance and display of an a male-defined heterosexuality, the need for homophilic relationships to shore up masculinity which rely on distancing women, the masculinity of management styles, the denial of inequality, the reluctance to examine cultures from an outsider's point of view, the silence on issues of violence and harassment – all these are aspects of masculinity in organizations which are troubling for women.

> I believe that the reason that the movement for women's equality remains only a partial victory has to do with men. In every arena – in politics, military, workplace, professions, and education – the single greatest obstacle to women's equality is the behaviors and attitudes of men.[25]

Organizational work on masculinity has so far been limited to attempts to engage men in 'helping' and speaking up for women. Indirectly the work on unconscious bias is addressing masculinity but allaying men's fears by saying that everyone has bias, it is part of the human tradition. Progress will be made when men and leaders begin to challenge aspects of masculinity that are unhelpful to the progress of both women and organizations.

AB Volvo has been working to further gender equality at management level in the company for over 20 years. Ten years ago, after a number of different training programs aimed at middle management, there was a realization that senior leadership needed to improve their skills and knowledge of gender relations in order to move beyond merely understanding 'women's' issues and helping them to progress. The then head of diversity, Louise Ekström, developed a 'Walk the Talk' program which ran from 2001 to 2006, focused on the training and development of senior male managers, and addressed the development of gender awareness with special attention on men and masculinity. It was a way of getting men to analyze the male norm, instead of focusing on the female minority. The head of each of Volvo's 12 divisions selected a senior male manager to participate in the program. The selected men gathered off site six times over a year, with a minimum of two days for each meeting. During this process the men were exposed to alternative role models, received a female mentor, and kept journals. The men were supported following the course in the form of a network, and graduates met twice a year. Some of the men are now part of an executive network that continues some of the work on gender. As all diversity professionals know, getting top leadership to attend training that takes up anything more than half a day, is virtually impossible, but this was 15 days in one year.[26]

Pia Höök, diversity director of AB Volvo, said that the sponsorship and engagement of the CEO, Leif Johansson, was vital in getting full participation from the rest of senior leadership. It was presented as an elite development course for an exclusive group with a high status. The group got to meet with prominent people in Swedish society, and some years the training included trips abroad. Among other things, the training involved reflection on their development as men and was at times intense, inevitably resulting in the formation of close bonds. One of the criticisms of the program from women in Volvo was about this eliteness. Paradoxically, in spite of all the good intentions and some good results, the training was seen by some to be perpetuating and strengthening the privilege of an all-male elite group. Some of the participants are now part of an 'executive network' that continues to work on gender, and new ways of training are being developed by Höök.

While academics are researching and writing about masculinity of management, it is harder to bring this into diversity training – yet without a critical examination of it, the focus will remain on the 'other': that is, women and minority groups. Amanda Sinclair has written about the difficulty of introducing discussions of masculinities as a teacher in a business school – the resistance to talk about something that is invisible to most men working in organization.[27]

The work on men and masculinities is only just beginning. Who will take up the challenge?

10

ON THE ROAD TO CHANGE

To use the expression of Simone de Beauvoir, women are still 'the second sex,' and mankind is still, well, a man.[1] The chapters in this book have, I hope, explored some of the ways in which a male-dominated society still determines the ways in which our organizations are run, the values they hold, the skills they value, and how we work. But it is changing, and some believe the change is about to accelerate. Women's growing economic and social power is behind this change, along with their expectations and desire to participate in the decision making of this world.

Exasperation that there are still so few women in influential and powerful positions in society and with the persistent pay gap has led to calls for renewed efforts in the field of equality and diversity. Not only is there a paucity of women at the top levels of all our organizations, there are many women working far below the level of their abilities, skills, and qualifications. Calls for change are coming from different quarters: governments; lobbyists like Fawcett Society and Opportunity Now in the United Kingdom, Catalyst in Europe and the United States, professional women's networks, diversity and equality professionals, and women themselves, including a new third wave of young feminists.

In the inaugural speech at the Gender Work and Organization conference at Keele in 2001, US academic Joanne Martin outlined six approaches for women's advancement in organizations. They were:

- fix the women
- value the feminine
- add women and stir
- make small deep cultural changes
- women led organizations
- change gendered society.[2]

197

FIX THE WOMEN

Early on in the equality and diversity journey, initiatives tend to focus on equipping women with the skills and attributes thought necessary to progress the organization. Women's leadership and development courses are still popular with organizations, and offer useful opportunities for women to develop their skills as well as their confidence, enabling them to better navigate their way through the upper chambers of their companies. A part of their popularity with women themselves is that the supportive learning environment provides the opportunity for women to see their experiences as systemic symptoms rather than personal failures.

Senior women from different countries in the professional services firm Ernst & Young are being put through the women's leadership course, at the Centre for Women's Leadership Cranfield, Fleur Bothwick, director of diversity and inclusiveness for the EMEIA region, has been surprised by the similarity of issues raised by senior women in the firm, whatever country they are in. These issues are:

> Believing that doing a good job is enough to be rewarded, not paying enough attention to impression management, not investing enough time in networking and gaining key sponsorship, and not noticing the micro inequalities at work.[3]

There is now recognition that while a 'fix the women' approach may undoubtedly benefit a few women and has its place in a diversity strategy, it will leave the dominant culture intact. In the same way women's employee networks provide support and business opportunities but do not challenge the culture.

VALUE THE FEMININE /ADD WOMEN AND STIR

The next approach has been to value the feminine as well as to add women and stir. Efforts to add women are taking place particularly at senior levels for lateral hires. After failing to develop and retain their own women, many companies try to improve their numbers by parachuting them in. Both approaches are still woman-focused, but take a step towards acknowledging that organizations have been a male preserve and are imbued with masculine practices and cultures which make it harder for women to progress. These practices are not overtly challenged, but rather the approach asks that leadership and male managers acknowledge and value women's skills and talents, as well as accommodate their need for flexible working. This approach includes the 'women are different but equal approach,' with all the difficulties discussed in Chapter 4. As Michael Kimmel said, 'gender difference is the product of gender inequality and not the other way around.'[4]

SMALL DEEP CULTURAL CHANGES

The fourth approach – making small deep cultural changes – is where many organizations find themselves today.[5] This approach shifts focus from women to the culture, but stops short of directly addressing masculinity and resistance. Sarah Bond, global head of diversity at KPMG, says, 'When faced with the complexity of organizational structures – it is daunting but we can resolve a lot by small individual changes. Focusing on the individual is the mood at the moment. Making people think, turning on a light bulb in someone's mind when you can.'[6] There are myriad practices which can be shown to be male-biased, as has been seen in the preceding chapters, for instance assumptions around commitment, meetings after hours, and internal politics.

Training on unconscious bias comes into this fourth approach, as individual employees are 'helped' to see their own unconscious bias. This can make small ripples if the training is well received, eyes are opened, and the recipient may truly rethink their attitudes or at least reflect before making a snap decision, based on stereotypes. But not all discrimination and bias is unconscious, and there are plenty of material and cultural barriers outside people's minds. How and why men and women relate to one another involves a lot more than identifying stereotypes and unconscious bias – that's like jumping to the last chapter without telling the story.

At this point I want to reiterate the approach set out in this book, which builds on the small deep cultural change approach.

HOLISTIC AND SYSTEMATIC CULTURE CHANGE

I suggest that a systematic analysis of an organizational culture in its entirety leaves nothing to chance – enabling a holistic rather than piecemeal approach to change, and in a quantifiable and manageable way.

My intention in writing this book was to deepen our understanding of organizational culture and gender inequalities for the purposes of creating more inclusive workplace cultures. My aim was to introduce some of the vast range of academic research in an accessible way to add some rigor to the debates we have in organizations about what are by now familiar issues. The purpose was not just intellectual – I believe that a culture change approach informed by solid research has a greater chance of success.

Some of the book's content goes beyond what many diversity professionals and managers may be familiar (or comfortable) with, but such is the clamor for further progress on gender equality, I feel the book is timely. It is not a pessimistic message but a realistic one.

The human desire for identity, belonging, and power, mingled in with the changing nature of gender relations, makes for a complex subject. I have not offered any new words or slogans to repackage the topic in order to sell it. Am I offering a quick fix, a surefire way of achieving an inclusive culture? No. But I hope that by introducing some wider social theories, including power and resistance, we can at last have some honest conversations which in themselves will be liberating and lift us beyond the limited rationale of business imperatives.

I have argued for a psycho-social approach to culture, that is one that recognizes both the under-the-surface emotions and feelings of individuals, and the wider social landscape which informs organizational culture. Cultures serve a purpose, creating group identity and helping the group achieve its goals, and the dilemma for those involved in change is to loosen these boundaries without removing people's sense of security and identity. Not every culture is functional, as evidenced by many an organizational failure.

Although not a quick fix, the book outlines the key constituents of organizational culture as they relate to gender, and recommends a holistic approach to change. This model or list provides the parameters/boundaries required to contain data and so lead to manageable and actionable interventions. The subject matter is vast and complex, and this can lead to one intervention being taken after another without any clear understanding of what one is hoping to achieve. Undertaking a culture audit using the model will provide the relevant data required for specific actions to be taken.

As stated at the beginning of the book, the assumption of every organization, unless it has a majority of women at the top, should be that life for most women at senior levels will be less comfortable than for most men.

FOLLOWING THE AUDIT

Having taken account of the history and geography of the organization the first step is to assess the level of gender awareness. This includes the history of equality and diversity, the level of knowledge and ways in which gender is discussed, and the role of the business case. This is a useful exercise to take stock of the ways women feel in the organization – welcomed or not? It's a simple and easy question to ask.

An analysis of style gives further opportunity to deconstruct derogative stereotypes held by both men and women, and to ask whether there are behaviors and ways of communication that might be more helpful to the business. Chapter 4 showed the pitfalls of perpetuating stereotypes by focusing on difference rather than critically examining the masculinity of management and leadership. Data derived from a survey as well as the ideas discussed can be used to design a workshop for mixed groups of managers.

In Chapter 5, an analysis of the ideology of work or the public/ private divide provides information about assumptions around meanings of work; work–home conflict, and the boundaries between home and work. All these were shown to have a gendered impact. Having established the ways in which employees in your organizations feel about home and work, flexible working, and the number of hours they work, who works them and why, leadership can set their own example in challenging some of these norms. Establishing excellence in results, productivity and good service does not have to mean 14-hour days. The corporate social responsibility which companies readily embrace in providing service and support to community projects, can be applied in a much more relevant way – to ensuring that the family lives of its own employees are not being damaged by its work practices.

The exclusion of some men and many women from the informal life of an organization, particularly at senior levels, is not going to be solved by any leadership decision or blanket ban. Information on its importance can be accessed via the audit, and the revelation itself may dilute its power. However it will require much higher numbers of women at the top of organizations, who no doubt will form their own informal networks in time that will reduce the power of the old boys' network.

Lastly comes the most challenging constituent of culture to both research and address internally – sexuality. Chapter 8 showed how certain aspects of male sexuality which objectify women spill over into behaviors, talk, and humor into the workplace. All cultures are sexualized in different ways. The risk of a lawsuit means that standards of behavior do need to be laid down, and most organizations have their own internal harassment policies. However brave questioning and analysis may reveal that certain behaviors (whether legal or not) are inhibiting women's progress, and the results of this part of the audit can be used in a well-facilitated discussion. Like BT and Barclays Wealth, other organizations can also take a stand against the sexualization of culture.

By taking this holistic systematic approach to culture change, addressing the key constituents at the three levels of change – organizational, interpersonal, and individual – with committed leadership real change will occur. I argued in Chapter 9 that the next phase for moving forward is for men, and particularly leaders, to play their part, and engage in changing workplaces, which accommodate the needs of both men and women. The involvement of senior leadership at every step of this process is crucial.

The content of the chapters can be used as reference points, ideas for questions and material for workshops or other interventions, which will vary depending on the results of the audit and the culture of the organization.

RESISTANCE

The desire to protect group interests, and the need to retain identity, are both strong, and mean that there will always be resistance to change. Whilst this is acknowledged in change literature, it is rarely applied to diversity culture change, when the resistance will be even greater, impacting our identities in much deeper ways than in other commercial change programs. The book has shown how resistance to diversity change is expressed in many ways, through cultural discourse and practice.

The most difficult form of resistance is passive resistance. Denial of inequality and refusal or reluctance to acknowledge that there is an issue, and therefore an insistence that there is no rationale for any change, is hard to challenge. Few people today would publicly oppose women's equality in the workplace. However, they might at the same time say that mothers should stay at home and look after their children, or that women are not in senior positions because they have children. These are socially legitimate points of view, and indeed convey the dominant ideology of our day. These dominating discourses of reproduction and difference, combined with the discourse of free choice, effectively silence those who want change. They can be seen as providing resistance. On an organizational scale resistance is hard to identify precisely because of the availability of 'common-sense' explanations for women's inequality such as biological difference or motherhood.

The current focus on women's difference from men can also be seen as resistance to furthering equality. It perpetuates the accepted masculine norm from which others are deemed 'different,' and casts doubt on the abilities and skills of women and other groups to actually improve on the ways in which our organizations are managed.

Chapter 6 on the long-hours culture showed how this practice is possibly the number one barrier for women who most often have the main domestic responsibility. It too can be seen as resistance coming at a time when women can offer almost everything else equally with men, but they often cannot match them on the resource of time.

We require a wider explanation of men's dominance over women in society, and thus in the shaping of language and discourse, in order to challenge some of these discourses.

On an individual level in my work I have seen resistance expressed by refusing to participate in diversity training workshops, or attending in silence, the power of which is far more unnerving for the facilitator than vociferous vocal opposition. Resistance in these settings can also be identified by people undermining the content of the workshops with humor or by domination of the agenda, 'Resistance can be expressed through jokes, allowing the teller a license to express something uncomfortable and risky.'[7]

The cultural barriers identified in the book will not disappear overnight. But by shining a light on them, both practices and values hitherto taken for granted as neutral or natural can be revealed as privileging men over women, and together we can embark on meaningful change.

WOMEN-LED ORGANIZATIONS

If organizations do not adapt and men do not change at a greater rate than they are doing at present, they will either face increasing regulation from government, or more women will leave and start their own organizations where they can put in their own values and create their own workplace cultures. There are increasing numbers of female-led businesses to provide examples of this fifth approach. Women leave corporate life, because as Carolyn Lee, head of diversity at Herbert Smith, says, 'they get tired of the macho culture, they get tired of the politics, they get tired of arguing for equal recognition and pay. And they reach a point where they are just not prepared to do it any more.'[8]

The reluctance of UK corporate leadership to engage on a more personal level increases the likelihood that further legislation will be passed to force change. European law has been the driver for all diversity and equality work in UK organizations, which might now appreciate the business benefits that they did not see 10 or 20 years ago. The pressure from Europe for the increased participation of women in the workforce is certainly spurring on organizations in continental Europe.

As well as the introduction of quotas at board level, some companies are introducing quotas for the numbers of women at senior level. In Germany in the autumn of 2010, Deutsche Telekom announced that its goal was to more than double women-held upper and middle management jobs before 2016, and that it planned to fill 30 percent of its middle and upper management jobs with women by the end of 2015 under quotas it is imposing.[9] It may just be that quotas are what are needed to bump up the required number of women at the top in order to change cultures for good.

CHANGE GENDERED SOCIETY

The last and most radical of the six approaches outlined at the start of this chapter – change gendered society – is beyond the scope of the individual organization. However gender relations in the West and beyond are undergoing something of a revolution. All organizations are part of this wider social change, reflecting the progress as well as the backlash and anxiety. It is up to each one to decide what part they want to play.

NOTES

Context

1   Rutherford (1999, 2001a, 2001b, 2002).
2   Rutherford and Ollerearnshaw (2002, 2004), Rutherford, Schneider, and Walmsley (2006).

Introduction

1   The most recent female FTSE report (2010) shows that 12.5 percent of FTSE 100 boards are made up of women. This has stayed at the same level for three years now. In the wider FTSE250 the situation is worse, with over half (52.4 percent) of boards having no women at all. Only 7.8 percent of all directors of FTSE 250 are women (Vinnicombe et al., 2010).
2   For example, Knights, Kerfoot, and Sabelis (1991).

1 Women in society

1   *Daily Telegraph,* January 23, 1936, quoted in Virginia Woolf, *The Three Guineas* (1977, p. 60).
2   The report structured by Yvette Cooper and conducted by the Commons library was reported in the *Guardian,* 5 July 2010.
3   Banyard (2010).
4   Equality and Human Rights Commission (2009a).
5   Banyard and Lewis (2009).
6   Westaway and McKay (2007).
7   Vinnicombe et al. (2010).
8   UNIFEM <www.unifem.org/gender_issues/women_poverty_economics/facts_figures.php>.
9   Source: Women's Learning Partnership.
10 United Nations General Assembly (2006).
11 www.womankind.org – see for further statistics of violence against women around the world its report 'Tackling Violence Against Women' at <www.womankind.org.uk/wp-content/uploads/2011/02/2007-Tackling-Violence-Against-women-a-worldwide-approach.pdf> (accessed April 11, 2011).
12 Walby and Allen (2004).
13 Home Office Statistics on Violence (2007).
14 <www.caadv.org.uk>.

15 Walter (2010, p. 33).

16 For a history of men's magazines see www.magforum.com/mens.htm.

17 A review into the sexualization of young people was published by the Labour government in April 2010. The review formed part of the government's strategy to tackle 'Violence Against Women and Girls (VAWG),' and looked at how sexualized images and messages may be affecting the development of children and young people and influencing cultural norms. It also examined the evidence for a link between sexualization and violence. See www.homeoffice.gov.uk/../sexualisation-young-people.html This was followed by the announcement in December 2010 of a review into sexualized products aimed at children. See www.guardian.co.uk/society/2010/dec/06/david-cameron-review-sexualised-products-children.

18 *Daily Mail,* June 14, 2010.

19 Melrose (2000).

20 Jarvinen, Kall, and Miller (2008).

21 Gutek and Cohen (1987).

22 Wolff (1977, p.20).

23 A recent Fawcett Society campaign to end the negative association included T-shirts with 'This is what a feminist looks like,' which were then worn by a range of public figures, male and female (www.fawcettsociety.org).

24 Urwin (2010).

25 See websites The F-Word and Feministing, and personal blogs C. Elliot, 'Too much to say for myself,' J. Smith, 'Political blonde feministing', and A.Clarke, 'Women's views on news.'

26 <www.ukfeminista.org,uk>.

27 Banyard (2010).

2 Belonging: meanings of organizational culture

1 Hunt (1989, p. 33).

2 Marshall (1984).

3 McFall (2010, p. 3).

4 Catalyst and Opportunity Now (2000), MacDowell (1997), Gambles, Lewis, and Rapoport (2006).

5 Hammond (1993), Rigg and Sparrow (1994), Lewis (1997).

6 Pemberton (1995), Itzen (1995).

7 Peters and Waterman (1982), Deal and Kennedy (1982), Handy (1985), Schien (1985), Trompenaars (1993), Hampden-Turner (1990), Brown (1995).

8 Elton Mayo, founder of the Human Relations Movement, undertook a series of experiments in the 1930s in an industrial company. These became known as the Hawthorne Studies. For analysis see Sonnenfeld (1985).

9 Brown (1995, p. 2).

10 Ouchi (1981), Peters and Waterman (1982), Deal and Kennedy (1982).

11 Brown (1995), Schein (2010).

12 Cockburn (1991).

13 Schein (2010).
14 For a discussion on unconscious bias see Kandola (2009).
15 Durkheim (1961) .
16 Douglas (1966).
17 Grint (1995, p. 166).
18 Deal and Kennedy (1982, p. 67).
19 Cockburn (1991).
20 Stapley (1991, p. 43), Hirshchorn (1990) , Gabriel (1999).
21 Stapley (1991, p. 43).
22 Stapley (1991, p. 153).
23 Schein (2010, p. 29).
24 Prime and Moss-Racusin (2009) .
25 Stapley (1991, p.153).
26 Weber (1947, p. 152).
27 Kanter (1977b, p. 200).
28 Walby (1990, p. 20).
29 Cockburn (1991, p. 17).
30 The concept of hegemony was developed by Antonio Gramsci, the Italian Marxist, in the 1920s. His concern was the way in which the ruling class was together able to produce a social and cultural environment in which capitalist relations of exploitation appeared quite normal and acceptable to ordinary people. This explains why coercive force is not always necessary for a dominant group to continue to rule. It also explains why force is necessary in any uprising where hegemony has not been achieved by the dominant group.
31 Smith (1987, p. 34).
32 Maddock (1999, p.192).
33 Acker (1990).
34 Pemberton (1995, pp. 108–25), Itzen (1995).
35 Watson (1990) on the Civil Service; Lewis and Lewis (1996) on family-friendly issues; Palmer (1996) on HM Customs and Excise. Some writers discuss culture in relation to a particular organizational issue: Alimo-Metcalfe (1994) on leadership.
36 McDowell (1997), Gherardi (1995), Maddock (1999), Wacjman (1998), Alvesson and Due Billing (1992). Alvesson and Due Billing (1994) develop a theory which incorporates discrimination into organizational cultures by showing the gender symbolism of various functions, professions and positions. They use gender as a metaphor, and usefully show the variety of different cultures which may exist within one organization.
37 Jung (1944).
38 Gherardi (1994, p. 599).
39 Maddock and Parkin (1993).
40 Collinson and Hearn (1996).
41 See Itzin (1995), Maddock (1999), (Wacjman 1998).
42 Adapted from Stapley (1991).
43 Still (1994).

44 Brown, (1995, p. 32).
45 Schein (2010), Brown (1995), Handy (1995). Charles Handy identified four different types of management style. Zeus, the dynamic entrepreneur, rules over companies of the club culture; Apollo, god of order and bureaucracy is the patron of the role culture. Athena, goddess of craftsmen, recognizes only expertise as the basis of power and influence: hers is the task culture. Dionysus is the god preferred by artists and professionals within the existential culture, people who owe little or no allegiance to a boss.
46 Hofstede (1980).
47 Schein (2010, p. 219).
48 Gagliardi (1990).

3 The gender agenda

1 Foucault (1972).
2 Sinclair (2000, pp. 83–101); quote from p. 94.
3 Wittenberg-Cox and Maitland (2008), Kandola (2009).
4 Liff (1995), Kingsmill (2000).
5 Equality Act 2005.
6 Elliott (2010).
7 MccGwire (1992).
8 Corcoran-Nantes and Roberts (1995).
9 Smith (1987), Acker (1990).
10 Lewis and Lewis (1996), Hochschild (1997).
11 See the latest maternity and paternity leave regulations on the CIPD website: www.cipd.co.uk/subjects/emplaw/maternity/matpat.htm.
12 Hewlett (2002a).
13 For a discussion of postmodernism, see Eagleton (1996).
14 Kandola and Fullerton (1998, p. 47).
15 Opportunity 2000 (1997).
16 Oakley and Mitchell (1997).
17 Taken from website http://www.ey.com/UK/en/About-us/Our-people/About-EY---Diversity-and-inclusiveness.
18 Liff (1997).
19 Kirton and Greene (2004).
20 Rigg and Sparrow (1994).
21 Wittenberg-Cox and Maitland (2008).
22 Wittenberg-Cox and Maitland (2008, p. 24).
23 Conversation with the author, September 20, 2010.
24 Joan Smith in conversation with Mary Ann Sieghart on *Woman's Hour* (BBC Radio 4, July 21, 2010): www.bbc.co.uk/programmes/b00t17k0.
25 McFall Treasury Select Committee on Women in the City (2010), the Equality and Human Rights Commission Inquiry into sex discrimination in the finance sector (2009), and the Davies Review on women on boards (2011).
26 Conversation with the author, November 4, 2010.
27 Rees (1998).

28   Conversation with the author, January 13, 2011.

29   'The case for making a strategic priority of the pursuit of equal opportunities grows year by year for business. A comprehensive approach widens not only the talent available to the business, but its understanding of the market place and its links with the community on which it depends' (Howard Davies, director-general of the CBI, 1995).

30   Chambers et al. (1998), Axelrod, Handfield-Jones, and Welsh (2001).

31   Reported in *Equal Opportunities Review* (2001), No. 90.

32   Shapiro and Allison (2007).

33   Marshall (1995b).

34   Rutherford and Ollerearnshaw (2002).

35   Rutherford and Ollerearnshaw (2002, p. 19).

36   Conversation with the author, 23 September 2010.

37   Information from conversation with Pam Farmer, British Telecom, November 10, 2011.

38   Conversation with the author, November 3, 2010.

39   Shell website: <www.shell.us/home/content/usa/aboutshell/who_we_are/diversity_inclusiveness/>.

40   Rutherford and Ollerearnshaw (2002).

41   Shapiro and Allison (2007).

42   Private conversation with the author .

43   Opportunity Now (2010b, p. 10).

44   Conversation with the author, November 4, 2010.

45   Conversation with the author, November 8, 2010.

46   Thomas (2004, pp. 1–11).

47   Conversation with the author, November 5, 2010.

48   Conversation with the author, September 10, 2010.

49   Goldman Sachs has never participated in the DiversityInc Top 50 Companies for Diversity® survey, so DiversityInc has no way of assessing the diversity of its management demographics. However, according to the complaint in a recent sex discrimination lawsuit, women make up only:
• 29 percent of the firm's vice presidents (2009)
• 17 percent of the firm's managing directors (2009)
• 14 percent of its partners (2008).
Today, only four members of its 30-person management committee (roughly 13 percent) are women, the complaint says. And of its nine executive officers, just one is a woman. For further information on the lawsuit see <www.diversityinc.com/article/8030/Goldman-Sachs-Sued-for-Gender-Discrimination/>.

50   'Womenomics: Japan's hidden asset' (October 19, 2005) <www2.goldmansachs.com/ideas/..change/womenomics.html>.

51   Daly (2007).

52   www.onlinewomeninpolitics.org/statistics.htm.

53   Silverstein and Syre (2009).

54   Catalyst (2004).

55   Desvaux, Devillard-Hoellinger, and Baumgarten (2007).

56 Kramer, Konrad, and Erkut (2006).
57 Peston (2009).
58 McSmith (2009).
59 McFall (2010).
60 Walby (2009).
61 Conversation with the author, September 10, 2010.
62 Personal communication, July 27, 2010.
63 Kandola (2009, p. 36).
64 Kandola (2009, p. 14).
65 Meyerson and Scully (1995).
66 Kirton, Greene, and Dean (2005).
67 Shapiro and Allison (2007).
68 Shapiro and Allison (2007, p. 29).
69 Conversation with the author, October 5, 2010.
70 Conversation with the author, October 5, 2010.
71 Private conversation with the author.
72 Private conversation with the author.
73 Conversation with the author, September 20, 2010.
74 Personal communication, July 27, 2010.
75 Kandola (2009).
76 Personal conversation with the author.
77 Personal conversation with the author.
78 Conversation with the author, September 10, 2010.
79 Wetherell, Stiven, and Potter (1989, pp. 59–71).
80 Rutherford and Ollerearnshaw (2002).
81 Rutherford and Ollerearnshaw (2002).
82 Personal communication, July 27, 2010.
83 Private conversation with the author.
84 The author's PhD research, 1999.
85 Roper (1994, p. 199).
86 Interview with a broker aged 27. Conversation with the author, October 2010.
87 Catalyst and Opportunity Now (2000), Opportunity Now (2010).
88 Gutek (1989, pp. 56–71).
89 Brescoli, Dawson, and Uhlmann (2010, p. 1640).
90 Ryan and Haslam (2007, pp. 1–26).
91 Sinclair (2000, pp. 83–101).
92 Male director, Investco investment management division .
93 Cockburn (1991).
94 Kanter (1977 b).
95 Cockburn (1991, p. 143).
96 Conversation with the author, 13 September 2010.
97 Investco research, PhD, 1997.
98 Female manager, Corporate Finance (from PhD research).
99 Female assistant director, Corporate Finance (from PhD research).
100 McDowell (1997).

101 Sealy, Vinnicombe, and Doldor (2009).
102 Personal conversation, December 2010.
103   Airco research, PhD, 1999.
104 Wetherell et al. (1989).
105 Opportunity Now (2010).

4 Style matters

1   Handy (1995).
2   Handy (1985), Schein (2010), Brown (1995).
3   Opportunity Now (2010).
4   Kerfoot and Knights (1996, pp. 78–99).
5   Gray (1992), Moir and Moir (1998).
6   Gerth and Wright Mills (1958, p. 215).
7   Taylor (1911).
8   Merchant (1982).
9   Acker (1990), Pringle (1989).
10   Pringle (1989).
11   Kerfoot and Knights (1996, pp. 78–99).
12   Cockburn (1986).
13   Willis (1977).
14   Collinson and Knights (1986).
15   Phillips and Taylor (1980, pp. 79–88).
16   Fine (2010: see p. 46).
17   Elliott (2010).
18   See <http://leytr.blogspot.com/2010/04/train-driver-rates-of-pay.html>; <www.nhscareers.nhs.uk/details/Default.aspx?Id=766>.
19   Philips and Taylor (1980, pp. 79–88).
20   Willmott (1993, pp. 515–42).
21   Marshall (1995a) .
22   Schein (1973, p. 95–100). Schein, Mueller, and Jacobson (1989, pp. 103–10), Powell (1988), Carr-Ruffino (1993, pp. 10–16).
23   Schein (2010, p. 49).
24   Schein (2010, p. 49).
25   Rigg and Sparrow (1994); Coyle (1993).
26   Conversation with the author.
27   Hammond (1993), Rosener (1990), Schwartz (1989, pp. 65–78).
28   Rosener (1990, pp. 119–125), Hegelson (1990), Fagenson (1993).
29   Savage (1992).
30   Still (1994, pp. 3–10).
31   Grint (1995).
32   Handy (1985), Schein (2010), Anthony (1994), Brown (1998).
33   Wahl (1998).
34   Wajcman (1998, p. 62).
35   Rutherford(2001a).
36   Reported in McElhinny (2006).
37   Rutherford (2001a).

38   Rutherford (2001a).
39   Rutherford (2001a).
40   Rutherford (2001a).
41   Thomson (1998).
42   The tenth edition is cited herein: Goleman (2006).
43   A glance at the list of books on emotional intelligence on Amazon will show that the majority of them are written by men.
44   Gherardi (1995, p. 153).
45   Thomson (1998, p. 101).
46   Hochschild (1983).
47   Airco PhD research 1999.
48   Parker and Hall (1993).
49   McDowell (1997).
50   Airco PhD research 1999.
51   Airco PhD research 1999.
52   Airco PhD research 1999 .
53   Linstead (1995, pp. 192–205).
54   Airco PhD research 1999.
55   Kelan (2009, p. 103).
56   Roper (1994).
57   Fineman (1993), Giddens (1992).
58   Swan (1994).
59   Airco PhD research 1999.
60   Airco PhD research 1999.
61   Rutherford (2001a).
62   Opportunity Now (2010a).
63   Private conversation with Fleur Bothwick.
64   Collinson and Hearn (1996).
65   Airco PhD research 1999.
66   PhD research 1999.
67   Helgeson (1990), Rosener (1990).
68   Catalyst and Opportunity Now (2000).
69   Catalyst and Conference Board (2001).
70   Opportunity Now (2010).
71   Rutherford (2001a), Still (1994), Wajcman (1998).
72   Airco PhD research 1999.
73   Wittenberg-Cox and Maitland (2008).
74   Babcock et al. (2003).
75   Bowles, Babcock and Lei (2007, pp. 84–103).
76   Holmes (2006), p35.
77   Brescoli, Dawson, and Uhlmann (2010) p. 1640.
78   Weisel (1991, pp. 45–51).
79   Gherardi (1995).
80   Private conversation with the author.
81   PhD research, 1999.
82   Conversation with the author.

83   Conversation with the author.
84   Rosener (1990), Hegelson (1990).
85   Gray (1992).
86   Tannen (1990, 1994).
87   Lakoff (1975).
88   For a discussion on the approaches to gender differences in language see Cameron (2007).
89   Taken from a GenderSpeak workshop by Pat Heim, www.heimgroup.com/ GenderSpeak_Workshop.asp.
90   Rutherford (2005).
91   Conversation with the author, 9 December 2010.
92   Conversation with the author, 9 December 2010.
93   Cameron (2007).
94   Holmes (2006, p. 141).
95   Gherardi (1995, p. 138).
96   Shaw (2006).
97   Catalyst and Opportunity Now (2000).
98   Shaw (2006).
99   Simpson (2004, p. 349–68).
100 Simpson (2004, p. 361).
101 Baron-Cohen (2003a), Moir (1989), Moir and Jessell (1998), Brizendene (2006). In *The Female Brain* (2006), Brizendene says that the human female brain is affected both by hormones, and difference in architecture of the brain that regulates such hormones and neurotransmitters.
102 Private conversation with the author.
103 Baron-Cohen (2003b).
104 Baron-Cohen (2003b, p. 185).
105 Discussion with Professor Simon Baron Cohen on the *Today* programme (November 17, 2010).
106 Gurian and Annis (2008).
107 <www.genderiq.tv/>.
108 Bleier (1984, p. 76).
109 Walter (2010), Cameron (2007), Fine (2010), Rippon (2010).
110 Fine (2010).
111 Maudsley (1874, pp. 466–83) Quoted in Walter (2010, p. 203).
112 Rippon (2010). Professor Rippon set out her views at the British Science Festival in Birmingham on 13 September 2010.
113 Milkman (1987).
114 Spencer, Steele, and Quinn (1999, pp. 93–113).
115 Fine (2010, p. 235).
116 For an interesting thesis on the effects of transgenerational prejudice see Schutsenberger (1998).
117 Cameron (2007, p. 172).
118 Fine (2010, p. 154).
119 Wajcman (1998).
120 Bacchi (1990).

5 The public/private divide

1   Private interview with the author .
2   Acker (1990, pp. 139–58).
3   Hochschild (1990).
4   Halford, Savage, and Witz (1997).
5   Walby (1990).
6   Acker (1990).
7   Massey (1997, pp. 115).
8   Gutek (1989, pp. 56–71).
9   Investco PhD research 1999.
10 Private interview with the author.
11 Kelan (2009).
12 Private interview with the author.
13 Acker (1992, pp. 248–61).
14 Airco PhD research 1999.
15 McDowell (1997).
16 Conversation with the author.
17 Airco PhD research 1999.
18 Hochschild (1990).
19 Lewis and Lewis (1996).
20 Massey (1993).
21 Desvaux et al. (2007, p. 22).
22 Pearson (2002). See also Opinion columns in the *Daily Mail*.
23 There is an interesting discussion of western women's dependence on poorer women's labour in Ehrenreich and Hochschild (2002).
24 World Economic Forum (2010).
25 Hewlett and Rashid et al. (2010).
26 Reported in the *Evening Standard*, 24 April 1995.
27 The report is part of the European Union's ongoing European Working Conditions Survey. Door-to-door surveys were carried out in all 27 EU member states, in which over 30,000 employed and self-employed workers were asked about their job, their wellbeing, and aspects of their lives outside work. From this, scholars from Cambridge and Manchester universities were able to draw up a detailed picture of people's working lives.
28 Gratton (2007).
29 Equality and Human Rights Commission (2009b).
30 Working Families (2010).
31 Fawcett Society website: http://www.fawcettsociety.org.uk/index.asp?PageID=644 (accessed on October 4, 2010).
32 Investco PhD research 1999.
33 Cheston (2010).
34 Investco PhD research 1999.
35 Investco PhD research 1999.
36 Interview with the author, 5 November 2010.
37 McFall (2010, p. 12). Treasury Select Committee on Women in the City.
38 Brandth and Kuande (2001, pp. 251–67).

39   Kuande (2009).
40   www.dpm.cabinetoffice.gov.uk/news/parenting-speech (accessed 13 April 2011).
41   <www.weforum.org/issues/corporate-gender-gap>.
42   Conversation with the author, September 23, 2010.
43   McFall (2010, p. 12), Treasury Select Committee on Women in the City.
44   Tom Bradshaw of Fathers Direct, quoted in Reeves (2002).
45   Airco PhD research 1999.
46   Airco PhD research 1999.
47   Private interview with the author.
48   Desvaux et al. (2007).
49   Gratton (2007).
50   Hewlett (2002b, pp. 66–73).
51   Massey (1994).
52   Airco PhD research 1999.
53   Conversation with the author, September 23, 2010.
54   Hochschild (1997).
55   Horlick (1998).
56   Airco PhD research 1999.
57   Airco PhD research 1999.
58   Gherardi (1994, pp. 591–691) or Gherardi (1995).
59   Bittman et al. (2003, pp. 186–214).
60   BNP Paribas (2008, pp. 7).

6 Are you going home already? The long-hours culture

1   <www.thefreelibrary.com/City+banker+'sacked+for+putting+her+family+first'- a0109705291>.
2   Buswell and Jenkins (1994).
3   Hochschild (1997, p. 56).
4   Office for National Statistics (2008).
5   Kodz et al. (2003).
6   Waterfield (2010).
7   ONS (1997).
8   Philpott (2010).
9   Kodz et al. (1998).
10   Airco PhD research 1999.
11   As quoted in Rutherford (2001b, pp. 259–76).
12   Collinson and Collinson (2004).
13   Collinson and Collinson (2004, p. 230).
14   Collinson and Collinson (2004, p. 231).
15   Airco PhD research 1999.
16   Massey (1997).
17   Massey (1997, p. 110).
18   Simpson (2004).
19   Working Families (2008a) This research examines culture and practice in 13 leading law firms, and establishes arguments and approaches to culture

change. It highlights successful projects and initiatives, and proposes additional measures that could work for the sector.

20 Private interview with the author 2010.
21 Conversation with the author, September 23, 2010.
22 Rutherford (2001b).
23 Investco PhD research 1999.
24 Investco PhD research 1999.
25 Massey (1997).
26 Curtis (2010).
27 Opportunity Now (2010).
28 Airco PhD research 1999.
29 Investco PhD research 1999.
30 Kodz et al. (2003).
31 Airco PhD research 1999.
32 Investco PhD research 1999.
33 Lewis and Taylor (1996, p. 121).
34 Opportunity Now (2004, p. 31).
35 Interview with the author, November 3, 2010.
36 Marshall (1995).
37 Doughty (2000).
38 Airco PhD research 1999.
39 Airco PhD research 1999.
40 Airco PhD research 1999.
41 Airco PhD research 1999.
42 Investco PhD research 1999.
43 Private interview, October 2010.
44 Quoted in Reeves (2002).
45 Private interview with the author, October 2010.
46 Gratton (2007).
47 Office for National Statistics: <www.statistics.gov.uk/cci/nugget.asp?id=167>.
48 Department of Work and Pensions (2009, p. 21).
49 OECD (2008).
50 Connolly and Gregory (2008).
51 Working Families (2005).
52 Doughty (2000), Hammers (2003).
53 Lewis, Rapoport, and Gambles (2003, pp. 824–41).
54 Maushart (2002, pp. 161).
55 Smithson and Stokoe (2005, pp. 147–68).
56 Perrons (2003, pp. 65–93).
57 Department of Work and Pensions (2009, pp.17).
58 From *The Times,* January 22, 2010: <http://business.timesonline.co.uk/tol/business/industry_sectors/support_services/article6997724.ece>.
59 PhD research 1999.
60 Personal interview with the author, October 11, 2010.
61 Flexible Working Task Force paper 2009: <www.dwp.gov.uk/docs/family-friendly-task-force-report.pdf> (accessed April 14, 2011).

62 Personal interview with the author, October 11, 2010.

63 BT.com: 'Society and environment.'

64 Dame Stephanie Shirley, taken from a speech given to the Computer Conservation Society, October 20, 1998. Found at <www.steveshirley.com/popuppage.asp?pageid=99>.

65 Personal interview with the author, September 23, 2010.

66 Personal interview with the author, October 11. 2010.

67 Working Families <www.workingfamilies.org.uk/articles/new-thinking/fathers-research-project/fathers-research> (accessed April 13, 2011).

68 Working Families, 10 March 2010: <www.workingfamilies.org.uk/articles/new-thinking/fathers-research-project/fathers-at-work> (accessed April 13, 2011).

69 Working Families (2010).

70 Reeves (2002).

71 Department of Work and Pensions (2009).

72 Equality and Human Rights Commission (2009b).

73 Bowden (2009).

74 Halford (2006, pp. 383–402).

75 Kelan (2009, pp. 90).

76 Sturges, and Guest (2004, pp. 5–20).

77 Opportunity Now (2010a).

78 Philpott (2010).

79 Working Families (2008b).

80 Quoted in Flexible Working Task Force Paper 2009 <www.dwp.gov.uk/docs/family-friendly-task-force-report.pdf> (accessed April 14, 2011).

81 <www.peoplemanagement.co.uk/pm/articles/2008/08/downturn-means-more-demand-for-women-who-work-part-time.htm> (accessed April 13, 2011).

82 Private interview with the author, October 2010.

83 Private interview with the author, 2009.

84 Philpott (2010).

85 Personal interview with the author, October 11, 2010.

86 Opportunity Now (2010a).

7 Let's have a drink! Informal networking and socializing

1 Kanter (1977b, p. 164).

2 Tomlinson, Brockbank, and Traves (1997).

3 Tomlinson et al. (1997, pp. 218–30).

4 Tomlinson et al. (1997, pp. 218).

5 Clegg and Dunkerley (1980, p. 132).

6 Peters and Waterman (1982), Deal and Kennedy (1982), Scase and Goffee (1989).

7 Collinson, Knights, and Collinson (1990).

8 Collinson et al. (1990, p. 144).

9 Interview with the author, published in 'Towards Equality,' April 1994, Fawcett Society newsletter, now only available in hard copy in the Women's Library, Aldgate, London.

10 Lorber (1989).
11 Schein (1992), Kanter (1977b), Marshall (1984).
12 Kanter (1977b, p. 49).
13 Kanter (1977b, p. 225).
14 Kanter (1977a, pp. 965–90).
15 Yoder (1991, pp. 178–92), Reskin and Roos (1990).
16 Gruber and Morgan (2005).
17 Coe (1992, p. 22).
18 McCarthy (2004).
19 Ernst & Young (2004).
20 Management-issues.com (2006) <www.management-issues.com/../research/ the- old-boy-network-is-alive-and-well.asp> (accessed April 14, 2011).
21 See Vinnicombe et al. (2010).
22 Kandola (2009).
23 Rogers (1988).
24 Benschop (2009).
25 Private interview with the author September 2010.
26 Ibarra (2010).
27 Investco PhD research 1999.
28 Investco PhD research 1999.
29 Ibarra (1997).
30 Conversation with the author, 10 September 2010.
31 Wittenberg-Cox (2010, p. 63).
32 Ibarra (1995).
33 Vinnicombe, Singh, and Kumra (2005).
34 Kelan (2009).
35 Conversation with the author, October 15, 2010.
36 Epstein (1989), Lorber (1989).
37 Kanter (1977b, p. 184).
38 Epstein (1989).
39 Duggary (1994).
40 Airco PhD research 1999.
41 Roper (1994, p. 102).
42 Airco PhD research 1999.
43 Ibarra, Carter, and Silva (2010).
44 Hewlett (2010).
45 Personal communication, November 11, 2010.
46 Airco PhD research 1999.
47 Airco PhD research 1999.
48 Private conversation with the author, September 2009.
49 Knights and Morgan (1990, pp. 181–200).
50 Cockburn (1991, p. 153).
51 Rogers (1988).
52 Private interview with the author, 2009.
53 Kanter (1977b).
54 Investco PhD research 1999.

55 Investco PhD research 1999.
56 Airco PhD research 1999.
57 Knoppers (2009).
58 Singh (2008, p. 25).
59 Rogers (1988).
60 Korda (1973, p. 54).
61 Private conversation with the author, September 2010.
62 Airco PhD research 1999.
63 Airco PhD research 1999.
64 Airco PhD research 1999.
65 Arthur, DelCampo, and van Buren (2010).
66 Collinson, Knights, and Collinson (1990, p. 145).
67 Private interview with the author, November 2010.
68 Radford and Balls (1998).
69 Banyard and Lewis (2009).
70 Banyard and Lewis (2009).
71 Private conversation with the author, November 2009.
72 Conversation with the author, November 5, 2010.
73 From a conversation with Craig Jones, November 5, 2010.
74 Dangerfield (2010).
75 Airco PhD research 1999.
76 Private interview, October 2010.
77 The latest *Female FTSE report 2010* notes that the figure has remained largely the same for three years in a row.
78 McFall (2010, Evidence, p. 3 Q. 29).
79 McFall (2010, p. 9).
80 The *Female FTSE 2009* opted instead to recommend a 30 percent voluntary target. The latest report of 2010 favoured a comply or explain rule for companies failing to reach 20 percent of women directors.
81 Kingsmill (2000).
82 Financial Reporting Council (2010).
83 Lewis and Rake (2008).
84 <http://www.bis.gov.uk/assets/biscore/business-law/docs/w/11-745-women-on-boards.pdf>
85 *2010 Female FTSE* report (Vinnicombe et al. 2010).
86 Nielsen (2010), Lewis and Rake (2008).

8 Sex in the office

1 For information on the work done in organizations on sexual orientation see UK lobby group Stonewall at www.stonewall.org.uk.
2 Private interview with the author.
3 Hearn and Parkin (1995).
4 Farley (1978), MacKinnon (1979), EEC guidelines on Sexual Harassment 1991, Rubinstein (1987), Sex Discrimination Act 1975, Equality Act 2010.
5 Gutek (1989), Stanko (1988), Stockdale (1991), Collinson and Hearn (1996),

Thomas and Kitzinger (1994, 1997), Nicholson (1996), Mott and Condor (1997), Cairns (1997).

6   Herbert (1979).

7   Hearn et al. (1989).

8   Gherardi (1995), Pringle (1989).

9   Pringle (1989, p. 31).

10   Gheradi (1995).

11   Collinson and Collinson (1989, pp. 91–110).

12   Adkins (1995).

13   Private interview with the author.

14   MacKinnon (1979, p. 25).

15   Pringle (1989).

16   Cairns (1997), Thomas and Kitzinger (1995, 1997).

17   Gagliardi (1990).

18   Rutherford, Schneider, and Walmsley (2006).

19   Rutherford (2001a).

20   Banyard and Lewis (2009).

21   Banyard (2010).

22   Ward et al. (2005, pp. 81, 467–71), cited in Walter (2010, pp. 55).

23   Banyard and Lewis (2009).

24   Dines (2010).

25   <www.guardian.co.uk/lifeandstyle/2010/jul/../gail-dines-pornography> (accessed April 13, 2011)

26   O'Carroll and Boshoff (2000).

27   Collinson and Hearn (1996).

28   Airco PhD research 1999.

29   Quoted in Gardner (2009).

30   Gardner (2009).

31   Investco PhD research 1999.

32   www.bbc.co.uk/news/business-12023033 (accessed 13 April 2011).

33   Private interview September 2010.

34   Private interview September 2010.

35   Collinson and Hearn (1996).

36   Dodd (2010).

37   Cockburn (1991), Collinson, Knights, and Collinson (1990), Collinson and Hearn (1996).

38   See Baigent (2005), Yount (2005).

39   Rutherford et al. (2006, p. 13).

40   Rutherford et al. (2006, p. 13).

41   Cockburn (1983).

42   Investco PhD research 1999.

43   Investco PhD research 1999.

44   Rutherford et al. (2006).

45   Cockburn (1991, p. 154).

46   Rutherford et al. (2006).

47   Harlow, Hearn, and Parkin (1995, pp. 91–108).

48 Rutherford et al. (2006).
49 Wardrop (2010).
50 Private interview with the author.
51 Cockburn (1991).
52 Private interview with the author.
53 Private interview with the author.
54 Rutherford et al. (2006, p. 14).
55 Rutherford et al. (2006).
56 Mott and Condor (199, pp. 49–91).
57 Thomas and Kitzinger (1995, pp. 151–62), Thomas and Kitzinger (1997).
58 Rutherford et al. (2006).
59 European Commission (1987).
60 Rutherford et al. (2006).
61 Thomas and Kitzinger (1995).
62 Rutherford et al. (2006).
63 Wright et al. (2006, pp. 465–70).
64 See website www.stonewall.org.uk.
65 Stonewall (2009).
66 Gherardi (1996).
67 Airco PhD research, 1999.
68 Thomas and Kitzinger (1995).
69 Collinson and Collinson (1989).
70 Willis (1977), Collinson (1992), Cockburn, (1983).
71 Airco and Investco PhD and other research.

9 Leaders and men

1   Schein (2010, pp. 249).
2   Opportunity Now (2010b, p. 8).
3   Opportunity Now (2004).
4   Personal interview with the author, September 20, 2010.
5   Personal interview with the author, December 8, 2010.
6   Personal interview with the author, November 8, 2010.
7   As quoted in Rutherford (2004, p. 32).
8   Shapiro and Allison (2007).
9   Griffiths (2010).
10 Shapiro and Allison (2007).
11 Personal interview with the author, November 10, 2010.
12 Personal interview with the author, November 10, 2010.
13 Personal interview with the author, September 23, 2010.
14 Personal interview with the author, November 3, 2010.
15 Personal interview with the author, December 8, 2010.
16 Wittenburg-Cox and Maitland (2008, p. 13).
17 Personal interview with the author, December 10, 2010.
18 Prime, Moss-Racusin, and Foust-Cummings (2009a), Prime and Moss-Racusin (2009b).
19 Personal interview with the author, December 2, 2010.

20   Opportunity Now (2004, p. 4).
21   European Commission (2008).
22   ORSE (2010, p. 12).
23   ORSE (2010, p. 12).
24   Collinson and Hearn (1996), Kimmel (2009), Hearn (1992), Roper (1994).
25   Kimmel (2001).
26   Interview with Pia Höök, diversity director of Volvo AB, January 21, 2011.
27   Sinclair (2000).

10 On the road to change

1   Beauvoir (1984).
2   Martin (2001a); see also Martin (2001b).
3   Interview with the author, January 13, 2011.
4   Kimmel (2009, p. 341).
5   Meyerson and Fletcher (2000, pp. 127–36).
6   Conversation with the author, October 5, 2010.
7   Gabriel (1999, p. 198).
8   Personal communication, July 27, 2010.
9   BBC News, 'Deutsche Telekom sets gender quotas', March 15, 2010 <http://
      news.bbc.co.uk/1/hi/business/8568066.stm>.

REFERENCES

Acker, J. (1990) 'Hierarchies, jobs and bodies: a theory of gendered organizations,' *Gender and Society,* Vol. 4, pp. 139–58.

Acker, J. (1992) 'Gendering organisational theory,' pp. 248–61 in A. Mills and P. Tancred (eds), *Gendering Organisational Analysis.* Newbury Park, Calif.: Sage.

Adams, L. (2010) 'Leading change: insights and inspiration from successful leaders,' *Opportunity Now*, p. 10.

Adkins, L. (1995) *Gendered Work: Sexuality, Family and the Labour Market.* Buckingham: Open University Press.

Alimo-Metcalfe, B (1994) 'Waiting for fish to grow feet: removing organizational barriers to womens' entry into leadership positions,' in M.Tanton (ed.), *Women in Management: A Developing Presence* London: Routledge.

Alvesson, M. and Due Billing, Y. (1992) 'Gender and organization: towards a differentiated understanding,' *Organization Studies,* Vol. 13, No. 2, pp. 73–102.

Alvesson, M. and Due Billing, Y. (1994) *Gender, Managers and Organizations.* Berlin and New. York: de Gruyter.

Anthony, P. (1994) *Managing Culture.* Buckingham: Open University Press.

Arthur, M. M., DelCampo, R. G., and Van Buren, H. J. III (2010) 'The impact of gender-differentiated golf course structures on women's networking abilities,' *Gender in Management*, Vol. 26, No. 1, pp. 108–28.

Axelrod, E. L., Handfield-Jones, H. and Welsh, T. A. (2001) 'The war for talent part 2,' *McKinsey Quarterly*, May.

Babcock, L., Laschever, S., Gelfand, M., and Small, D. (2003) 'Nice girls don't ask,' *Harvard Business Review*, October.

Bacchi, C. (1990) *Same Difference? Feminism and Sexual Difference.* Sydney: Allen & Unwin.

Baigent, D. (2005) 'Fitting in: the conflation of firefighting, male domination and harassment' pp. 45–65 in J. E. Gruber and P. Morgan (eds), *In the Company of Men.* Boston, Mass.: NorthEastern University Press

Banyard, K. (2010) *The Equality Illusion: The Truth about Men and Women Today.* London: Faber.

Banyard, K. and Lewis, R. (2009) *Corporate Sexism: The Sex Industry's Infiltration of the Modern Workplace.* London: Fawcett Society, September.

Baron-Cohen, S. (2003a) *The Essential Difference.* New York: Basic Books.

Baron-Cohen, S. (2003b) 'You just can't help it,' *Guardian*, April 17.

Beauvoir, S. de (1984) *The Second Sex*, trans. and ed. H. M. Parshley. Harmondsworth: Penguin.

Benschop, Y. (2009) 'The micro politics of gendering in networking,' *Gender Work and Organization*, Vol. 16, No. 2 (March).

Bittman, M., England, P., Sayer, L., Folbre, N., and Matheson, G. (2003) 'When does gender trump money? Bargaining and time in household work,' *American Journal of Sociology*, Vol. 109, No. 1, pp. 186–214.

Bleier, R. (1984) *Science and Gender: A Critique of Biology and its Theories on Women*. London: Pergamon.

BNP Paribas (2008) *Involving Men*. Paris: Observatoire sur la Responsibilite Societale des Entreprises (ORSE).

Bowden, P. (2009) 'Flexible working; benefits and barriers. Perceptions of working parents.' Government Equalities Office (GEO) research report. <www.dwp.gov.uk/docs/family-friendly-task-force-report.pdf> (accessed April 2, 2011).

Bowles, H. R., Babcock, L., and Lei, L. (2007) 'Social incentives for gender differences in the propensity to initiate negotiations: sometimes it does hurt to ask,' *Organizational Behaviour and Human Design Processes*, Vol. 103, No. 1 (May).

Brandth, B. and Kuande, E. (2001) 'Flexible work and flexible fathers.' *Work, Employment and Society*, Vol. 15, No. 2, pp. 251–67.

Brescoli, V., Dawson, E., and Uhlmann, E. (2010) '"Hard won and easily lost": the fragile status of leaders in gender stereotype – incongruent occupations,' *Psychological Science*, Vol. 21, No. 12, pp. 1640–2.

Brizendene, A. L. (2006) *The Female Brain*. New York: Morgan Road.

Brown, A. (1995) *Organisational Culture*. London: Pitman.

BT (2010) Sustainability Report 2010 <www.btplc.com/Responsiblebusiness/Ourstory/Sustainabilityreport/section/index.aspx?sectionid=c5ed3088-f0d4-4476-a6e0-63c17edbcb30> (accessed 7 April 2011).

Buswell, C. and Jenkins, S. (1994) Equal opportunity policies: employment and patriarchy,' *Gender, Work and Organisation*, Vol. 1, No. 2 (April), pp. 83–93.

Cairns, K. (1997) '"Femininity" and women's silence to response to sexual harassment and coercion,' in A.Thomas and C. Kitzinger (eds), *Sexual Harassment: Contemporary Feminist Perspectives*. Buckingham: Open University Press.

Cameron, D. (2007) *The Myth of Mars and Venus*. Oxford: Oxford University Press.

Carr-Ruffino, N. (1993) 'US women: breaking through the glass ceiling,' *Women in Management Review and Abstracts*, Vol. 6, No. 5, pp. 10–16.

Catalyst (2004) 'The bottom line: connecting corporate performance and gender diversity' <www.catalyst.org/.../the-bottom-line-connecting-corporate-performance-and-gender-diversity> (accessed April 2, 2011).

Catalyst and Conference Board (2001) 'Women in leadership: a European business initiative' <www.catalyst.org/.../women-in-leadership-a-european-business-imperative> (accessed April 4, 2011).

Catalyst and Opportunity Now (2000) *Breaking the Barriers: Women in Senior Management in the UK*. December.

Chambers, E. G., Foulon, M., Handfield-Jones, H., Hankin, S. M., and Michaels, E. G. (1998) 'The war for talent,' *McKinsey Quarterly*, August.

Cheston, P. (2010) 'Banker seeks 13.5m after losing her job because of baby,' *Evening Standard*, August 11 <www.thisislondon.co.uk/standard/article-

23865944-banker-seeks-pound-13.5-million-after-losing-her-job-because-of-baby.do> (accessed October 4, 2010).

Clarke, A. (nd) *Women's Views on News.* www.womensviewsonnews.org (website/blog).

Clegg, S. and Dunkerley, D. (1980) *Organisation, Class and Control.* London: Routledge & Kegan Paul

Cockburn, C. (1983) *Brothers: Male Dominance and Technological Change.* London: Pluto.

Cockburn, C. (1986) 'The gendering of jobs: workplace relations and the reproduction of sex segregation,' pp. 29–42 in S. Walby (ed.), *Gender Segregation at Work.* Milton Keynes: Open University Press.

Cockburn, C. (1991) *In the Way of Women: Men's Resistance to Sex Equality in Organizations.* Basingstoke: Macmillan.

Coe, T. (1992) *Key to the Men's Club: Opening the Doors to Women in Management.* Corby, Northants: Institute of Management.

Collinson, D. L. (1992) *Managing the Shopfloor: Subjectivity, Masculinity and Workplace Culture.* Berlin: Walter de Gruyter,

Collinson, D. L. and Collinson, M. (1989) 'Sexuality in the workplace: the domination of men's sexuality, 'pp. 91–110 in J. Hearn, D. Sheppard et al. (eds), *The Sexuality of the Organization.* London: Sage.

Collinson, D. L. and Collinson, M. (2004) 'The power of time: leadership, management and gender,' pp. 520–45 in C. F. Epstein and A. L. K. Russell (eds), *Fighting for Time: Shifting Boundaries of Work and Social Life.* New York: Sage.

Collinson, D. and Hearn, J. (eds) (1996) *Men as Managers, Managers as Men: Critical Perspectives on Men, Masculinities and Management.* London: Sage.

Collinson, D. and Knights, D. (1986) 'Men only: theories and practice of job segregation in insurance,' in D. Knights and H. Wilmot (eds), *Gender and the Labour Process.* Aldershot: Gower.

Collinson, D. L., Knights, D., and Collinson, M. (1990) *Managing to Discriminate.* London, Routledge.

Connolly, S. and Gregory, M. (2008) 'Moving down: women's part time work and occupational change in 1991–2001,' *Economic Journal*, Vol. 118 (February).

Corcoran-Nantes, Y. and Roberts, K. (1995) 'We've got one of those; the peripheral status of women in male dominated industries,' *Gender, Work and Organisation*, Vol. 2, No. 1 (January), pp. 21–33.

Coyle, A. (1993) 'Gender, power and organizational change: the case of women managers,' IRRU workshop paper, December. Coventry: University of Warwick.

Curtis, P. (2010) 'Paid more than the prime minister: 170 highest earning civil servants revealed,' *Guardian*, June 1 <www.guardian.co.uk/politics/2010/jun/01/top-earning-civil-servants-named> (accessed April 2, 2011).

Daly, K. (2007) 'Gender inequality, growth and global ageing,' Goldman Sachs Global Economics Paper No. 154.

Dangerfield, A. (2010) 'Too much sex in the city, say London's councils,' BBC News, November 12 <www.bbc.co.uk/news/uk-england-london-11733974> (accessed April 2, 2011).

Davies of Abersoch, Lord (2011) *Women on Boards*. London: Department for Business Innovation and Skills <http://www.bis.gov.uk/assets/biscore/business-law/docs/w/11-745-women-on-boards.pdf> (accessed June 13, 2011).

Deal, T. and Kennedy, A. (1982) *Corporate Cultures: The Rights and Rituals of Corporate Life*. Reading, Mass.: Addison-Wesley.

Department of Work and Pensions (2009) *Flexible Working: Working for Families, Working for Business*. Report by the Family Friendly Working Hours Taskforce <www.dwp.gov.uk/docs/family-friendly-task-force-report.pdf> (accessed April 4, 2011).

Desvaux, G., Devillard-Hoellinger, S., and Baumgarten, P. (2007) 'Women matter: gender diversity, a corporate performance driver,' New York: McKinsey.

Dines, G. (2010) *Pornland: How Porn has Hijacked our Sexuality*. Boston, Mass.: Beacon.

Dodd, V. (2010) 'Firearms policewoman wins record damages in sexism case,' *Guardian,* June 18 <www.guardian.co.uk/uk/2010/jun/18/barbara-lynford-tribunal-sexism-award> (accessed April 6, 2011).

Doughty, S. (2000) 'Britain family friendly firms face staff backlash; childless workers want extra time off as well,' *Daily Mail*, July 24.

Douglas, M. (1966) *Purity and Danger*. London: Routledge.

Duggary, G. (1994) *The Executive Tart and Other Myths: Media Women Talk Back*. London: Virago.

Durkheim, E. (1961) *Moral Education*. New York: Free Press.

Eagleton, T. (1996) *The Illusions of Postmodernism*. Oxford: Blackwell.

Ehrenreich, B. and Hochschild, A. R. (eds) (2002) *Global Women: Nannies, Maids and Sex Workers in the New Economy*. New York: Henry Holt.

Elliott, C. (nd) 'Too much to say for myself,' blog <http://toomuchtosayformy-self.com/>.

Elliott, C. (2010) 'Equal pay: today Birmingham, tomorrow the world,' *Guardian*, April 28.

Epstein, C. (1989) *Deceptive Distinctions: Sex, Gender and the Social Order*. New Haven, Conn.: Yale University Press.

Equality and Human Rights Commission (EHRC) (2009a) *Financial Services Inquiry: Sex Discrimination and the Gender Pay Gap*. October. London: EHRC.

EHRC (2009b) *Working Better – Fathers, Family and Work*. London: EHRC.

Ernst & Young (2004) 'Non-executive directors and their contribution to board performance,' non-executive director research <http://bettythayer.com/downloads/publications/board_performance.pdf> (accessed April 4, 2011).

European Commission (1991) Guidelines on Sexual Harassment <http://europa.eu/legislation_summaries/employment_and_social_policy/equality_between_men_and_women/c10917b_en.htm>.

European Commission (2008) Report from the Commission to the Council, the European Parliament, the European Economic and Social Committee and the Committee of the Regions, Equality between Women and Men. January 23, COM (2008). Brussels: European Commission. <http://europa.eu/legisla-tion_summaries/employment_and_social_policy/equality_between_men_and_women/c10167_en.htm> (accessed April 7, 2011).

F-word, The (nd) blog

Fagenson, E. (1993) 'Diversity in management: introduction and importance of women in management,' pp. 248–60 in E. Fagenson (ed.), *Women in Management: Trends, Issues and Challenges in Managerial Diversity.* Newbury Park, Calif.: Sage.

Farley, L. (1978) *Sexual Shakedown: The Sexual Harassment of Women on the Job.* New York: McGraw Hill.

Feministing (nd) blog <www.feministing.com>

Financial Reporting Council (2010) *The Walker Review of Corporate Governance of the UK Banking Industry.* www.frc.org.uk/corporate/walker.cfm (accessed November 24, 2010).

Fine, C. (2010) *The Delusion of Gender: The Real Science behind Sex Differences.* London: Icon.

Fineman, S. (ed.) (1993) *Emotions in Organizations.* London: Sage.

Foucault, M. (1972) *The Archeology of Knowledge.* London: Tavistock.

Gabriel, Y. (ed.) (1999) *Organizations in Depth.* London: Sage.

Gagliardi, P. (1990) *Artifacts and Symbols: Views of the Corporate Landscape.* Berlin: de Gruyter.

Gambles, R, Lewis, S., and Rapoport, R. (2006) *The Myth of Work-Life Balance: The Challenge of our Time. Men, Women, and Societies.* Oxford: John Wiley.

Gardner, C. (2009) 'Bank of England accused of institutional sexism,' *The Scotsman*, February 2.

Gerth, H. and Wright Mills, C. (eds) (1958) *From Max Weber: Essays in Sociology.* London: Routledge & Kegan Paul

Gherardi, S. (1995) *Gender, Symbolism and Organisational Cultures.* London: Sage.

Gherardi, S (1994) 'The gender we think, the gender we do in our everyday organisational lives,' *Human Relations Special Edition,* pp. 591–691.

Giddens, A. (1992) *The Transformation of Intimacy: Sexuality, Love and Eroticism in Modern Societies.* Brighton: Harvester.

Goldman Sachs (2005) 'Womenomics: Japan's hidden asset,' 19 October <www2.goldmansachs.com/ideas/...change/womenomics.html> (accessed April 4, 2011).

Goleman, D. P. (2006) *Emotional Intelligence*, 10th edn. New York: Bantam.

Gratton, L. (2007) *Innovative Potential: Men and Women in Teams.* London: Centre for Women in Business, London Business School <www.london.edu/assets/documents/publications/Innovative_Potential_NOV_2007(1).pdf > (accessed April 4, 2011).

Gray, J. (1992) *Men are from Mars: Women are from Venus.* New York: Harper Collins.

Griffiths, C. (2010) 'Simmons female representation: lady billers,' *The Lawyer*, October <www.thelawyer.com/focus-simmons-female-representation-lady-billers/1005883.article> (accessed April 4, 2011).

Grint, K. (1995) *Management: A Sociological Introduction.* Oxford: Polity.

Gruber, J. E. and Morgan, P. (eds) (2005) *In the Company of Men. Male Dominance and Sexual Harassment.* Boston, Mass.: Northeastern University Press.

Gurian, M. and Annis, B. (2008) *Leadership and the Sexes: Using Gender Science to Create Success in Business.* San Francisco, Calif.: Jossey-Bass.

Gutek, B. (1989) 'Sexuality in the workplace: key issues in social research and organizational practice,' pp. 56–71 in J. Hearn, D. Sheppard, P. Tancred-Sheriff, and G. Burrell (eds), *The Sexuality of the Organization*. London: Sage.

Gutek, B. A. and Cohen, A. G. (1987) 'Sex ratios, sex role spillover, and sex at work: a comparison of men's and women's experiences,' *Human Relations,* Vol. 40, No. 2, pp. 97–115.

Halford, S. (2006) Collapsing the boundaries: organization, fatherhood and home-working,' *Gender Work and Organization*, Vol. 13, Issue 4, pp. 383–402.

Halford, S., Savage, M., and Witz, A. (1997) *Gender, Careers and Organisations*. Basingstoke: Macmillan.

Hammers, M. (2003) 'Family-friendly' benefits prompt non-parent backlash,' *Workforce Management,* 1 August.

Hammond, V. (1993) 'Opportunity 2000 – a culture change approach to equal opportunity,' *Women in Management Review,* Vol. 17, No. 7, pp. 56–71.

Hampden-Turner, C. (1990) *Corporate Culture: From Vicious to Virtuous Circles.* London: Economist Books.

Handy, C. (1985) *Understanding Organisations.* London: Penguin.

Handy, C. (1995) *The Gods of Management: The Changing Work of Organisation.* London: Arrow.

Harlow, E., Hearn, J., and Parkin, W. (1995) 'Gendered noise: organizations and the silence and din of domination,' pp. 91–108 in C. Itzin and J. Newman (eds), *Gender, Culture and Organizational Change: Putting Theory into Practice.* London: Routledge.

Hearn, J. (1992) *Men in the Public Eye: The Construction and Deconstruction of Public Men and Public Patriarchies.* London/New York: Routledge.

Hearn, J. and Parkin, D. (1995) *'Sex' at Work: The Power and the Paradox of Organisational Sexuality*, rev. edn. Hemel Hempstead: Prentice Hall.

Hearn, J., Sheppard, D., Tancred-Sheriff, P., and Burrell, G. (eds) (1989) *The Sexuality of the Organization.* London: Sage.

Hegelson, S. (1990) *The Female Advantage: Women's Ways of Leadership.* New York: Doubleday.

Herbert, C. (1989) *Talking of Silence: The Sexual Harassment of Schoolgirls.* London: Farmer.

Hewlett, S. (2010) 'A final push can break the glass ceiling,' *Financial Times,* 17 November.

Hewlett, S. A. (2002a) *Creating a Life: Professional Women and the Quest for Children.* New York: Hyperion.

Hewlett, S. A. (2002b) 'Executive women and the myth of having it all,' *Harvard Business Review*, Vol. 80 (April), pp. 66–73.

Hewlett, S. A. and Rashid, A. R. with Fredman, C., Jackson, M., and Sherbin, S. (2010) 'The battle for female talent in emerging markets,' *Harvard Business Review* (May), pp. 101–6.

Higgs, D. (2003) *Review on the Role and Effectiveness of Non-Executive Directors,* April <www.berr.gov.uk/files/file23012.pdf> (accessed April 13, 2011).

Hirshchorn, L. (1990) *The Workplace Within: The Psychodynamics of Organizational Life.* Cambridge, Mass.: MIT Press..

Hochschild, A. R. (1983) *The Managed Heart: The Commercialization of Human Feeling.* Berkeley, Calif. University of California Press.

Hochschild, A. R. (1990) *The Second Shift: Working Parents and the Revolution at Home.* London: Piatkus.

Hochschild, A. R. (1997) *The Time Bind: When Work Becomes Home and Home Becomes Work.* New York: Metropolitan Books.

Hofstede, G. (1980) *Cultures Consequences: International Differences in Work Related Values.* Beverly Hills, Calif./London: Sage.

Holmes, J. (2006) *Gendered Talk in the Workplace.* Oxford: Blackwell.

Home Office (2007) *Cross Government Action Plan on Sexual Violence and Abuse* <www.homeoffice.gov.uk/documents/Sexual-violence-action-plan> (accessed April 4, 2011).

Horlick, N. (1998) *Can You Have It All?* London: Pan.

Hunt, J. C. (1989) *Psychoanalytic Aspects to Field Work.* London: Sage.

Ibarra, H. (1995) 'Race,opportunity, and diversity of social circles in managerial networks', *Academy of Management Journal*, Vol. 38, No. 3, pp. 673–703.

Ibarra, H. (1997) 'Paving an alternative power. gender differences in managerial networks,' *Social Psychology Quarterly*, Vol. 60, No. 1 (March).

Ibarra, H. (2010) 'How leaders create and use networks,' *Harvard Business Review* (January) <http://hbr.org/2007/01/how-leaders-create-and-use-networks/ar/1> (accessed 4 April 2011).

Ibarra, H. H., Carter, N. M., and Silva, C. (2010) 'Why men still get more promotions than women,' *Harvard Business Review* (September), pp. 80–5.

Itzen, C. (1995) 'The gender culture in organisations,' pp. 30–54 in C. Itzen and J. Newman (eds), *Gender, Culture and Organisational Change: Putting Theory into Practice.* London: Routledge.

Jarvinen, J., Kall, A., and Miller, I. (2008) *Hard Knock Life* <www.endviolence-againstwomen.org.uk/data/files/hard_knock_life.pdf> (accessed 28 March 2011).

Jung, C. (1944) *Psychology and Alchemy.* London: Routledge.

Kandola, B. (2009) *The Value of Difference: Eliminating Bias in Organisations.* Oxford: Pearn Kandola.

Kandola, R. and Fullerton, J. (1998) *Diversity in Action: Managing the Mosaic.* London: Institute of Personnel and Development.

Kanter, R. M. (1977a) 'Some effects of proportions of group life: skewed sex ratios and responses to token women,' *American Journal of Sociology*, Vol. 82, pp. 965–90.

Kanter, R. M. (1977b) *Men and Women of the Corporation.* New York: Basic Books.

Kelan, E. (2009) *Performing Gender at Work.* Basingstoke: Palgrave Macmillan:

Kerfoot, D. and Knights, D. (1996) 'The best is yet to come? The quest for embodiment in managerial work,' pp. 78–99 in D. Collinson and J. Hearn (eds), *Men as Managers, Managers as Men: Critical Perspectives on Men, Masculinities and Managements.* London: Sage.

Kimmel, M. (2001) 'Gender equality: not for women only,' lecture for

International Women's Day Seminar, European Parliament, Brussels, March 8 <www.europrofem.org/audio/ep_kimmel/kimmel.htm> (accessed April 4, 2011).

Kimmel, M. (2009) *The Gendered Society*. Oxford: Oxford University Press.

Kingsmill, D. (2000) *Kingsmill Review on Women's Pay and Employment*, December. London: Department of Trade and Industry.

Kirton, G. and Greene, A.-M. (2004) *The Dynamics of Managing Diversity. A Critical Approach*. Oxford: Elsevier Butterworth-Heinemann.

Kirton, G., Greene, A.-M., and Dean, D. (2005) 'British diversity professionals as change agents: radicals, tempered radicals or liberal reformers?' paper presented at Gender Work and Organization Conference, Keele University. Repr. in (2007) *International Journal of Human Resource Management*, Vol. 18, No. 11, pp. 1979–94.

Knights, D., Kerfoot, D., and Sabelis, I. (eds) (1991) *Gender, Work and Organization*. Oxford: Wiley Blackwell.

Knights, D. and Morgan, G. (1990) 'Gendering jobs: corporate strategy, managerial control and the dynamics of job segregation,' *Work, Employment and Society*, Vol. 5, No. 2, pp. 181–200.

Knoppers, A. (2009) 'Giving meaning to sport involvement in managerial work,' *Gender Work and Organization*, September <http://onlinelibrary.wiley.com/doi/10.1111/j.1468-0432.2009.00467.x/full> (accessed April 4, 2011).

Kodz, J., Davis, S., Lain, D., Strebler, M., Rick, J., Bates, P., Cummings, J., and Meager, N. (2003) *Working Long Hours: A Review of the Evidence*. Employment Relations Research Series ERRS16. London: Dept of Trade and Industry <www.employment-studies.co.uk/pubs/summary.php?id=errs16> (accessed April 4, 2011).

Kodz, J., Kersley, B., Strebler, M., and O'Regan, S. (1998) 'Breaking the long hours culture,' Institute of Employment Studies report no. 352, December <www.employment-studies.co.uk/pubs/summary.php?id=3524th> (accessed April 4, 2011).

Korda, M. (1973) *Male Chauvinism! How it Works*. New York: Ballantine.

Kramer, V. W., Konrad, A. M., and Erkut, S. U. (2006) *Critical Mass on Corporate Boards: Why Three or More Women Enhance Governance*. Report no. WCW11. Wellesley, Mass.: Wellesley Centers for Women.

Kuande, E. (2009) 'Work life balance for fathers in knowledge work: some insights from the Norwegian context,' *Gender Work and Organization*, Vol. 16, No. 1 (January).

Lakoff, R. (1975) *Language and A Woman's Place*. Oxford: Oxford University Press.

Lewis, R. and Rake, K. (2008) 'Breaking the mould for women leaders: could boardroom quotas hold the key?' Fawcett Society think piece for Gender Equality Forum, October.

Lewis, S. (1997) '"Family friendly" employment policies: a route to changing organisational culture of playing about at the margins?,' *Gender, Work and Organisation*, Vol. 4, No. 1, pp. 13–24.

Lewis, S. and Lewis, J. (eds) (1996) *The Work–Family Challenge: Rethinking Employment*. London: Sage.

Lewis, S., Rapoport, R., and Gambles, R. (2003) 'Reflections on the integration of paid work with the rest of life,' *Journal of Managerial Psychology*, Vol. 18, pp. 824–41.

Lewis, S. and Taylor, K. (1996) 'Evaluating the impact of family-friendly employment policies: a case study,' p. 121 in S. Lewis and J. Lewis (eds), *The Work–Family Challenge*. London: Sage.

Liff, S. (1995) 'Equal opportunities: continuing discrimination in a context of formal equality,' in P. Edwards (ed.), *Industrial Relations*. Oxford: Blackwell.

Liff, S. (1997) 'Two routes to managing diversity: individual differences or social group characteristics,' *Employee Relations,* Vol. 19, Issue 1, pp. 11–26.

Linstead, S. (1995) 'Averting the gaze: gender and power on the perfumed picket line,' *Gender, Work and Organisation*, Vol. 2, No. 4, pp. 192–205.

Lorber, C. J. (1989) 'Trust, loyalty and the place of women in the informal organisation of work,' in J. Freeman (ed.), *Women: A Feminist Perspective*. Mountain View, Calif.: Mayfield.

MacDowell, L. (1997) *Capital Culture: Gender at Work in the City*. Oxford: Blackwell.

MacKinnon, C. (1979) *Sexual Harassment of Working Women: A Case of Sex Discrimination*. New Haven, Conn.: Yale University Press.

Maddock, S. (1999) *Challenging Women. Gender, Culture and Organization*. London: Sage.

Maddock, S. and Parkin, D. (1993) 'Gender strategies and women's choices and strategies at work,' *Women in Management Review*, Vol. 8, Issue 2, pp. 3–9.

Management-issues.com (2006) 'The old boy network is alive and well' </www.management-issues.com/2006/8/24/research/the-old-boy-network-is-alive-and-well.asp> (accessed April 4, 2011).

Marshall, J. (1984) *Women Managers: Travellers in a Male World*. Chichester: Wiley.

Marshall, J. (1995a) 'Gender and management: a critical review of research,' *British Journal of Management*, Vol. 6 (Special issue, December), pp. 53–62.

Marshall, J. (1995b) *Women Managers Moving On*. London: Routledge.

Martin, J. (2001a) Keynote speech, Rethinking Gender, Work and Organisation Conference, Keele University, 27–29 June.

Martin, J. (2001b) *Organizational Culture: Mapping the Terrain*. Thousand Oaks, Calif.: Safe.

Massey, D. (1993) 'Scientists, transcendence and the home/work boundary,' in *Organisations, Gender and Power: Papers from an IRRU Workshop*, University of Warwick.

Massey, D. (1994) *Space, Place, and Gender*. Minneapolis, Minn.: University of Minnesota Press.

Massey, D. (1997) 'Masculinity, dualisms and high technology,' in N. Duncan (ed.), *BodySpace*. London: Routledge.

Maudsley, H. (1874) 'Sex in mind and education,' *Fortnightly Review,* No. 15, pp. 466–83. Discussed in <http://brain.oxfordjournals.org/content/130/2/585.full#xref-ref-8-1> (accessed April 4, 2011).

Maushart, S. (2002) *Wifework: What Marriage Really Means for Women*. London: Bloomsbury.

McCarthy, H. (2004) 'Girlfriends in high places: how women's networks are changing the workplace.' London: Demos.

McDowell, L. (1997) *Capital Culture: Gender at Work in the City.* Oxford: Blackwell.

McElhinney, B. (2006) 'Challenging hegemonic masculinities: female and male police officers handling domestic violence,' in K. Hall and M. Bucholz (eds), *Gender Articulated: Language and the Socially Constructed Self.* London: Routledge.

McFall, J. (2010) *Women in the City.* Treasury Select Committee. 10th Report of Session 2009/2010 <www.publications.parliament.uk/pa/cm200910/cmse lect/cmtreasy/482/482.pdf> (accessed April 5, 2011).

McGwire, S. (1992) *Best Companies for Women: Britain's Top Employers.* London: Pandora.

McSmith, A. (2009) 'What if women ruled the banks?' <www.independent. co.uk/news/business/news/what-if-women-ruled-the-banks-1681064.html> (accessed April 3, 2011).

Melrose, M. (2000) 'Ties that bind – young people and the prostitution labour market in Britain,' paper presented at Fourth Feminist Research Conference, Bologna, September 2000 <www.women.it/cyberarchive/files/melrose.htm> (accessed 4 April 2011).

Merchant, C. (1982) *The Death of Nature: Women, Ecology and the Scientific Revolution.* New York: Harper & Row.

Meyerson, D. E. and Fletcher, J. K. (2000) 'A modest manifesto for shattering the glass ceiling,' *Harvard Business Review* (Jan/Feb), pp. 127–36.

Meyerson, D. E. and Scully, M. A. (1995) 'Tempered radicalism and the politics of ambivalence and change,' *Organization Science*, Vol. 6, No. 5, pp. 585–600.

Milkman, R. (1987) *Gender at Work: The Dynamics of Job Segregation by Sex During World War II.* Urbana, Ill.: University of Illinois Press.

Moir, A. (1989) *Sex Matters.* New York: Michael Joseph.

Moir, A. and Jessell, D. (1991) *Brain Sex.The Real Difference between Men and Women.* New York: Dell.

Moir, A. and Moir, W. (1998) *Why Men Don't Iron: The Real Science of Gender Studies.* London: Harper Collins.

Mott, H. and Condor, S. (1997) 'Sexual harassment and the working lives of secretaries,' pp. 49–91 in A. Thomas and C. Kitzinger (eds), *Sexual Harassment: Contemporary Feminist Perspectives.* Buckingham: Open University Press.

Nicholson, P. (1996) *Gender, Power and Organisation: A Psychological Perspective.* London: Routledge

Nielsen, T. (2010) 'Breaking into the boardroom: is it time for gender quotas?' *Director*, May <www.director.co.uk/magazine/2010/5_May/women_board room_ 63_09.html> (accessed April 4, 2011).

O'Carroll, L. and Boshoff, A. (2000) 'Frostrup may be hired to front a one-off *Panorama*,' *Daily Mail* (London), September 6.

Oakley, A. and Mitchell, J. (1997) *Who's Afraid of Feminism? Seeing Through the Backlash.* London: Hamish Hamilton.

Observatoire sur la Responsibilité Societale des Entreprises (ORSE) (2010) *Involving Men in the Challenges of Gender Equality.* <www.orse.org> (accessed April 13, 2011).

Office for National Statistics (2008) *Labour Force Survey.* London: ONS. <www.statistics.gov.uk/pdfdir/lmsuk1108.pdf> (accessed April 4, 2011).

Opportunity 2000. *Report 1997.* London: Opportunity Now.

Opportunity Now (2004) *Diversity Dimensions : Integration into Organisational Culture.* London: Opportunity Now.

Opportunity Now (2010a) *What Holds Women Back: Women and Men's Perceptions of the Barriers to Women's Progression.* <www.opportunitynow.org.uk/research/what_holds_women_back_/index.html> (accessed April 4, 2011).

Opportunity Now (2010b) *Leading Change: Insights and Inspiration from Successful Leaders.* London: Opportunity Now.

Organisation of Economic Cooperation and Development (OECD) (2008) 'The reversal of gender inequalities in higher education: an on-going trend,' in *Higher Education to 2030, Volume 1 – Demography.* Paris: OECD. <www.oecd.org/.../0,3746,en_2649_39263238_41788555_1_1_1_1,00.html> (accessed April 4 , 2011).

Ouchi, W. (1981) *Theory Z: How American Business Can Meet the Japanese Challenge.* Reading, Mass.: Addison-Wesley.

Palmer, A. M. (1996) 'Something to declare: women in HM Customs and Excise,' pp. 125–52 in S. Ledwith and F. Colgan (eds), *Women in Organisations: Challenging Gender Politics.* London: Macmillan.

Parker, V. A. and Hall, D. T. (1993) 'Workplace flexibility. faddish or fundamental?' pp. 122–55 in P. Mirvis (ed.), *Building the Competitive Workforce.* New York: Wiley.

Pearson, A. (2002) *I Don't Know How She Does It.* London: Vintage.

Pemberton, C. (1995) 'Organisational culture and equalities work,' pp. 108 –25 in J. Shaw and D. Perrons (eds), *Making Gender Work: Managing Equal Opportunities.* Buckingham: Open University Press.

Perrons, D. (2003) 'The new economy and the work–life balance; conceptual explorations and a case study of new media,' *Gender Work and Organization,* Vol. 10, Issue 1, pp. 65–93.

Peston, R. (2009) 'Why men are to blame for the crunch' <www.bbc.co.uk/blogs/thereporters/robertpeston/2009/07/why_men_are_to_blame_for_the_c.html> (accessed April 4, 2011).

Peters, T. and Waterman, R. H. (1982) *In Search of Excellence.* New York: Harper & Row.

Phillips, A. and Taylor, B. (1980) 'Sex and skill: notes towards a feminist economics,' *Feminist Review,* No. 6, pp. 79–88.

Philpott, J. (2010) 'Working hours in the recession,' August. London: Chartered Institute for Personnel and Development (CIPD). <www.cipd.co.uk/press office/_articles/workauditworkinghours.htm> (accessed 4 April 2011).

Powell, G. N. (1988) *Women and Men in Management.* California: Sage.

Prime, J. and Moss-Racusin, C. A. (2009) *Engaging Men in Gender Initiatives: What Change Agents Need to Know.* New York: Catalyst.

Prime, J., Moss-Racusin, C. A. and Foust-Cummings, F. (2009) *Engaging Men in Gender Initiatives: Stacking the Deck for Success.* New York: Catalyst. <www.catalyst.org/file/314/engaging_men_in_gender_initiatives_2.pdf> (accessed April 5, 2011).

Pringle, R. (1989) *Secretaries Talk: Sexuality, Power and Work*. London and New York: Verso.

Radford, J. and Balls, E. H. (1998) 'The body and violence against women,' paper presented at BSA Conference, York, April.

Rees, T. (1998) *Mainstreaming Equality in the European Union: Education, Training and Labour Market Policies*. London: Routledge.

Reeves, R. (2002) 'Dad's Army: the case for father-friendly workplaces.' London: Work Foundation.

Reskin, B. and Roos, P. (1990) *Job Queues, Gender Queues: Explaining Women's Inroads into Men's Organizations*. Philadelphia, Pa.: Temple University Press.

Rigg, C. and Sparrow, J. (1994) 'Gender, diversity and working styles, in women,' *Management Review*, Vol. 9, No. 1, pp. 9–16.

Rippon, G. (2010) 'Sorry, boys – women are on the same wavelength,' *Sunday Times*, September 12. Also reported in <www.telegraph.co.uk/.../Women-and-men-have-virtually-identical-brains- scientist-claims.html> (accessed April 4, 2011).

Rogers, B. (1988) *Men Only: An Investigation into Men's Organisations*. London: Pandora.

Roper, M. (1994) *Masculinity and the British Organization Man Since 1945*. Oxford: Oxford University Press.

Rosener, J. (1990) 'Ways women lead,' *Harvard Business Review*, Vol. 68, pp. 119–25.

Rubinstein, M. (1987) *The Dignity of Women at Work. A Report on the Problem of Sexual Harassment in the Member States of the European Community* Directive V/4/2/87, October. Brussels: European Commission.

Rutherford, S. (1999) *Organisational Cultures, Women Managers and Patriarchal Closure*. PhD thesis, Bristol University.

Rutherford, S. (2001a) 'Any difference/men women and management styles,' *Gender, Work and Organisation,* Vol. 8. No. 3 (July), pp. 326–45.

Rutherford, S. (2001b) '"Are you going home already?" The long hours culture, women managers and the patriarchal closure,' *Time and Society*, Vol. 10, No. 2/3 (September), pp. 259–76.

Rutherford, S. (2001c) 'Towards equality,' Fawcett Society newsletter.

Rutherford, S. (2002) 'Organizational culture, women managers and exclusion,' *Women in Management Review*, Vol. 8.

Rutherford, S. (2004) 'Diversity dimensions: integration into organisational culture,' report. London: Opportunity Now.

Rutherford, S. and Ollerearnshaw, S. (2002) *The Business of Diversity*. Hampshire: Schneider-Ross. Summary available for download at <www.schneider-ross.com/resources.press.php> (accessed April 4, 2011).

Rutherford, S. (2005) 'Different but equal,' pp. 332–46 in R. Burke and M. Matthis (eds), *Supporting Women's Career Advancement: Challenges and Opportunities*. Cheltenham: Edward Elgar.

Rutherford, S. and Ollerearnshaw, S. (2004) 'Integration into organisational culture,' *Opportunity Now*, June.

Rutherford, S., Schneider, R., and Walmsley, A. (2006) *Quantitative and*

Qualitative Research into Sexual Harassment in the Armed Forces <www.mod.uk/
NR/rdonlyres/538E55EE-9CA4.../20060522SRReport.pdf> (accessed April 2,
2011).

Ryan, M. K. and Haslam, S. A. (2007) 'The glass cliff: exploring the dynamics
surrounding the appointment of women to precarious leadership
positions,' *Academy of Management Review*, Vol. 32, No. 2, pp. 1–26.

Savage, M. (1992) 'Women's expertise, men's authority: gendered organisations
and the contemporary middle classes,' pp. 124–55 in M. Savage and A. Witz
(eds), *Gender and Bureaucracy*. Oxford: Blackwell.

Scase, R. and Goffee, R. (1989) *Reluctant Managers: Their Work and Lifestyles.*
London: Unwin Hyman.

Sealy, R., Vinnicombe, S., and Doldor, E. (2009) *The Female FTSE Board Report
2009.* International Centre for Women Leaders, Cranfield School of
Management.

Schein, E. H. (1985) *Organizational Culture and Leadership.* San Francisco, Calif.:
Jossey-Bass.

Schein, E. H. (1992) 'Coming to a new awareness of organisational culture,' in
G. Salaman (ed.), *Human Resources Strategies.* Beverly Hills, Calif.: Sage.

Schein, E. H. (2010) *Organizational Culture and Leadership*, 4th edn. San Francisco,
Calif.: Jossey-Bass.

Schein, V. E. (1973) 'The relationship between sex role stereotypes and requisite
management characteristics,' *Journal of Applied Psychology*, Vol. 57, No. 2, pp.
95–100.

Schein, V. E. (1994) 'Managerial sex typing: a persistent and pervasive barrier to
women's opportunities,' p. 49 in M. Davidson and R. Burke (eds), *Women in
Management.* London: Routledge.

Schein, V. E., Mueller, R., and Jacobson, C. (1989) 'The relationship between sex
role stereotypes and requisite management characteristics,' *Sex Roles*, Vol. 20,
Nos 1–2, pp. 103–10.

Schutsenberger, A. (1998) *The Ancestor Syndrome.* London: Routledge.

Schwartz, F. N. (1989) 'Management women and the new facts of life,' *Harvard
Business Review* (Jan/Feb), pp. 65–78.

Sealy, R., Vinnicombe, S., and Doldor, E. (2009) *The Female FTSE Board Report
2009.* International Centre for Women Leaders, Cranfield School of
Management.

Shapiro, G. and Allison, M. (2007) 'Reframing diversity: when diversity adds
value,'<www.reframingdiversity.com> (accessed 2 April 2010).

Shaw, S. (2006) 'Governed by the rules? The female voice in parliamentary
debates,' pp 81–102 in J. Baxter (ed.), *Speaking Out: The Female Voice in Public
Contexts.* Basingstoke: Palgrave Macmillan.

Silverstein, M. J. and Syre, K. (2009) 'The female economy: companies ignore
women, "the largest market opportunity in the world",' *Harvard Business
Review*, September, pp. 46–53.

Simpson, R. (2004) 'Masculinity at work: the experiences of men in female
dominated occupations,' *Work Employment & Society*, Vol. 18, No. 2 (June),
pp. 349–68.

Sinclair, A. (2000) 'Teaching managers about masculinities: are you kidding?' *Management Learning,* Vol. 31, No. 1, pp. 83–101.

Singh, V. (2008) 'Transforming boardroom cultures in science, engineering and technology organizations,' International Centre for Women Business Leaders, Cranfield University, July.

Smith, D. (1987) *The Everyday World as Problematic: A Feminist Sociology.* Milton Keynes: Open University Press.

Smith, J. (nd) Political blonde. blog <www.politicalblonde.com>.

Smithson, J. and Stokoe, E. H. (2005) 'Discourses of work–life balance: negotiating 'genderblind' terms in organizations,' *Gender, Work and Organization,* Vol. 12, Issue 2, pp. 147–68.

Sonnenfeld, J. (1985) 'Shedding light on the Hawthorn Studies,' *Journal of Organizational Behaviour,* Vol. 2, pp. 111–30.

Spencer, S. J., Steele, C. M., and Quinn, D. M. (1999) 'Stereotype threat and women's math performance,' *Journal of Experimental Social Psychology,* Vol. 35, No. 1, pp. 93–113.

Stanko, E (1988) 'Keeping women in and out of line: sexual harassment and occupational segregation,' pp. 91–9 in S. Walby (ed.), *Gender Segregation at Work.* Milton Keynes: Open University Press.

Stapley, L. (1991) *The Personality of the Organisation A Psycho-Dynamic Explanation of Culture and Change.* London: Free Association Books.

Still, L. V. (1994) 'Where to from here? Women in management: the cultural dilemma,' *Women in Management Review,* Vol. 9, No. 4, pp. 3–10.

Stockdale, J. (1991) 'Sexual harassment at work,' pp. 53–65 in J. Firth-Cozens and M. West (eds), *Women at Work.* Cambridge: Cambridge University Press.

Stonewall (2009) *The Double-Glazed Glass Ceiling: Lesbians in the Workplace* <www.stonewall.org.uk/documents/doubleglazed_glass_ceiling.pdf> (acessed April 4, 2011).

Sturges, J. and Guest, D. (2004) 'Working to live or living to work? Work/life balance early in the career,' *Human Resource Management Journal,* Vol. 14, Issue 4, pp. 5–20.

Swan, E. (1994) 'Managing Emotion' in M. Tanton (ed.), *Women in Management: Developing a Presence.* London: Routledge

Tannen, D. (1990) *You Just don't Understand: Men and Women in Conversation.* New York: Morrow.

Tannen, D. (1994) *Talking 9 to 5: Men and Women at Work,* New York: Harper.

Taylor, F. W. (1911) *Theory of Scientific Management.* New York and London: Harper & Brothers.

Thomas, A. and Kitzinger, C. (1994) 'It's just something that happens: the invisibility of sexual harassment in the workplace,' *Gender Work and Organisation,* Vol. 1, No. 3, pp. 151–61.

Thomas, A. and Kitzinger, C. (1995) 'It's just something that happens: the invisibility of sexual harassment in the workplace,' *Gender, Work and Organizations,* Vol. 2, No. 4, pp. 151—62.

Thomas, A. and Kitzinger, C. (1997) *Sexual Harassment: Contemporary Feminist Perspectives.* Buckingham: Open University Press.

Thomas, D. A. (2004) 'Diversity as strategy,' *Harvard Business Review* (Sept), pp. 1–11.

Thomson, K. (1998) *Emotional Capital: Capturing Hearts and Minds to Create Lasting Business Success.* Oxford: Capstone.

Tomlinson, F., Brockbank, A., and Traves, J. (1997) 'The feminization of management? Issues of "sameness" and "difference" in the roles and experiences of female and male retail managers,' *Gender, Work and Organization*, Vol. 4, No. 4, pp. 218–30.

Trompenaars, F. (1993) *Riding the Waves of Culture: Understanding Cultural Diversity in Business.* London: Nicholas Brealey.

United Nations General Assembly (2006) *In-Depth Study on All Forms of Violence against Women: Report of the Secretary General.* A/61/122/Add.1. 6 July. New York: UN General Assembly. <www.un.org/womenwatch/daw/vaw/violenceagainstwomenstudydoc.pdf> (accessed April 4, 2011).

Urwin, R. (2010) 'New feminism has started the fight-back at last,' *This is London*, 7 June. www.thisislondon.co.uk/standard/article-23841968-new-feminism-has-started-the-fight-back-at-last.do (accessed April 4, 2011).

Vinnicombe, S., Sealy, R., Graham, J., and Doldor, E. (2010) *Female FTSE 2010: Opening Up the Appointments Process.* International Centre for Women Leaders, Cranfield School of Management, November.

Vinnicombe, S., Singh, V., and Kumra, S. (2005) *Making Good Connections: Best Practice for Women's Corporate Networks.* Cranfield Centre for Developing Women Leaders in association with Opportunity Now.

Wachman, R. (2009). Mining gets dirty with sexist rant at Anglo's Carroll,' *Guardian*, July 9 <http://www.guardian.co.uk/business/2009/jul/09/boustred-attacks-carroll> (accessed April 6, 2011).

Wacjman, J. (1998) *Managing Like a Man.* Cambridge: Polity Press.

Wahl, A. (1998) 'Surplus femininity,' paper given at conference, 9–10 January, Manchester.

Walby, S. (1990) *Theorizing Patriarchy.* Oxford: Blackwell.

Walby, S. (2009) 'The future of financial services supervision in the EU: Recommendations for the inclusion of gender.' www.lancs.ac.uk/fass/doc_library/.../Walby_Larosiere_consultation.pdf (accessed April 4, 2011).

Walby, S. and Allen, J. (2004) *Domestic Violence, Sexual Assault and Stalking: Findings from the British Crime Survey.* London: Home Office Research, Development and Statistics Directorate.

Walter, N. (2010) *Living Dolls: The Return of Sexism.* London: Virago.

Ward, H. et al. (2005) 'Who pays for sex? An analysis of the increasing prevalence of female commercial sex contacts among men in Britain,' *Sexually Transmitted Infections*, Vol. 81, pp. 467–71.

Wardrop, M. (2010) 'HBOS manager loses sexual harassment claim,' *Daily Telegraph*, May 15 <www.telegraph.co.uk/news/uknews/7725854/HBOS-manager-loses-sexual-harassment-claim.html> (accessed April 4, 2011).

Waterfield, B. (2010) 'Britain's Working Time Directive "opt out" under threat,' *Daily Telegraph*, January 25 <www.telegraph.co.uk/news/worldnews/europe/7066898/Britains-working-time-directive-opt-out-under-threat.html> (accessed April 4, 2011).

Watson, S. (1990) 'Is Sir Humphrey dead? The changing culture of the civil service,' Working Paper 103, School of Advanced Urban Studies, University of Bristol.

Weber, M. (1947) (1947) *The Theory of Social and Economic Organization*, trans. A. M. Henderson and Talcott Parsons. New York: Free Press.

Weisel, M. (1991) 'Employer's burden of proof in "mixed motives" title vii litigation and available remedies: Hopkins v Price Waterhouse one year later,' *Labor Law Journal*, Vol. 42, No. 1, pp. 45–51.

Wetherell, M., Stiven, H., and Potter, J. (1989) 'Unequal egalitarianism: a preliminary study of discourses concerning gender and employment opportunities,' *British Journal of Social Psychology*, Vol. 26, pp. 59–71.

Westaway, J. and McKay, S. (2007) 'Women's financial assets and debts,' Fawcett Society, November <www.fawcettsociety.org.uk/documents/Fawcett%20 Assets%20Report.pdf> (accessed 4 April 2011).

Willis, P. (1977) *Learning to Labour*. Farnborough: Saxon House.

Willmott, H. (1993) 'Strength is ignorance, slavery is freedom: managing culture in organizations,' *Journal of Management Studies*, Vol. 30, No. 2, pp. 515–42.

Wittenberg-Cox, A. (2010) *How Women Mean Business*. Chichester: John Wiley.

Wittenberg-Cox, A. and Maitland, A. (2008) *Why Women Mean Business: Understanding the Emergence of our Next Economic Revolution*. Chichester: Wiley.

Wolff, J. (1977) 'Women in organizations,' in S. Clegg and D. Dunkerley (eds), *Critical Issues in Organizations*. London: Routledge.

Woolf, V. (1977) *The Three Guineas*. London: Penguin.

Working Families (2005) 'Hours to suit; the hidden brain drain,' www.working-families <www.workingfamilies.org.uk/asp/.../zone/.../hourstosuit-brochure.pdf> (accessed April 4, 2011).

Working Families (2008a) 'Legal lives: retaining talent through a balanced culture,' <www.workingfamilies.org.uk/asp/.../legal_lives_programme.pdf> (accessed April 4, 2011).

Working Families (2008b) 'Flexible working in a challenging economic climate.' briefing, November 1 <www.workingfamilies.org.uk/...briefings/flexible-working-in-a-challenging-economic-climate> (accessed April 4, 2011).

Working Families (2010) *Work–Life Balance. Working for Fathers?* Interim report, November. <www.workingfamilies.org.uk/admin/uploads/Fathers %20research%20project%20interim%20report.pdf> (accessed April 5, 2011).

World Economic Forum (2010) *The Corporate Gender Gap* <www.weforum.org/ women-leaders-and-gender-parity> (accessed June 16, 2011).

Wright, T., Colgan, F., Creegany, C., and McKearney, A. (2006) 'Lesbian, gay and bisexual workers: equality, diversity and inclusion in the workplace,' *Equal Opportunities International*, Vol. 25, Issue 6, pp. 465–70.

Yoder, J. D. (1991) 'Rethinking tokenism: looking beyond numbers,' *Gender and Society*, Vol. 5, No. 2, pp. 178–92.

Yount, K. (2005) 'Sexualization of work roles among men miners: structural and gender-based origins of "harazzment",' pp. 65–92 in J. E. Gruber and P. Morgan (eds), *In the Company of Men*. Boston, Mass.: Northeastern University Press.

INDEX